WHAT WE BELIEVE

Published in 2010 by
Veritas Publications
7–8 Lower Abbey Street
Dublin 1, Ireland
Email publications@veritas.ie
Website www.veritas.ie

ISBN 978 1 84730 214 4

Copyright © Patrick Mullins OCarm, 2010

Scripture taken from the *New Revised Standard Version* Bible, published by
Thomas Nelson, Inc., Nashville, Tennessee, 1990. Used with permission.

10 9 8 7 6 5 4 3 2 1

A catalogue record for this book is available from the British Library.

Designed by Paula Ryan

Printed in the Republic of Ireland by ColourBooks Ltd, Dublin

Veritas books are printed on paper made from the wood pulp of managed
forests. For every tree felled, at least one tree is planted, thereby renewing
natural resources.

WHAT WE BELIEVE

Understanding the Faith that We Share with the Saints

Patrick Mullins OCarm

VERITAS

CONTENTS

INTRODUCTION: THEY PROCLAIM OUR FAITH

This book is an introduction to what the Catholic Church believes. Although it may prove useful to others, it is intended primarily for those who would like to understand their own faith better and to participate in the Church's life of faith more fully.

The introductory chapter, 'Faith in Christ', outlines the nature of faith and the way in which it enables Christians to share the priestly, kingly and prophetic dimensions of Christ's role and mission.

Chapters two, three, four and five are concerned with prayer, the sacraments, the commandments and the creed. These chapters correspond, respectively, to parts four, two, three and one of the *Catechism of the Catholic Church* (1992). Chapter two of this book, 'Faith and Prayer', outlines the teaching of the *Catechism* on prayer. Taking St Thérèse of Lisieux, St Teresa of Avila and St John Chrysostom as guides, it presents prayer as a personal relationship with God, in which we are gradually brought to the full maturity of spiritual childhood, recognising God as 'Our Father'.

Chapter three, 'Faith and Worship', presents the *Catechism's* teaching on the public liturgy and worship of the Church. Taking St Thomas Aquinas, St Ignatius of Antioch and St Teresia Benedicta a Cruce (Edith Stein) as models, it recognises all prayer as a sharing in the priestly prayer of Jesus, our Lord. The formal prayer of the liturgy enables us to unite the spiritual sacrifices of our lives with Christ's sacrifice, in order that we may receive from God the grace of becoming truly one with him in Eucharistic communion.

In chapter four, 'Faith and Righteousness', St Augustine, St Catherine of Siena and Bl. John XXIII are witnesses to the teaching of the *Catechism* on righteousness. The incarnate Word suffered and died for us while we are still sinners, in order to unite us to himself for ever. He is the model and source of our righteousness. Any righteousness of ours is the fruit of our faith, hope and love, and it takes the form of a committed solidarity with all our sisters and brothers in all their needs.

Chapter five, 'Faith and Belief', illustrates the teaching of the *Catechism* on the profession of our faith using St Irenaeus, St Joan of Arc and Bl. Elizabeth of the Trinity as examples. Our belief in God, Father, Son and Holy Spirit, is closely bound up with what we believe about ourselves and our spiritual destiny. We have been created in God's image and likeness, but it is only in Christ that the full grandeur and glory that God has intended for us from the beginning can be realised.

The final chapter, 'A Living Faith for Today', tries to identify the most significant elements of the teaching of the *Catechism* for our times. These key elements provide the basis on which our lives of faith, hope and love can be built.

Chapter 1

FAITH IN CHRIST

This introductory chapter is an exploration of the meaning of Christian faith. It begins by describing the main characteristics of the Old Testament faith of Abraham and Moses, and of the Old and New Testament faith of Mary, the Mother of Jesus. It then identifies Priest, King and Prophet as three of the dimensions of our faith concerning Jesus the Messiah-Christ, and it outlines the way in which we are given a share in his priestly, royal and prophetic offices through faith and the sacraments. With the subdivision of the priestly office into prayer and worship, these three offices are then presented as the basis for the four sections in the Catechism, on which chapters two, three, four and five of this book are based.

ABRAHAM, MOSES AND MARY AS MODELS OF FAITH

We can identify the essential characteristics of our own faith in the Old Testament figures of Abraham and Moses, who are recognised as models of faith by Judaism, Christianity and Islam. Abrahamic faith provided the essential model for both New Testament faith and for Muslim faith but, although their common ground is considerable, New Testament faith departs radically from both Judaism and Islam in its recognition of Jesus of Nazareth as God incarnate. His mother, the Jewess Mary of Nazareth, is held in high esteem by both Islam and Christianity. The Catholic

Church considers her to be the outstanding model and example of faith, hope and love for all the disciples of her divine Son. In her, the faith of Abraham and the faith of Moses find their finest flowering and fulfilment.

Abraham, Our Father in Faith

In the opening chapters of the Book of Genesis, we read how God created all things, including humankind, and that God looked on all that was created and saw that it was 'very good'. Humankind sinned against God, however, and chapters 3-11 of the Book of Genesis tells the sad story of our gradual and increasing turning away from God: Cain killing Abel, Noah and the Flood, the Tower of Babel. Everything seems to be going from bad to worse and there seems to be no one left who is genuinely trying to do God's will. All this changes, however, when we begin chapter 12 of Genesis with the story of Abram (Abraham).

> Now the LORD said to Abram, 'Go from your country and your kindred and your father's house to the land that I will show you. I will make of you a great nation, and I will bless you, and make your name great, so that you will be a blessing. I will bless those who bless you, and the one who curses you I will curse, and in you all the families of the earth shall be blessed.'

Abram's journey of faith begins with God, who takes the initiative, rather than with Abram himself. The first thing that God demands of Abram is that he be willing to separate himself from those things that provide alternative means of support and security (living in his father's house, among his own relations and in his own country). He is to leave his own people, but he is not free to go where he chooses; he must go to the land that God chooses for him.

To appreciate the importance of what God promises Abram, we need to remember the situation in which he found himself. Abram's great-great-great-grandfather was called Peleg, and Peleg was the great-great-great-grandson of Noah. Abram's father, Terah, came from Ur of the Chaldeans (modern-day Iraq) and had moved with his family to Haran (in modern-day Syria) where they settled, a journey of some six hundred miles north-west up the river Euphrates. In Ur, Abram married Sarai, but she was barren and had no children. At the time God makes this promise to Abram, Abram is seventy-five years old and the promise is that he will be blessed by God and become a great nation, i.e. have such a large family that they will form a nation. This was surely a most extraordinary prophesy to make to a man in Abram's position.

Despite the extraordinary nature of what God tells him, Abram does not question God. He takes God at his word and does what God has told him to do. With nothing to guide him but what God has told him, he leaves Haran to go wherever the LORD will lead him.

> So Abram went, as the LORD had told him; and Lot went with him. Abram was seventy-five years old when he departed from Haran. Abram took his wife Sarai and his brother's son Lot, and all the possessions that they had gathered, and the persons whom they had acquired in Haran, and they set forth to go to the land of Canaan.

When his father, Terah, had left Ur, he took his son and daughter-in-law, Abram and Sarai, and his grandson, Lot, with him. He had intended to go to the land of Canaan but stayed in Haran instead. When Abram leaves Haran, he takes with him his wife, Sarai, his nephew, Lot, and all the possessions and people (servants, presumably) they had acquired while in Haran. When Abram leaves Haran he heads for the land of

Canaan (where his father had originally intended to go). Canaan is roughly two hundred miles south-west of Haran.

The story of Abram, later renamed as Abraham, has always been seen as a model for the way that we are called to respond to what God asks of us in faith. In the Letter to the Hebrews (11:8-12), Abraham is praised for his faith for four reasons. First, he obeyed God's command to migrate to another country (see Gen 12:1, 4). Second, his confidence that his descendants would possess that land even though he himself, together with Isaac and Jacob (see Gen 26:4; 35:12), would never be more than sojourners there (see Gen 15:16, 18). Third, he lived as a nomad, living in a tent rather than in a house, the reason for this being that he would not have a permanent house except in heaven (Gen 12:22; 13:14). Finally, his faith enabled him to have children, despite his age and the fact that his wife was barren. Abraham believed that the God who had promised him that he would be the father of a great nation was faithful, and by believing he received the power of procreation – despite the fact that he was 'as good as dead' (i.e. so old). He had so many descendants that they became as many as the stars or as the grains of sands on the seashore.

> By faith Abraham obeyed when he was called to set out for a place that he was to receive as an inheritance; and he set out, not knowing where he was going. By faith he stayed for a time in the land he had been promised, as in a foreign land, living in tents, as did Isaac and Jacob, who were heirs with him of the same promise. For he looked forward to the city that has foundations, whose architect and builder is God. By faith he received power of procreation, even though he was too old – and Sarah herself was barren – because he considered him faithful who had promised. Therefore from one person, and this one as good as dead, descendants were born, 'as many as

the stars of heaven and as the innumerable grains of sand by the seashore'.

Abraham has always been seen as a model for the way we respond to what God asks of us in faith. He is described as our 'Father in Faith' (see Rom 4:12) because of the way he responded to what God asked of him.

Moses, Man of Faith

At the end of the book of Genesis, we are told that Abraham's grandson, Jacob, came down into Egypt to be with his son, Joseph, who had a position of importance there. In the opening chapters of the Book of Exodus we read that, after Joseph's death in Egypt, the people of Israel were oppressed by a king (pharaoh) who did not know Joseph. Used as forced labourers to keep them under control and commanded to kill all new-born males to keep their numbers down, they cried for help to God. It is through the call of Moses, described in chapter 3 of the Book of Exodus, that God responds to the cry for help of the Israelites. After murdering an Egyptian who had abused his fellow Egyptians, Moses fled from Egypt to the Sinai Peninsula where the Midianites (who, like the Israelites, were Semites) lived. There Moses had married a Midianite woman called Zipporah, the daughter of Jethro, a Midianite priest. Some time afterwards, Moses had an experience (see Exod 3:1–10) near Mount Horeb (also known as Mount Sinai) that so transformed his life and the lives of his fellow Israelites that the mountain became known as 'the mountain of God'.

> Moses was keeping the flock of his father-in-law Jethro, the priest of Midian; he led his flock beyond the wilderness, and came to Horeb, the mountain of God. There the angel of the LORD appeared to him in a flame of fire out of a bush; he looked, and the bush was blazing, yet it was not consumed. Then Moses said, 'I must turn

aside and look at this great sight, and see why the bush is not burned up.' When the LORD saw that he had turned aside to see, God called to him out of the bush, 'Moses, Moses!' And he said, 'Here I am.' Then he said, 'Come no closer! Remove the sandals from your feet, for the place on which you are standing is holy ground.' He said further, 'I am the God of your father, the God of Abraham, the God of Isaac, and the God of Jacob.' And Moses hid his face, for he was afraid to look at God.

Attracting Moses' attention by the strange sight of a bush that was blazing but not burnt up, God calls to Moses from the bush and Moses answers. God reveals himself as the God of Moses' ancestors and tells Moses that he is aware of the desperate situation of the Israelites in Egypt:

> Then the LORD said, 'I have observed the misery of my people who are in Egypt; I have heard their cry on account of their taskmasters. Indeed, I know their sufferings, and I have come down to deliver them from the Egyptians, and to bring them up out of that land to a good and broad land, a land flowing with milk and honey, to the country of the Canaanites, the Hittites, the Amorites, the Perizzites, the Hivites, and the Jebusites. The cry of the Israelites has now come to me; I have also seen how the Egyptians oppress them. So come, I will send you to Pharaoh to bring my people, the Israelites, out of Egypt.'

God has not been blind to what has been happening to the Israelites in Egypt and he promises that, led by Moses, the people will be delivered from their slavery and given a land of their own, a land 'flowing with milk and honey'.

In the Letter to the Hebrews (11:24–28), Moses is presented as a model for our Christian faith because he decided to live

14

in solidarity with his own people, the Israelites, and to suffer ill-treatment with them, rather than choosing to enjoy the privileges that could have been his because he was brought up in the household of Pharaoh, the king of Egypt. The text implies that Moses chose to live like this because of some awareness that the future Messiah would come from them:

> By faith, Moses, when he was grown up, refused to be called a son of Pharaoh's daughter, choosing rather to share ill-treatment with the people of God than to enjoy the fleeting pleasures of sin. He considered abuse suffered for the Messiah to be greater wealth than the treasures of Egypt, for he was looking ahead to the reward. By faith he left Egypt, unafraid of the king's anger; for he persevered as though he saw him who is invisible. By faith he kept the Passover and the sprinkling of blood, so that the destroyer of the firstborn would not touch the firstborn of Israel.

Moses is also praised for having been 'unafraid of the king's anger', leading the Israelites out of Egypt and persevering as though he were being personally led by Jesus himself. God revealed to Moses that in order to convince Pharaoh to allow the people of Israel to go, he should sprinkle the blood of a lamb on the door-posts of the Israelite houses so that the destroyer of the firstborn would 'pass over' the firstborn of Israel. Although it must have seemed a strange and unusual thing to do, the people followed the instructions given to them by Moses and the firstborn of the Israelites were, in fact, spared.

Mary, Woman of Faith
In Luke's Gospel, the birth of Jesus is foretold (1:26-38):

> In the sixth month the angel Gabriel was sent by God to a town in Galilee named Nazareth, to a virgin

engaged to a man whose name was Joseph, of the house of David. The virgin's name was Mary. And he came to her and said, 'Greetings, favoured one! The Lord is with you.' But she was much perplexed by his words and pondered what sort of greeting this might be. The angel said to her, 'do not be afraid, Mary, for you have found favour with God. And now, you will conceive in your womb and bear a son, and you will name him Jesus. He will be great, and will be called the Son of the Most High, and the Lord God will give to him the throne of his ancestor David. He will reign over the house of Jacob forever, and of his kingdom there will be no end.'

In the previous section of Luke's Gospel, it is to Zechariah, rather than to Elizabeth his wife, that the angel appears to announce the birth of John the Baptist. In this section, however, the announcement is made to a betrothed virgin, Mary, who was perplexed and did not understand the angel's greeting. It implied that she was especially graced or favoured by God and she did not understand why this should be so, or in what way she was especially favoured. The angel explains that she is to conceive and bear a son named Jesus (literally, 'the Lord saves') who will be 'great' (see Tob 12:22; Pss 48:2; 86:10; 96:4) and called the 'Son of the Most High' (see Gen 14:19-22; Sir 24:2), and who will rule forever on the throne of his ancestor, King David. Joseph was of the house of David (verse 27) and, through marriage, both Mary and her son would belong to the Davidic line.

Mary said to the angel, 'How can this be, since I am a virgin?' The angel said to her, 'The Holy Spirit will come upon you, and the power of the Most High will overshadow you; therefore the child to be born will be holy; he will be called Son of God. And now, your relative Elizabeth in her old age has also conceived a son; and this is the sixth month for her who was said to be barren. For nothing will be impossible with God.' Then Mary said, 'Here am I, the servant of the Lord; let it be with me according to your word.' Then the angel departed from her.

Mary asks how all this could come about since, even though she was engaged to Joseph, she was still a virgin. She may have been thinking of the law forbidding sexual relations till the year of engagement was completed, or it may be that she had made a vow of virginity and that Joseph had accepted that arrangement. In answer to Mary's question, the angel makes it clear that Joseph will not be the father of the child; he will be the Son of God and conceived through the power of the Holy Spirit. Apparently aware that this 'explanation' of how the child was to be conceived must sound strange, the angel then tells Mary that her elderly and barren cousin, Elizabeth, has also conceived. Recognising in faith that nothing will be impossible 'with God', even the conception of a child independently of sexual intercourse, Mary declares herself to be the Lord's servant and submits herself to all that the angel has told her.

In 1987, Pope John Paul II issued an encyclical letter on the Blessed Virgin Mary in the life of the Pilgrim Church, *Redemptoris Mater,* in which he presents Mary as a model for our faith (nn. 13–14). He put particular emphasis on Mary's 'yes' to God, her 'Let it be done' (in Latin *'fiat'*) according to God's word:

> The mystery of the Incarnation was accomplished when Mary uttered her *fiat*: 'Let it be to me according to your word', which made possible, as far as it depended upon her in the divine plan, the granting of her Son's desire. Mary uttered this *fiat in faith*. In faith she entrusted

herself to God without reserve and 'devoted herself totally as the handmaid of the Lord to the person and work of her Son.'[1] And, as the Fathers of the Church teach, she conceived this Son in her mind before she conceived him in her womb: she conceived him, in other words, 'in faith'![2] It is therefore right for Elizabeth to praise Mary with the words: 'and blessed is she who believed *that there would be a fulfilment* of what was spoken to her from the Lord.'

Mary's 'yes' to God was an expression of her faith, the entrusting of herself to God and her dedication to his service. It was also an expression of her willingness to accept the word of God as trustworthy and to believe that what God's messenger had said to her was true. Pope John Paul II compared the role of Mary in the New Testament to that of Abraham in the Old:

Mary's faith can also be *compared to that of Abraham*, whom Saint Paul calls 'our father in faith' (see Rom 4:12). In the salvific economy of God's revelation, Abraham's faith constitutes the beginning of the Old Covenant; Mary's faith at the Annunciation inaugurates the New Covenant. Just as Abraham '*in hope believed against hope*, that he should become the father of many nations' (see Rom 4:18), so Mary, at the Annunciation, having professed her virginity ('How can this be, since I have no husband?'), *believed* that through the power of the Most High, by the power of the Holy Spirit, she would become the Mother of God's Son in accordance with the angel's revelation: 'The child to be born will be called holy, the Son of God' (Lk 1:35).

The Pope also underlined the sense of 'abandoning oneself' in our relationship with God and the recognition that God's ways are not our ways, which is an intrinsic part of authentic faith. He also pointed out that, because we cannot understand the mind of God, the 'light' that faith gives us is always 'dim' and difficult for us to fully comprehend, even for someone like Mary:

> To believe means 'to abandon oneself' to the truth of the word of the living God, knowing and humbly recognising 'how unsearchable are his judgments and how *inscrutable his ways*' (Rom 11:33). Mary, who by the eternal will of the Most High stands, one may say, at the very centre of those 'inscrutable ways' and 'unsearchable judgments' of God, conforms herself to them in the dim light of faith, accepting fully and with a ready heart everything that is decreed in the divine plan.

JESUS AS KING, PROPHET AND PRIEST

Having outlined the main characteristics of the faith of Abraham, Moses and Mary, I will now outline the way in which the faith of the New Testament recognises Jesus as the fulfilment of Old Testament expectations about the Messiah-Christ, and the way in which it describes different individuals as sharing in his teaching, preaching and healing ministry.

After the exile in Babylon, the Jewish people began to focus their hopes on the coming of a future Messiah, who would restore the purity and fervour of their religion and establish a new Golden Age like that under King David and King Solomon. Although presented in different ways by different writers, the coming Messiah was generally seen as a king, a prophet or a priest.

Following a much earlier tradition than its final editing, probably after the exile in Babylon, the Second Book of

Samuel describes the prophet Nathan as telling King David that God would establish one of his descendants as an eternal king:

> When your days are fulfilled, and you lie down with your ancestors, I will raise up your offering after you, who shall come forth from your body, and I will establish his kingdom. He shall build a house for my name, and I will establish the throne of his kingdom forever. I will be his father to him, and he shall be a son to me. When he commits iniquity, I will punish him with a rod such as mortals use, and with blows inflicted by human beings. But I will not take my steadfast love from him, as I took it from Saul, whom I put away from before you. Your house and your kingdom shall be made sure for ever before me: your throne shall be established for ever. (2 Sam 7:12-16)

The Book of Sirach looks forward to the return of the prophet Elijah who would restore the relationship between the tribes of Jacob-Israel and their God:

> You were taken up by a whirlwind of fire, in a chariot with horses of fire. At the appointed time, it is written, you are destined to calm the wrath of God before it breaks out in fury, to turn the hearts of parents to their children, and to restore the tribes of Jacob. (Sirach 48:9-10)

The prophet Malachi looked forward to the coming of a divine messenger who would judge and purify the corrupt Jewish priesthood:

> For the lips of a priest should guard knowledge … But you are turned aside from the way … you have corrupted the covenant of Levi, says the LORD of

Hosts. See, I am sending my messenger to prepare the way before me, and the Lord whom you seek will suddenly come to his temple … he is like a refiner's fire and like fuller's soap; he will sit as a refiner and purifier of silver, and he will purify the descendants of Levi … until they present offerings to the Lord in righteousness. (Mal 2:7-8; 3:1-3)

The New Testament presents Jesus, who is king, prophet and priest, as the fulfilment of these Messianic expectations.

In Matthew's Gospel, the awaited royal Messiah–Christ, born of David's line (see 2 Sam 7:12-16) through the marriage of his mother, Mary, is recognised as the 'king of the Jews', like his ancestor David:

'Where is the child who has been born king of the Jews? For we observed his star at its rising, and have come to pay him homage.' When King Herod heard this, he was frightened, and all Jerusalem with him. (Mt 2:2-3)

In John's Gospel, Jesus makes it clear to Pilate that he is the king of the Jews, but that his kingship is 'not of this world':

Then Pilate entered the headquarters again, summoned Jesus, and asked him, 'Are you the King of the Jews?' … Jesus answered, 'My kingship is not from this world …' Pilate asked him, 'So you are a king?' Jesus answered, 'You say that I am a king. For this I was born, and for this I came into the world, to testify to the truth. Every one who belongs to the truth listens to my voice.' (Jn 18:33-37)

The implication of Jesus being the king of the Jews but having a kingship that 'is not from this world' is that Jesus is, in fact,

God. For, as the enthronement psalms (Pss 93, 95-99) with their refrain 'The LORD is king' imply, God is the true king of Israel. Because his kingship is theological, Jesus rejected any attempt to make himself king in the political sense:

> When Jesus realized that they were about to come and take him by force to make him king, he withdrew again to the mountain by himself. (Jn 6:15)

The kings of Israel were regarded as shepherds who acted on behalf of God, the principal shepherd of his people, and in John's Gospel Jesus is presented as showing his kingly authority through his self-sacrificing pastoral care:

> I am the good shepherd; I know my own and my own know me, just as the Father knows me and I know the Father. And I lay down my life for the sheep. (Jn 10:14-15)

The New Testament presents Jesus as the fulfilment of the prophecy about an Elijah-like prophet who would 'restore the tribes of Jacob' (Sir 48:10). Elijah raised a widow's son from the dead (see 1 Kings 17:23) and, after Jesus does the same, he is described as 'a great prophet' like Elijah:

> The dead man sat up and began to speak ... and they glorified God, saying, 'A great prophet has risen among us!' and 'God has looked favourably on his people!' (Lk 7:15-17)

When he is rejected at Nazareth, Jesus compares himself to Elijah:

> [N]o prophet is acceped in the prophet's hometown ... there were many widows in Israel in the times of Elíjah ... yet Elíjah was sent to none of them except to a widow of Zarephath in Sidon. (Lk 4:24-26)

John the Baptist recognised that he himself was not the expected Messiah or Elijah returned or another prophet like Moses. He implies, however, that Jesus fulfils and is greater than any of these roles:

> They asked him, 'Why then are you baptizing if you are neither the Messiah [Christ], nor Elijah, nor the prophet?' John answered them, 'I baptize with water. Among you stands one whom you do not know, the one who is who coming after me; I am not worthy to untie the thong of his sandal.' (Jn 1:21–27)

Jesus is greater than the greatest of the prophets, because he not only proclaims God's Word but is, in fact, God's Word become flesh:

> And the Word became flesh and lived among us, and we have seen his glory, glory as of a father's only son, full of grace and truth. (Jn 1:14)

The Letter to the Hebrews presents Jesus as the only and eternal High Priest of the new covenant, but also as one who has been tempted just as we are:

> Since, then, we have a great high priest who has passed through the heavens, Jesus, the Son of God, let us hold fast our confession. For we do not have a high priest who is unable to sympathize with our weaknesses, but we have one who in every respect has been tempted as we are, yet without sin. Let us therefore approach the throne of grace with boldness, so that we may receive mercy and find grace to help in time of need. Every high priest chosen from among mortals is put in charge of things pertaining to God on their behalf, to offer gifts and sacrifices for sins. (Heb 4:14–5:1)

Jesus' high priesthood is permanent and his single perfect sacrifice of himself for our sins makes him the only priest of the new Covenant:

> Furthermore, the former priests were many in number ... because they were prevented by death from continuing in office; but he holds his priesthood permanently, because he continues forever ... Unlike the other high priests he has no need to offer sacrifices day after day ... this he did once for all when he offered himself. (Heb 7:23–28)

At his death, the veil separating the Holy of Holies was torn in two, implying that he, himself, had become the new 'Holy of Holies':

> Jesus ... breathed his last. At that moment the curtain of the temple was torn in two, from top to bottom. (Mt 27:50–51)

Jesus' Ministry of Teaching, Preaching and Healing

Matthew's Gospel describes the public ministry of Jesus as being made up of three elements: teaching, preaching and healing:

> Jesus went throughout Galilee, teaching in their synagogues and porclaiming the good news of the kingdom and curing every disease and every sickness among the people. (Mt 4:23)

> Then Jesus went about all the cities and villages, teaching in their synagogues and proclaiming the good news of the kingdom, and curing every disease and every sickness. (Mt 9:35)

Jesus is presented as teaching in the synagogues (see Mt 4:23; Jn 6:59), in the cities (see Mt 11:1), in the temple (see Mt 21:23; Jn 7:14; Jn 8:20) and even daily (see Mt 26:55). Matthew seems to interpret the teaching of Jesus as an expression of his kingly authority. Although he is recognised and addressed as 'Teacher',[3] he discourages the use of this term for others because he is the common Master/Teacher of all people (see Mt 23:8). He teaches with authority (see Mt 7:29; 13:54) and he presents himself as the authorised interpreter and the fulfilment of the Old Testament law (see Mt 5:17).

Jesus continues his kingly ministry of authoritative teaching in and through 'the Twelve' chosen as apostles and through their successors. He commissioned the Eleven to 'make disciples of all nations ... teaching them to observe everything' that he had commanded them (see Mt 28:19-20). Those who followed Jesus and accepted his teaching (see Mt 10:24, 25) were known as his disciples (see Mt 5:1; 8:21, 23; 9:10, 11, 14, 19, etc.) and they included the Twelve (see Mt 10:1; 12:1). Following the death and resurrection of Jesus, the term 'disciple' was used to describe those who came to believe in Jesus, thanks to the teaching ministry of the Twelve (see Acts 6:1-2; 9:10-26). Their teaching (see Acts 2:42; 5:28) and that of the other apostles and elders was recognised as sound instruction or doctrine (see 1 Tim 1:10; 4:6; 6:3; 2 Tim 4:3; Tit 1:9; 2:1). The principal teacher of the Church after Pentecost (Jn 14:26) is, however, the Holy Spirit, with whom all Christians are anointed (see 1 Jn 2:20, 27). It is the Holy Spirit who is responsible for the charism of teaching that enables an individual to interpret the Scriptures and to give moral exhortation (see Rom 12:7; 1 Cor 4:26).

Only Matthew uses the phrase 'the gospel of the kingdom' to describe the content of Jesus' preaching (see Mt 4:23; 9:35; 24:14). It suggests that Jesus saw himself as having been commissioned to bring the victory message of the coming Kingdom of God in the same way that victorious generals freed a slave chosen from their ranks, who was then sent to bring the victory message (*eu-angelion*) to the king and all his subjects. Although both John the Baptist and Jesus preached that 'The kingdom of heaven is at hand' (see Mt 3:1; 4:17), the prophetic mission of Jesus surpassed that of John because it was fulfilled in his own coming.

Jesus continues his prophetic ministry of preaching in and through the Twelve he chose as apostles and through their successors. He commissioned them to preach the same message he had himself preached (see Mt 10:7) and he sent out the Eleven to preach this gospel to the whole world (see Mt 24:14; 26:13). It was not only the Eleven and their successors who were sent out to preach, however, and Luke records that Jesus sent out seventy-two of his disciples, two by two, to proclaim the kingdom (see Lk 10:1-9). After he commissioned them, he said to them:

> Whoever listens to you listens to me, and whoever rejects you rejects me, and whoever rejects me rejects the one who sent me. (Lk 10:16)

Certain individuals (see Agabus in Acts 11:28) receive an informal, charismatic gift of prophecy (see 1 Cor 14:1-15) from the Holy Spirit. This gift helps them to reveal divine secrets (see 1 Cor 13:2) and to exhort, console and build up the community (see 1 Cor 14:3). Like the apostles, prophets have a foundational role in the Church (see 1 Cor 12:28-29; Eph 2:20; 4:11) and St Paul describes authentic prophecy as being in accordance with apostolic authority (see 1 Cor 14:17, 33).

The parable of the sower (see Mk 4:1-20) identifies the seed with the Word that Jesus preaches (see Mk 4:14) and the parable twice invites those present to 'listen' (Mk 4:3, 9). The implication would seem to be that listening to the preaching of God's Word should lead to understanding the Word and to conversion. Presumably, all those who hear the preaching of the Word must also be willing to listen and be converted, if the ministry of those who share in Christ's prophetic office is to be fruitful.

For Matthew, Jesus' healing ministry was the fulfilment of a prophecy in Isaiah 53:4:

> That evening they brought to him many who were possessed with demons; and he cast out the spirits with a word, and cured all who were sick. This was to fulfil what had been spoken through the prophet Isaiah, 'He took our infirmities and bore our diseases.' (Mt 8:16-17)

The way that Luke's Gospel describes the healing of the woman who had been bent double for eighteen years suggests that Jesus understood all physical illness as being held bound by Satan:

> And ought not this woman, a daughter of Abraham whom Satan bound for eighteen years, be set free from this bondage on the Sabbath day? (Lk 13:16)

This association between healing and liberation from Satan's power suggests that the healing ministry of Jesus was seen as part of his sanctifying or priestly role.

Jesus continues his own priestly ministry of healing and sanctification in and through the Twelve he chose as apostles and through their successors. He commissioned the Twelve to 'cure every disease and every sickness' (Mt 10:1), telling them, 'Cure the sick' (Mt 10:8). It was not only the Twelve and their successors who were sent out to heal, however, and Luke records that Jesus sent out seventy-two of his disciples, two by two, to heal the sick (see Lk 10:1-9). St Paul recognises that the Holy Spirit also gives 'gifts of healing' to particular individuals (see 1 Cor 12:9).

Faith in Christ's priestly authority over the effects of evil in our world was needed in order to be healed by him. Jesus said to Jairus, 'Only believe, and she will be saved' (Lk 8:50). On three occasions, Luke records Jesus as telling those who have been healed that it was their faith that made them well (see Lk 8:48; 17:19; 18:42). Faith in Christ's authority over evil is also, presumably, a necessary condition of being healed through those who today share in Christ's priestly office of healing.

Kingly Service, Prophetic Witness and Priestly Worship in the Catechism

Although they are often remembered and celebrated, those who have received a recognised hierarchical or charismatic sharing in Christ's teaching, preaching or healing ministry are, and have always been, a minority among the People of God. Being incorporated into Christ and into the Church through Baptism, Confirmation and Eucharist gives us all a share in his kingly service, prophetic witness and priestly worship. For the majority, however, it does not involve the formal conferring of an ordained ministry or the public recognition of a particular charismatic gift. It is rather in their experience of participating in the priestly prayer and worship of Christ that they share in Christ's priesthood. They share in his kingly authority by their victory over the power of sin and by their participation in his obedience to the command to love God and neighbour. And it is through their declaration by word and deed that they believe in him that they share in his prophetic witness. Their sharing in Christ's office of king, prophet and priest mirrors the hidden years before Jesus began his public ministry, rather than the few public years that are the primary focus of the Gospels.

Vatican II's two Constitutions on the Church, *Lumen gentium* and *Gaudium et spes*, outline the priestly, prophetic and kingly dimensions of the laity's vocation in the following excerpts:

All the laity's works, prayers and apostolic undertakings ... become spiritual sacrifices acceptable to God through Jesus Christ (see 1 Pet 2:5), which, in the Eucharistic celebration, together with the sacrifice of the Lord's Body, are most fittingly offered to the Father. Thus the laity too, as worshippers doing good everywhere, consecrate the world itself to God. (*Lumen gentium* 34)

[Lay people] are called ... to be witnesses to Christ in all circumstances and at the very heart of the community of mankind. (*Gaudium et spes* 43.4)

[Christ] ... both establishes the laity as witnesses and provides them with the appreciation of the faith (*sensus fidei*) and the grace of the word (see Acts 2:17-18; Rev 19:10) so that the power of the Gospel may shine out in daily family and social life. (*Lumen gentium* 35)

Even by their secular activity the laity must help one another to greater holiness of life, so that the world may be filled with the spirit (*spiritu*) of Christ and more effectively bring about its destiny in justice, in love and in peace ... Moreover, by uniting their forces, let the laity so remedy the institutions and conditions of the world when the latter are an inducement to sin, that these may be conformed to the norms of justice, favouring rather than hindering the practice of virtue. (*Lumen gentium* 36)

The priestly, prophetic and kingly aspects of Christian life are described in greater detail in the *Catechism of the Catholic Church* (1992). Like the *Catechism of the Council of Trent*, the 1992 *Catechism* has a four-part structure that might be described as Creed, Cult, Code and Canticle.[4] The sections on Cult (worship) and Canticle (prayer) correspond to the priestly dimensions of the life of faith and the sections on

Creed and Code correspond, respectively, to the prophetic and kingly dimensions. The first part of the *Catechism*, on the Profession of Faith, outlines the way in which those who believe in Christ share in his prophetic witness. Part two, the celebration of the Christian mystery, describes the way in which the Church's liturgy facilitates our sharing in his priestly worship. The third part, Life in Christ, which includes the Ten Commandments, outlines the way in which Christ's faithful share in his victory and kingly authority over sin and death. Part four, on Christian prayer, focuses on the way in which Christ's disciples share in his priestly prayer.

In his introduction to part four of the *Catechism of the Catholic Church* (1992), Christoph Schönborn[5] notes that 'a *catechism* does not cite theologians but rather saints, whether they be theologians or "simple believers"'. He also points out that it had been proposed that 'one begin reading the *Catechism*' with the last part on Christian Prayer.[6] Picking up on both of these suggestions, I will begin by outlining what the Catholic Church believes about prayer and focus on what Schönborn calls 'the witness of the saints, in whom the faith becomes present and real'.[7] Although the often exceptional charisms they receive from the Holy Spirit distinguish them from the great majority of Christ's disciples, whose gifts and graces are generally of a less spectacular kind, the faith experience of the saints is an important gift to the People of God. Allowing for the diversity of circumstances and temperaments, both in the saints concerned and in our own lives, their experience provides a reliable norm for our lives of faith, hope and love.

Notes

1. Vatican II's Dogmatic Constitution on the Church, *Lumen gentium* 56.
2. See *Lumen gentium* 53, 56.

3. See Mt 8:19; 9:11; 12:38; 17:24; 19:16; 22:16, 24, 36; 26:18.
4. See the *Catechism*, n. 13.
5. Christoph Schönborn OP, then professor of theology at Freiburg in Switzerland and later Cardinal Archbishop of Vienna, was head of the editorial committee that prepared the draft of the 1992 *Catechism of the Catholic Church*.
6. Joseph Ratzinger and Christoph Schönborn, *Introduction to the Catechism of the Catholic Church* (San Francisco: Ignatius Press, 1994), 95.
7. Ibid.

Chapter 2

FAITH AND PRAYER

Part four of the Catechism, Christian prayer, focuses on the way in which the faith of Christ's disciples enables them to share in his priestly prayer. This chapter outlines the guidance that the Catechism gives us about prayer. Three witnesses to the prayer tradition of the Church have been chosen to give an example of what that guidance might mean in practice.

CHRYSOSTOM, TERESA AND THÉRÈSE AS MODELS OF PRAYER

The three writers most frequently cited in the section on prayer in the *Catechism* are St Augustine of Hippo (354–430), cited ten times,[1] St Cyprian, cited six times,[2] and St John Chrysostom, also cited six times.[3] The only women cited are the two Carmelite Doctors of the Church, St Teresa of Jesus, cited twice,[4] and St Thérèse of the Child Jesus, cited only once.[5] In choosing three of these saints as witnesses to the Church's faith tradition, I want, as far as possible, to balance the genders and to include representatives of the traditions of the early Church, both Eastern and Western, some important figures of the Middle Ages, as well as some more contemporary saints. Given that very few women are cited in the *Catechism*, I have chosen to include both St Teresa and St Thérèse among the models of prayer presented in this chapter. For reasons of gender balance, and in order to include a representative of the Eastern tradition, I have chosen another

Doctor of the Church, St John Chrysostom, as the third witness to the prayer tradition of the Church. St Augustine will be one of the models chosen in a later chapter. I will also consider the prayer experience of the three models of faith that we explored in the opening chapter: Abraham, Moses and the Blessed Virgin Mary.

St John Chrysostom (349–407)[6]

St John Chrysostom was born at Antioch and was raised by his mother when his father, a high-ranking military officer, died soon after his birth. He received Baptism in his late teens or early twenties and was tonsured after he received the minor ecclesiastical order of reader. Trained in rhetoric by the pagan teacher Libanius, he studied theology under Diodore of Tarsus before becoming a hermit in his mid-twenties. The extreme asceticism of his hermit lifestyle damaged his stomach and kidneys and he was forced to return to Antioch about two years later. Following his ordination as a deacon in 381 and as a presbyter (priest) in 386, he became famous as a preacher (Chrysostom means 'golden mouth'). His *Homilies* on various books of the Bible show his concern for the spiritual and material needs of the poor:

> Do you wish to honour the body of Christ? Do not ignore him when he is naked. Do not pay him homage in the temple clad in silk, only then to neglect him outside where he is cold and ill-clad. He who said: 'This is my body' is the same who said: 'You saw me hungry and you gave me no food', and 'Whatever you did to the least of my brothers you did also to me' … What good is it if the Eucharistic table is overloaded with golden chalices when your brother is dying of hunger? Start by satisfying his hunger and then with what is left you may adorn the altar as well.[7]

In 398, at the age of forty-nine, Chrysostom was persuaded, somewhat unwillingly, to become Archbishop of Constantinople, a position that gave him a status that was higher than most of the officials in the imperial court. During his time as archbishop, he set about harmonising the liturgical life of the Church by revising the prayers and rubrics for the celebration of the Eucharist. To this day, the Divine Liturgy of St John Chrysostom is the norm for celebrating the Eucharist among Eastern Orthodox and most Eastern Catholic Churches.

In 401, Chrysostom deposed six bishops who were guilty of simony at a synod held in Ephesus. When Chrysostom refused to host the lavish parties that the wealthy and powerful expected, and when he criticised the lavish lifestyle of the imperial court, he made many enemies, including Aelia Eudoxia, the wife of the Eastern Emperor, Arcadius. His appointment as archbishop had been opposed by Patriarch Theophilus of Alexandria, who accused him of supporting the discredited opinions of Origen. Together with Aelia Eudoxia, Patriarch Theophilus and more than thirty other bishops brought twenty-nine charges against Chrysostom at the Synod of the Oak in 403 and he was deposed and exiled to Bithynia. There was an accident in the palace on the night of his arrest, prompting pangs of conscience in Aelia Eudoxia, and he was soon recalled and reinstated as archbishop.

When he denounced the dedication ceremonies of a silver statue of Aelia Eudoxia near his cathedral late in 403, however, he was banished to the Caucasus in Armenia. Pope Innocent I protested to the Emperor about his banishment and, in 405, a papal delegation was sent to Constantinople to secure Chrysostom's release, but to no avail. By means of his letters, Chrysostom continued to exert considerable influence in Constantinople and, as a result, he was sent to an even more remote exile in Pitiunt in Abkhazia. St John Chrysostom never reached his place of exile because he died at Comana in 407 on his way there.

The body of extant writings that St John Chrysostom left behind is the largest among the Greek Fathers. Although his best known work is probably his treatise on *The Priesthood*, his writings consist mostly of homilies on Scripture, including a commentary on the Lord's Prayer in the Gospel of Matthew. In one of his homilies on prayer, we read:

> Prayer is the light of the soul, giving us true knowledge of God. It is a link mediating between God and man. By prayer the soul is borne up to heaven and in a marvellous way embraces the Lord. This meeting is like that of an infant crying on its mother, and seeking the best of milk. The soul longs for its own needs and what it receives is better than anything to be seen in the world. Prayer is a precious way of communicating with God, it gladdens the soul and gives repose to its affections. You should not think of prayer as being a matter of words. It is a desire for God, an indescribable devotion, not of human origin, but the gift of God's grace.[8]

In 438, thirty years after Chrysostom died, his successor, St Proclus, brought his remains to Constantinople. The relics of St John Chrysostom were looted by some Crusaders during the sack of Constantinople in 1204 and taken to Rome, but they were returned to the Orthodox Church by Pope John Paul II exactly a thousand years later in 2004. His silver and jewel-encrusted skull and his right hand are now kept in the Vatopedi Monastery on Mount Athos and a number of miraculous healings have been attributed to them.

St Teresa of Avila (1515–1582)

Teresa Muñoz Cepeda de Ahumada, known to history as St Teresa of Avila, entered the Carmelite monastery of the Incarnation at Avila in 1536 when she was twenty-one. For nearly twenty years she struggled because she was unable to choose between what she owed God and her attachments to the world:

> When I was experiencing the enjoyments of the world, I felt sorrow when I recalled what I owed to God. When I was with God, my attachments to the world disturbed me. This is a war so troublesome that I don't know how I was able to suffer it even a month, much less for so many years.[9]

Her 'conversion' began during Lent of 1554, when she was about thirty-nine years old:

> It happened one day entering the oratory, I saw a statue they had borrowed for a certain feast to be celebrated in the house. It represented the much wounded Christ and was very devotional so that beholding it I was utterly distressed in seeing him that way, for it well represented what He suffered for us. I felt so keenly aware of how poorly I thank Him for those wounds that, it seemed to me, my heart broke. Beseeching Him to strengthen me once and for all that I might not offend Him, I threw myself down before Him with the greatest outpouring of tears … I think I then said that I would not rise from there until He granted what I was begging Him for. I believe certainly this was beneficial to me, because from that time I went on improving.[10]

A few years later, during the Autumn of 1560, a group of sisters in the Convent of the Incarnation wondered about the possibility of reforming the mitigated Carmelite Rule observed in that convent to bring it more in line with the rule followed by the Discalced Franciscan nuns in Avila. Nothing definite was decided at that time, but Teresa says that, one day after communion, the Lord gave her 'the most explicit commands to work for this aim' with all her might.

In the first version of her autobiography, often known as her *Life* or as *The Book of Her Life* (1561), she outlines four different approaches to prayer, which she presents as four different ways of drawing water for our spiritual garden:

> Beginners must realize that in order to give delight to the Lord they are starting to cultivate a garden on very barren soil, full of abominable weeds. His Majesty pulls up the weeds and plants good seed. Now let us keep in mind that all of this is already done by the time a soul is determined to practice prayer and has begun to make use of it. As with the help of God we must strive like good gardeners to get these plants to grow and take pains to water them so that they don't wither but come to bud and flower and give forth a most pleasant fragrance to provide refreshment for this Lord of ours. Then he will often come to take delight in this garden and find His joy among these virtues.

> But let us see now how it must be watered so that we may understand what we have to do, the labor this will cost us, whether the labor is greater than the gain, and for how long it must last. It seems to me the garden can be watered in four ways. You may draw water from a well (which is for us a lot of work). Or you may get it by means of a water wheel and aqueducts in such a way that it is obtained by turning the crank of the water wheel. (I have drawn it this way sometimes – the method involves less work than the other, and you get more water.) Or it may flow from a river or a stream. (The garden is watered much better by this means because the ground is more fully soaked, and there is no need to water so frequently – and much less work for the gardener.) Or the water may be provided by a great deal of rain. (For the Lord waters

the garden without any work on our part – and this way is incomparably better than all the others mentioned.)[11]

In 1562, a new foundation in Avila known as St Joseph's was established, and 'Teresa of Jesus', as she was now known, became its prioress. Her book, *Way of Perfection*, was written in 1565 in order to set down 'certain things about prayer' for her sisters. In 1569, the first convent of contemplative friars was formally opened at Duruelo by the Carmelite provincial who offered Mass and received the profession (according to the unmitigated Carmelite Rule of 1247) of three friars, one of whom was John de Yepes, who had entered the Carmelite convent of St Anne in 1563 at the age of twenty-one and who was to become known to history as St John of the Cross. In 1571, Teresa returned to her original Convent of the Incarnation to bring about its reform. About 1577, again for the benefit of her sisters, she wrote the *Interior Castle*, in which the spiritual life is presented as a journey through seven successive 'shells' or 'dwelling places' (*moradas*) to the centre of our 'interior castle', where Jesus our king dwells.

Having been beatified in 1614, Teresa of Avila became the first Carmelite saint to be officially canonised in 1622. Along with St Catherine of Siena, she was proclaimed one of the first two women Doctors of the Universal Church in 1970. In his homily on that occasion, Pope Paul VI quoted St Teresa's own words when he described her 'sublime and simple message of prayer' as an exhortation to

> understand the great good God does for a soul that willingly disposes itself for the practice of prayer ... For mental prayer in my opinion is nothing else than an intimate sharing between friends; it means taking time frequently to be alone with Him who we know loves us.[12]

St Thérèse of Lisieux (1873–1897)

Marie Françoise Thérèse Martin was born in Alençon, Normandy, on 2 January 1873, the youngest of nine children born to Louis and Zélie Martin, who were themselves beatified in 2008. Thérèse was a warm and affectionate child, and her early memories are happy ones:

> God was pleased all through my life to surround me with *love*, and the first memories I have are stamped with smiles and the most tender caresses. But although He placed so much *love* near me, He also sent much love into my little heart, making it warm and affectionate. I loved Mama and Papa very much and showed my tenderness for them in a thousand ways, for I was very expressive.[13]

In December 1876, Zélie Martin discovered that the 'fibrous tumour' in her breast was inoperable. When she died in 1877 at the age of forty-six, Thérèse looked on her older sister, Pauline, as her second 'mother' and she became very attached to her father, her dear 'King'. It was through him that she first became aware of the Carmelites:

> Each afternoon I took a walk with Papa. We made our visit to the Blessed Sacrament together, going to a different church each day and it was in this way we entered the Carmelite chapel for the first time ... Papa showed me the choir grille and told me there were nuns behind it. They were beautiful days for me, those days when my 'dear King' took me fishing with him. Sometimes I would try to fish with my little line, but I preferred to go *alone* and sit down on the grass bedecked with flowers, and then my thoughts became very profound indeed! Without knowing what it was to meditate, my soul was absorbed in real prayer ... Earth then seemed to be a place of exile and I could dream only of heaven.[14]

In 1882, when she was about eight and a half, she lost her 'second mother' when her sister Pauline entered the Carmel at Lisieux. Shortly afterwards, while on a visit to the Carmel, Thérèse told the prioress that she also had a vocation to Carmel. The following year she became very ill over a period of about three months, but she was instantly (and, she believed, miraculously) cured while praying before a statue of Our Lady of Victories and earnestly imploring the help of the Blessed Virgin:

> All of a sudden the Blessed Virgin appeared *beautiful* to me, so *beautiful* that never had I seen anything so attractive; her face was suffused with an ineffable benevolence and tenderness, but what penetrated to the very depths of my soul was the *'ravishing smile of the Blessed Virgin'*. At that instant, all my pain disappeared, and two large tears glistened on my eyelashes and flowed down my cheeks silently, but they were tears of unmixed joy.[15]

During 1884, following the conventions of the time, Thérèse made her First Communion and, about a month later, her Confirmation.

Up to the age of thirteen, there was little to distinguish Thérèse Martin from other young women of the time. She had always been affectionate and pious and, up to then, seems to have been a somewhat spoilt, sensitive and touchy child. Shortly before her fourteenth birthday, however, during Christmas 1886, she experienced the apparently instant, but profound change that she would later call 'the grace of leaving my childhood, in a word, the grace of my complete conversion'.[16] Accustomed to receiving presents that had been left in her slippers when she returned from Midnight Mass, she overheard her father saying, 'Well, fortunately, this will be the last year!' Recognising the situation as providential, and that

'Jesus desired to show me that I was to give up the defects of my childhood', she discovered the strength of soul to control the poundings of her heart and joyfully thanked her family for their presents.[17] She later commented:

> I felt charity enter into my soul and the need to forget myself and to please others ... I experienced a great desire to work for the conversion of sinners, a desire I hadn't felt so intensely before.[18]

She wanted to serve God in any way she could and to work for the conversion of souls in whatever way God might want. At one point, she thought of becoming a foreign missionary. At another, she felt she was called to suffer for the salvation of the world, like Jesus.

Early the following year, in 1887, Marie, her eldest sister, joined their sister Pauline when she also entered the Carmel in Lisieux. Soon afterwards, when a triple murderer by the name of Henri Pranzini was sentenced to death by guillotine, Thérèse took on the job of praying for his conversion. When she heard that he had embraced the crucifix on the scaffold she regarded it as proof that her prayers had been answered. Reflecting on what had happened, she gradually came to see that the best way she could help in the conversion of souls was to devote herself to contemplative prayer. And so, at the age of fourteen, she also applied to enter the convent of Discalced Carmelite nuns at Lisieux, where two of her sisters, Pauline (Sr Agnes of Jesus) and Marie (Marie of the Sacred Heart), were already nuns. After being initially rejected because she was too young, Thérèse was eventually allowed to enter the red-bricked Carmel in Lisieux on 9 April 1888 at the age of fifteen.

During her nine years there, Thérèse concentrated on her own life of prayer, quietly performing the duties assigned to her and following the Carmelite rule with great faithfulness. In 1893, when she was twenty, Thérèse was appointed acting mistress of novices, an office she held for the last four years of her life. In September 1894, Thérèse's older sister, Céline, entered the Carmel as Sr Genevieve of the Holy Face. As acting novice mistress, Thérèse was given responsibility for Céline's formation. In August 1895, when Thérèse's cousin Marie Guerin also entered the Carmel at Lisieux, Thérèse was again given responsibility for her formation.

Thérèse wrote the first section of the spiritual memoirs, *The Story of a Little White Flower*, as a feast day present for her blood-sister, Pauline (Mother Agnes of Jesus), between January 1895 and January 1896. She wrote the second section, a short spiritual essay for and at the request of her blood-sister, Marie (Sr Marie of the Sacred Heart), during September 1896. During June and July 1897, she wrote the third section for the newly re-elected prioress, Mother Gonzague. Shortly after she completed the third part of her memoirs, in conversation with Mother Agnes (her sister Pauline) on 17 July 1897, she explained what her 'Little Way' was all about:

> I feel that my mission is about to begin, my mission of making others love God as I love him, my mission of teaching my little way to souls … I want to spend my heaven in doing good on earth.[19]

During the last eighteen months of her life (April 1896 to September 1897), she underwent great physical pain and illness and a profound spiritual darkness. She described it as a 'dark tunnel', a time when she was covered in 'thickest darkness', tempted to suicide and blasphemy, wanting to believe but finding it almost impossible to do so.[20]

> Then suddenly the fog that surrounds me becomes more dense; it penetrates my soul and envelops it in such a way that it is impossible to discover within it the sweet image of my Fatherland; everything has disappeared!

When I want to rest my heart fatigued by the darkness that surrounds it by the memory of the luminous country after which I aspire, my torment redoubles; it seems to me that the darkness, borrowing the voice of sinners, says mockingly to me: 'You are dreaming about the light, about a fatherland embalmed in the sweetest perfumes; you are dreaming about the *eternal* possession of the Creator of all these marvels; you believe that one day you will walk out of this fog that surrounds you! Advance, advance; rejoice in death which will give you not what you hope for but a night still more profound, the night of nothingness.'[21]

In this situation, she adopted an attitude of spiritual weakness, resolving, like others faced with pain and suffering, to 'carry our crosses weakly ... suffer weakly and without courage'.

Thérèse died on 30 September 1898 and a version of her autobiography was published privately and mailed to a number of other Carmels the following year. Between 1898 and 1913, more than a million copies were printed in various languages. In 1914, Pope St Pius X called her 'the greatest Saint of modern times', and, because of her amazing popularity, the Vatican waived its usual fifty-year rule and allowed investigations for beatification to begin. Thérèse was beatified in 1923, twenty-six years after her death, and she was canonised as a Virgin in 1925. Two years later, in 1927, Pope Pius XI recognised the importance of her prayer and intercession for the missionaries when he declared Thérèse principal co-patron, with St Francis Xavier, of the Missions. When Pope John Paul II declared her a Doctor of the Universal Church in 1997, he described her as a master of 'the science of divine love' who had 'penetrated the mysteries' of the infancy of Jesus and whose Little Way was both 'unique' and at the same time 'the most basic and most universal truth'.[22] In his homily for Mission Sunday in 1997, the Pope said:

Among the Doctors of the Church, Thérèse of the Child Jesus and Holy Face is the youngest, but her spiritual itinerary shows such maturity and the intuitions of her faith expressed in her writings are so vast and so profound, that they merit a place among the great spiritual masters.

PRAYER IN THE CHRISTIAN LIFE[23]

It is principally for the witness of their lives of prayer, for the way in which their faith gave concrete shape to their relationships with God and for their teaching on prayer, that John Chrysostom, Teresa and Thérèse are honoured as Doctors of the Universal Church. The witness of their lives and of their teaching can help us to appreciate and understand the meaning of prayer in our own lives. For them, prayer is the gift by which our longing for God finds expression, the way in which we are to respond to God, the living expression of the inner life of the Church.

Discovering the Power of Prayer

Describing prayer as 'a vital and personal relationship with the living and true God', the *Catechism of the Catholic Church* begins its section on 'What is Prayer?' with the following quotation from St Thérèse of Lisieux:

> For me, prayer is an aspiration of the heart; it is a simple look turned to heaven, it is a cry of gratitude and love in the midst of trial as well as joy.[24]

Thérèse tells us that, after her mother's death, her older sister, Pauline, used to ask 'if I had raised my heart to God'[25] before dressing her every morning.[26] She says that, even as a child, her heart was filled 'with a sweet melancholy' when she heard 'the indistinct notes of some military music' and that 'Earth then seemed to be a place of exile and I could dream only of heaven'.[27] Her recognition of God's presence was a great joy to her:

> I remember one day when the beautiful blue sky became suddenly overcast and soon the thunder began to roll and the lighting to flash through the dark clouds. I saw it strike a short distance away, and, far from being frightened, I was thrilled with delight because God seemed to be so close![28]

Although the earth seemed a place of exile for her, Thérèse was not blind to the great beauty and grandeur of creation. Standing by the window during her train journey to Rome before entering Carmel, she remembered seeing

> Switzerland with its mountains whose summits were lost in the clouds, its graceful waterfalls gushing forth in a thousand different ways, its deep valleys literally covered with gigantic ferns and scarlet heather.[29]

She described 'these beauties of nature, poured out *in such profusion*' as raising her soul 'to heaven which was pleased to scatter such masterpieces on a place of exile destined to last only a day'.[30] At that time, she said to herself:

> When I am a prisoner in Carmel and trials come my way and I have only a tiny bit of starry heavens to contemplate, I shall remember what my eyes have seen today. This thought will encourage me and I shall easily forget my own little interest, recalling the grandeur and power of God, this God whom I want to love alone.[31]

For Thérèse, Carmel was the place where she could carry out her apostolate of prayer most effectively. Reflecting on the way her prayer for the triple murderer, Pranzini, had brought him to embrace the crucifix before being guillotined in 1887, she had come to a deep appreciation of the power of prayer, especially when we ask for what we want with the simplicity and confidence of a child. She had a thirst for the souls of 'great sinners' like Pranzini and she says that she 'burned with a desire to snatch them from the eternal flames'.[32] She tells us that she had originally struggled to understand the emphasis that St Teresa of Avila had placed on praying for priests: 'To pray for sinners attracted me, but to pray for the souls of priests whom I believed to be as pure as crystal seemed puzzling to me.' Her first-hand encounters with a number of priests during her journey to Rome had opened her eyes somewhat, and she came to realise that 'though their dignity raises them above the angels, they are nevertheless weak and fragile men'.[33] By the time she made her profession as a Carmelite, she was able to describe the purpose of her life in Carmel in the following terms: 'I came to save souls and especially to pray for priests'.[34]

Near the end of her life, she described the power of prayer as being like that of the influence of a queen on the divine King:

> How great is the power of *Prayer*! One could call it a Queen who has at each instant free access to the King and who is able to obtain whatever she asks. To be heard it is not necessary to read from a book some beautiful formula composed for the occasion. If this were the case... alas! I would have to be pitied! ... Outside the *Divine Office* which I am very unworthy to recite, I do not have the courage to force myself to search out *beautiful* prayers in books ... there are so many of them it really gives me a headache! ... I cannot recite them all and not knowing which to choose, I do like children who do not know how to read, I say very simply to God

what I wish to say, without composing beautiful sentences, and He always understands me ... For me, *prayer* is an aspiration of the heart, it is a simple glance directed to heaven, it is a cry of gratitude and love in the midst of trial as well as joy; finally it is something great, supernatural, which expands my soul and unites me to Jesus.[35]

The Revelation of Prayer[36]

The *Catechism of the Catholic Church* reminds us that 'God calls every being from nothingness into existence' and that, like the angels, human beings are 'capable of acknowledging "how majestic is the name of the Lord in all the earth"' (Ps 8:5) (n. 2566). We may have lost our likeness to God because of sin, but our hearts yearn for the One who called us into being. When we are drawn into the mysterious encounter with God that is prayer, we discover that we are not setting out in search of a God who, up to then, has been unaware of us. We are, rather, responding to the call that is implicit in our own existence. It is in the ongoing drama of that response and encounter that we come to know God and that we come to know ourselves as part of God's creation:

As God gradually reveals himself and reveals man to himself, prayer appears as a reciprocal call, a covenant drama. Through words and actions, this drama engages the heart. It unfolds throughout the whole history of salvation. (n. 2567)

Abraham, Moses and Mary, the three models of faith that we have already considered, illustrate the way in which the nature and practice of prayer has gradually been revealed to us by God.

Our response in prayer to God's call is not primarily verbal. The prayer of Abraham, our father in faith, is evident first of all in his obedience to the Word of God calling him to leave his own country and move to another country where he would become the father of a great nation:

> When God calls him, Abraham goes forth 'as the Lord had told him' (Gen 12:4) ... Only later does Abraham's first prayer in words appear: a veiled complaint reminding God of his promises which seem unfulfilled (see Gen 15:2–3). (n. 2570)

Abraham's fidelity to God's call was put to the test when he was asked to sacrifice his son and heir, Isaac. We are shocked that he was willing to do the awful deed, but the Letter to the Hebrews (11:19) recognises that he 'considered that God was able to raise men even from the dead' and that even the death of his son and heir could not prevent God fulfilling his promises. When the angel prevented him sacrificing his son, Abraham learned that God does not, in fact, want us to sacrifice our sons because 'God himself will provide the lamb for a burnt offering' (Gen 22:8). Confident of God's righteousness, Abraham interceded again and again for the people of Sodom:

> Then Abraham came near and said, 'Will you indeed sweep away the righteous with the wicked? Suppose there are fifty righteous within the city; will you then sweep away the place and not forgive it for the fifty righteous who are in it? Far be it from you to do such a thing, to slay the righteous with the wicked, so that the righteous fare as the wicked! Far be that from you! Shall not the Judge of all the earth do what is just?' And the LORD said, 'If I find at Sodom fifty righteous in the city, I forgive the whole place for their sake.' (Gen 18:23–26)

The *Catechism* describes Abraham's response to God in prayer 'as a battle of faith marked by trust in God's faithfulness and by certitude in the victory promised to perseverance' (n. 2592).

Just as God took the initiative in calling Abraham, God also addressed Moses from the midst of the burning bush. In the dialogue that follows, during which God confides in Moses that he is aware of the sufferings of his people, the Israelites, 'Moses also learns how to pray: he balks, makes excuses, above all questions: and it is in response to his question that the Lord confides his ineffable name, which will be revealed through his mighty deeds.'[37]

> But Moses said to God, 'If I come to the Israelites and say to them, "The God of your ancestors has sent me to you"; and they ask me, "What is his name?" what shall I say to them?' God said to Moses, 'I AM WHO I AM.' He said further, 'Thus you shall say to the Israelites this: "I AM has sent me to you."' (Exod 3:13-14)

According to the book of Exodus (33:11), 'The LORD used to speak to Moses face to face, as one speaks to a friend.' Thanks to his intimacy with God, Moses 'becomes the most striking example of intercessory prayer' in the Old Testament:

> He does not pray for himself but for the people whom God made his own. Moses already intercedes for them during the battle with the Amalekites and prays to obtain healing for Miriam (see Exod 17:8-12; Num 12:13-14). But it is chiefly after their apostasy that Moses 'stands in the breach' before God in order to save his people (Ps 106:23; see Exod 32:1-34:9). (n. 2577)

In what the *Catechism* describes as the 'mysterious battle' of his intercession with God on behalf of God's sinful people, Moses comes to recognise that God's own glory is at stake and that God 'cannot forsake the people that bears his name' (n. 2577). His commitment to us is unconditional. It is our response and commitment to God that is in doubt.

In her response to God in prayer, Mary of Nazareth, who became the Mother of God, draws together the lived experience of Israel's prayer. Her *Magnificat* (Lk 1:46-55) recognises that, through her, God was finally fulfilling the promises made 'to Abraham and to his descendants for ever'. Entrusting herself totally to God's call in faith, as Abraham and Moses had done, she declared her willingness to become the mother of God's incarnate Son: 'Here I am, the servant of the Lord; let it be with me according to your word' (Lk 1:38).

It is, however, only in Jesus, the incarnate Son of God, that the nature and meaning of prayer is revealed to us in all its fullness. Learning from his mother how to pray 'in the words and rhythms of the prayer of his people, in the synagogue at Nazareth and the Temple of Jerusalem', his prayer sprang, in fact, from an otherwise secret source, as he intimates at the age of twelve: 'I must be in my Father's house' (Lk 2:49). In him, 'the filial prayer, which the Father awaits from his children, is finally to be lived out by the only Son in his humanity, with and for men' (n. 2599). Jesus is not only the most perfect example of human prayer. Fully sharing our humanity, he is the only Son of the Father and his prayer is, therefore, at one and the same time both the prayer of the only Son who reveals the Father to us and the most perfect example of humanity's response to God in prayer. Committing himself humbly to the loving will of the Father, Jesus prays to the Father before the decisive moments of his mission, such as his Baptism by John, his Transfiguration and his Passion (see Lk 3:21; 9:28; 22:41-44).[38]

In the days of his flesh, Jesus offered up prayers and supplications, with loud cries and tears, to the one who was able to save him from death, and he was heard because of his reverent submission. Although he was a Son, he learned obedience through what he suffered, and having been made perfect, he became the source of eternal salvation for all who obey him. (Heb 5:7-9)

Jesus often prays in solitude and secret (see Mk 1:35; 6:46; Lk 5:16) and he teaches his disciples to pray with a purified and repentant heart (see Mt 5:23-24, 44-45), with lively and persevering faith (Mt 7:7-11) and with the boldness of a son and heir (see Mk 9:23; 11:24). He calls them to be watchful in prayer so that they do not fall into temptation (see Lk 21:34-36; 22:40, 46). And, in a radical departure that reflects his unique status as the only Son of the Father, Jesus invites his disciples to present their petitions to God in his name (see Jn 14:13).[39]

Following the Ascension, the disciples of Jesus 'were constantly devoting themselves to prayer' (Acts 1:14) as they awaited the outpouring of the Holy Spirit, whom the Father would send in his name and who would teach them everything and remind them of all that Jesus had said to them (see Jn 14:26). The Pentecost Spirit formed the early Christian community in its life of prayer, which is founded on the apostolic faith, authenticated by charity and nourished in the Eucharist (see Acts 2:42).[40] The Bible is the primary prayer book of Christians and the disciples of Christ have made their own those texts in the Law of Moses, the Prophets and the Psalms, which find their fulfilment in Christ (see Lk 24:27, 44). The different forms of prayer revealed in the apostolic and canonical Scriptures (blessing, petition, intercession, thanksgiving and praise) remain normative for Christians. The great liturgical and spiritual traditions of the Church show that the Holy Spirit also 'inspires new formulations of the unfathomable mystery of Christ at work in his Church's life, sacraments and mission'.[41]

The Church as a School of Prayer[42]

Shortly after the incident in the Temple in Jerusalem, when Jesus said to Mary and Joseph, 'I must be in my Father's house' (Lk 2:49), we read:

> Then he went down with them and came to Nazareth, and was obedient to them … And Jesus increased in wisdom and in years, and in divine and human favour. (Lk 2:51-52)

It was, presumably, under the influence of Mary and Joseph that Jesus learned the wisdom of the Jewish prayer tradition. His own prayer as God's only Son was the fulfilment of that tradition and, by means of the 'Our Father', he taught his disciples to continue his own, unique form of filial prayer. Thanks to the outpouring of the Pentecost Spirit, whom Jesus described as a spring of water 'gushing up to eternal life' (Jn 4:14), Christ's disciples learn how to participate in Christ's prayer to the Father. In this way, 'the believing and praying Church'[43] has become a living school of prayer. The Word of God, the liturgy of the Church and our daily lives of Christian faith, hope and love are among the many sources of prayer in the Church, 'wellsprings where Christ awaits us to enable us to drink of the Holy Spirit'.[44]

Led by the Holy Spirit, the Church has come to recognise the Trinitarian nature of the prayer of Christ and his disciples. Only the interior teaching of the Holy Spirit makes it possible for us to address God as 'Father' (see Rom 8:15)[45] or to recognise Jesus as Lord (see 1 Cor 12:3).[46] The Holy Spirit has also led the Church to recognise the Virgin Mary's 'singular cooperation with the action of the Holy Spirit' and to associate its prayer in a particular way with hers.[47] As a child, St Thérèse of Lisieux had been miraculously cured while earnestly imploring the help of the Blessed Virgin before a statue of Our Lady of Victories. Her last recorded written words express her 'union of heart with Mary and her total self-giving to her',[48] implying that even if her own power of intercession had enabled her to become Queen of Heaven, she would have greater trust in Mary's intercession than in her own:

> O Mary, if I were Queen of Heaven and you were Thérèse, I would want to be Thérèse so that you might be the Queen of Heaven!!![49]

In keeping with the long tradition of venerating and asking for the intercession of the saints in heaven, Thérèse describes a dream that she had on 10 May 1896, in which she saw the 'Venerable Mother' of the Teresian Carmel, St Teresa of Avila, and Venerable Anne Jesus, the Foundress of Carmel in France:

> I was, up until then, *absolutely indifferent to Venerable Mother Anne of Jesus*. I never invoked her in prayer and the thought of her never came to my mind except when I heard others speak of her, which was seldom. And when I understood to what a degree *she loved me*, how *indifferent* I had been towards her, my heart was filled with love and gratitude, not only for the Saint who had visited me but for all the blessed inhabitants of heaven.[50]

For Thérèse, 'PRAYER which burns with a fire of love' is the lever that enabled the saints of the past to lift the world to God, and she comments that 'it is in this way the saints still militant lift it, and that, until the end of time, the saints to come will lift it'.[51]

The many spiritualities that can be distinguished among the saints in heaven are described by the *Catechism* as 'refractions of the one pure light of the Holy Spirit'. Just as the 'spirit' of the Old Testament prophet Elijah was passed on to Elisha (see 2 Kings 2:9), and just as St Thérèse of Lisieux was given a share in the charism of St Teresa of Avila, the personal charism of some witnesses to God's love for his people can be passed on to give rise to a particular school of Christian spirituality. The Carmelite school, which I have highlighted in this chapter, is one of many different schools of spirituality with which the Church has been blessed. A school of spirituality can also emerge 'at the point of convergence of liturgical and theological currents, bearing witness to the integration of the faith into a particular human environment and its history.'[52] The particular traditions of the different forms of Consecrated Life, the collective charisms of the many New Ecclesial Movements and Communities, and the different ministries associated with ordained ministry, have further enriched the diversity of spiritualities in the Church.

The 'domestic Church' of the Christian family is normally the first place in which we are formed in the Church's tradition of prayer.[53] The many different circumstances of family life need to be recognised, however, and Vatican II's Decree on the Apostolate of the Laity, *Apostolicam actuositatem* 4, says:

> Lay spirituality will take its particular character from the circumstances of one's state in life (married and family life, celibacy, widowhood), from one's state of health and from one's professional and social activity.

Formation in Christian prayer should recognise that personal prayer and family prayer, and more formal liturgical prayer constitute a unity and that particular places are more suited to particular forms of prayer than others.

> The church, the house of God, is the proper place for the liturgical prayer of the parish community. It is also the privileged place for adoration of the real presence of Christ in the Blessed Sacrament.[54]

The *Catechism* points out that the most appropriate place for personal prayer

> [C]an be a 'prayer corner' with the Sacred Scriptures and icons, in order to be there, in secret, before our Father (see Mt 6:6). In a Christian family, this kind of little oratory fosters prayer in common. (n. 2691)

The Church provides formation in Christian prayer in various ways through its ordained ministers, through the various forms of the Consecrated Life, through catechesis and through 'Prayer Groups' of various kinds.[55] The practice of 'spiritual direction' or 'spiritual mentoring', based on the gifts of wisdom, faith and discernment that the Holy Spirit gives to certain of the faithful for the common good, has proved an invaluable help to many.

A Christian's Life of Prayer[56]

Psalm 34 begins, 'I will bless the LORD at all times; his praise shall continually be in my mouth', and 1 Thessalonians 5:17 tells us to 'Pray without ceasing, give thanks in all circumstances'. In Ephesians 6:18 we read, 'Pray in the Spirit at all times, in every prayer and supplication. To that end keep alert and always persevere in supplication for all the saints.'[57] In order to achieve the continual prayer of a life that is dedicated to responding to God's call, we all need to pray at specific times and to participate in the rhythm of prayer that characterises the life of the Church.

> The Tradition of the Church proposes to the faithful certain rhythms of praying intended to nourish continual prayer. Some are daily, such as morning and evening prayer, grace before and after meals, the Liturgy of the Hours. Sundays, centred on the Eucharist, are kept holy primarily by prayer. The cycle of the liturgical year and its great feasts are also basic rhythms of the Christian's life of prayer.[58]

Within this broad framework, the paths by which each believer is led in prayer are those that the Lord has chosen, those that express the personal resolve of that individual's heart. There are, nevertheless, three forms of prayer that can be regarded as characteristic of the Christian tradition:

> The Christian tradition comprises three major expressions of the life of prayer: vocal prayer, meditation, and contemplative prayer. They have in common the recollection of the heart. (n. 2721)

St John Chrysostom reminds us that it is not the number of prayers that we say, but the degree to which our hearts are present to God when we pray that determines whether our vocal prayers are heard: 'Whether or not our prayer is heard depends not on the number of words, but on the fervour of our souls'.[59]

The family background of St Thérèse of Lisieux is unique in that the sanctity of her parents, Blesseds Louis and Zélie Martin, has been formally recognised. Thérèse grew up in a devout family and she was familiar with the rhythm of morning and evening prayer. Each morning, after her older sister, Pauline, had dressed her, they used to kneel down to say their prayers together.[60] Last thing at night, the family went upstairs to say their night prayers together and, 'When prayer was ended we came according to age to bid Papa good night and receive his kiss'.[61] Her family normally attended Mass on Sunday mornings and Vespers followed by Compline and Benediction on Sunday evenings.[62] She would later recall the celebration of the great feasts, the Eucharistic processions and the May devotions of her childhood.[63]

Reciting the Liturgical Hours in the choir at the Carmel in Lisieux every day, Thérèse was familiar with the discipline of uniting her mind with her lips as she recited the Psalms. In her personal prayer, however, Thérèse tells us that she found it difficult to choose from among the sometimes elaborate prayers that were then in vogue. Instead she adopted a more direct approach: 'I say very simply to God what I want to say, without composing beautiful sentences, and he always understands me.'[64] She found that reciting the 'Our Father' and the 'Hail Mary' slowly helped her to pray at times when, as she put it, 'my mind is in such aridity that it is impossible to draw from it one single thought to unite me to God':

> I very slowly recite an 'Our Father' and then the angelic salutation [the 'Hail Mary']; then these prayers give me great delight; they nourish my soul much more than if I had recited them precipitately a hundred times.[65]

For Thérèse, meditation seems to have been primarily a matter of reflection, trying to relate the divine mysteries to her own life.[66] Commenting on her meditation on Jesus' statement that we can have no greater love than to lay down our lives for our friends (Jn 15:13), she wrote:

> [W]hen meditating upon these words of Jesus, I understood how imperfect was my love for my Sisters. I saw that I didn't love them as God loves them.[67]

She tells us, too, that, although she originally found the works of St John of the Cross helped her meditation, there came a time when it was only the Gospels that sustained her during her hours of prayer:

> Ah! how many lights have I not drawn from the works of our holy Father, St John of the Cross! At the ages of seventeen and eighteen I had no other spiritual nourishment; later on, however, all books left me in aridity and I'm still in that state. If I open a book composed by a spiritual author (even the most

beautiful, the most touching book), I feel my heart contract immediately and I read without understanding, so to speak. Or if I do understand, my mind comes to a standstill without the capacity of meditating. In this helplessness, Holy Scripture and the *Imitation* [*of Christ* by St Thomas a Kempis] come to my aid; in them I discover solid and very pure nourishment. But it is especially the gospels that sustain me during my hours of prayer, for in them I find what is necessary for my poor little soul. I am constantly discovering in them new lights, hidden and mysterious meanings.[68]

According to the *Catechism*:

Contemplative prayer is the simple expression of the mystery of prayer. It is a gaze of faith fixed on Jesus, an attentiveness to the Word of God, a silent love. It achieves real union with the prayer of Christ to the extent that it makes us share in his mystery. (n. 2724)

To help us to understand this kind of prayer, the *Catechism* quotes St Teresa of Avila, who describes mental or spiritual prayer (as distinct from vocal or meditative prayer) as being characterised by the kind of intimacy and sharing that is found in a loving friendship:

For mental prayer (*oración mental*) in my opinion is nothing else than an intimate sharing between friends; it means taking time frequently to be alone with Him who we know loves us. (n. 2709)[69]

Thérèse's experience of contemplative prayer is evident, perhaps, in the following text:

I have experienced it [the heat of Jesus' love]; when I *am feeling* nothing, when I am INCAPABLE *of praying*, of practising virtue, then this is the moment for seeking opportunities, *nothings*, which please Jesus more than mastery of the world or even martyrdom suffered with generosity. For example, a smile, a friendly word, when I want to say nothing, or put on a look of annoyance, etc., etc. (...) When I do not have opportunities, I want to tell Him frequently that I love Him; this is not difficult, and it keeps the *fire* going. *Even though* this fire of love would seem to me to have gone out, I would like to throw something on it, and Jesus could then relight it (...) I am not always faithful, but I never get discouraged; I abandon myself into the arms of Jesus.[70]

Both Teresa and Thérèse lived by the Carmelite Rule (1247), which describes human life as 'a trial' (Job 7:1) during which we should 'strive with all care to put on the armour of God' so that we 'may be able to hold out against the ambush of the enemy' (see Eph 6:11). The *Catechism* recognises that the resulting 'spiritual battle' means that prayer is also, necessarily, a battle:

> Prayer presupposes an effort, a fight against ourselves and the wiles of the Tempter. The battle of prayer is inseparable from the necessary 'spiritual battle' to act habitually according to the Spirit of Christ: we pray as we live, because we live as we pray. (n. 2752)

The trials and temptations of the battle of prayer include those that 'cast doubt on the usefulness or even the possibility of prayer' (n. 2753). Sometimes these arise from 'erroneous conceptions of prayer' that lead people to forget that prayer comes 'from the Holy Spirit and not from themselves alone'. For this reason, prayer is not a merely psychological activity, or the effort of concentration needed to reach a mental void, or the adoption of ritualised words or postures, or something that is necessarily incompatible with a busy and demanding lifestyle (n. 2726). For others, the temptation to give up the 'battle of prayer' comes from 'currents of thought' that cultivate a mentality that leaves no room for prayer because they ignore or downplay the spiritual dimension of all human life (n. 2753). We can be tempted to reject anything that cannot be objectively verified by reason or science, anything that is not objectively productive or anything that challenges our sensuality and comfort, and we can be 'taken in' by the view that prayer necessarily involves an escape from reality or a divorce from life (n. 2727).

For many, perhaps, it is our own experience of failure in prayer that makes us lose heart in the 'battle to gain humility, trust, and perseverance'. We may feel discouraged during a period of dryness, for example, we may despair about being liberated from inappropriate attachments and we may struggle to accept that prayer is also God's gift and not simply a matter of our own determination (n. 2728). When we have the sense that our prayers have not been heard, we need to remember that 'we do not know how to pray as we ought' and that 'the prayers that the Spirit makes for God's holy people are always in accordance with the mind of God' (see Rom 8:26-27). 'You ask and do not receive, because you ask wrongly, to spend it on your passions' (Jas 4:3), and we must all learn that God cannot answer us if we ask with a divided heart (see Jas 4:4), 'for he desires our well-being, our life' (n. 2737).

Like the *Catechism* (nn. 2754–5), St Thérèse recognised distractions, dryness, lack of faith and discouragement (*acedia*) as among the principal difficulties and temptations that we face in the battle of prayer. She normally prepared for receiving Holy Communion by inviting 'all the angels and saints to come and conduct a magnificent concert' in her soul so that, when Jesus descended into her heart, he would be 'content to find Himself so well received'. Happy that Jesus was content and disregarding the fact that she herself did not receive 'the least' consolation when making her thanksgivings after Mass, she adds that she frequently suffered from 'both distractions and sleepiness' during her thanksgiving.[71] Thérèse interpreted 'the most absolute aridity and almost total abandonment' that she describes as the normal state of her soul in terms of allowing Jesus to sleep in her 'little boat' (see Mt 8:23-27):

> Jesus was sleeping as usual in my little boat; ah! I see very well how rarely souls allow Him to sleep peacefully within them. Jesus is so fatigued with always having to take the initiative and to attend to others that He hastens to take advantage of the repose I offer to Him.[72]

Having always enjoyed such a living faith that she was 'unable to believe there were really impious people who had no faith', Thérèse went through a period of great spiritual darkness during her final illness. She describes God as permitting her soul 'to be invaded by the thickest darkness' so that even 'the thought of heaven, up until then so sweet' to her was 'no longer anything but the cause of struggle and torment'. During her trial of faith, Thérèse said that even though she did not have 'the joy of faith', she nevertheless tried 'to carry out its works at least'. As she struggled with discouragement and despair, Thérèse humbly put her trust in God. Despite the weakness of the flesh, her spirit was strong (see Jn 15:5) and, as she put it herself, 'I do not refuse the fight ... "He teaches my hands to fight, and my fingers to make war. He is my protector, and I have hoped in him!" (Ps 144:1-2).'[73]

Some fifteen hundred years earlier, St John Chrysostom presented prayer as our principal means of defence in our struggle to overcome sin:

> Nothing is equal to prayer; for what is impossible it makes possible, what is difficult, easy ... For it is

impossible, utterly impossible, for the man who prays eagerly and invokes God ceaselessly ever to sin.[74]

The *Catechism* also recognises that, as well as times dedicated particularly to prayer, St John Chrysostom recommended that we combine prayer with our other everyday activities:

It is possible to offer fervent prayer even while walking in public or strolling alone, or seated in your shop ... while buying or selling ... or even while cooking.[75]

The *Catechism* concludes its outline of the life of prayer with a section on the priestly prayer of Jesus that is recorded for us in chapter 17 of John's Gospel.[76] As the new High Priest about to enter the Holy of Holies through his passion, his resurrection and his ascension, Jesus unveils the mystery of the inner life of the Blessed Trinity and the indwelling of God in the soul as he prays for the sins of his people (see Lev 16). All the many dimensions of our lives of prayer find their inner unity in his priestly prayer, for it is only in union with his prayer that prayer becomes possible for us. After quoting a long series of extracts from John 17, Thérèse wrote: 'Yes, Lord, this is what I would like to repeat after You before flying into Your arms'.[77]

THE 'OUR FATHER'[78]

The lives and teaching of John Chrysostom, Teresa and Thérèse are presented to us by the Church as an authoritative witness to the nature of Christian prayer as revealed to us in Jesus, as it has developed in the prayer tradition of the Church, and as it continues uninterrupted in the daily life of the Church. Their lives of prayer can also be 'read' as a living and authoritative commentary on the 'Our Father', the definitive model for Christian prayer that Jesus gave in response to his disciples' request, 'Lord, teach us to pray' (Lk 11:1).[79]

The 'Our Father' is known as the 'Lord's Prayer' because 'it comes to us from the Lord Jesus, the master and model of our prayer' (n. 2775) and it is 'the quintessential prayer of the Church':

> It is an integral part of the major hours of the Divine Office and of the sacraments of Christian initiation: Baptism, Confirmation, and Eucharist. Integrated into the Eucharist it reveals the eschatological character of its petitions, hoping for the Lord, 'until he comes' (see 1 Cor 11:26). (n. 2776)

St Teresa of Avila describes it as providing us with all that we need for contemplation and the way of perfection:

> I marvel to see that in so few words everything about contemplation and perfection is included; it seems we need to study no other book than this one.[80]

St John Chrysostom presented the 'Our Father' as a prayer by and for the People of God as a whole:

> [The Lord] teaches us to make prayer in common for all our brethren. For he did not say 'my Father' who art in heaven, but 'our' Father, offering petitions for the common Body.[81]

In her commentary on the 'Our Father',[82] Teresa describes her sense of joy and wonder because Jesus has invited his disciples to address his Father as 'Our Father in heaven'.[83] Speaking directly to Jesus, she says:

> O Son of God and my Lord! How is it that you give so much all together in the first words? Since You humble Yourself to such an extreme in joining with us in prayer

and making Yourself the Brother of creatures so lowly and wretched, how is it that You give us in the name of Your Father everything that can be given? For you desire that He consider us His children, because Your word cannot fail.[84]

Acknowledging that (thanks to Baptism) we have become the adopted children of God the Father, the sisters and brothers of Jesus his Son,[85] the *Catechism* says that calling on God as our heavenly Father 'should develop in us the will to become like him and foster in us a humble and trusting heart' (n. 2800). Teresa says:

What son is there in the world who doesn't strive to learn who his father is when he knows he has such a good one with so much majesty and power?[86]

Just as discovering something about our family tree can reveal to us something about ourselves, discovering the identity and nature of our heavenly Father, as revealed to us by Jesus, helps us to appreciate the spiritual dimension of our being in a new and profound way.[87] When we acknowledge God as our Father, we acknowledge, too, that heaven, 'the Father's house, is the true homeland toward which we are heading and to which, already, we belong' (n. 2802).

The first three petitions of the 'Our Father' are concerned with the Father's glory, 'the sanctification of his name, the coming of the kingdom, and the fulfilment of his will' (n. 2857). When we pray for the sanctification of God's name[88] by us and in us, and by and in each and every person whatever their circumstances, we are aligning ourselves with the divine plan for the salvation of all humanity through, with and in Jesus Christ, our Lord.[89] When we pray for the coming of God's kingdom,[90] we are looking forward, not only to the growth of the reign of God in the 'here and now' of our own lives, but to the definitive establishment of that reign when Jesus returns in glory.[91] Chrysostom recognises our prayer that God's will be done 'on earth as it is in heaven' as a command to always pray universally, and not just for any sectional interest:

> Consider how [Jesus Christ] teaches us to be humble, by making us see that our virtue does not depend on our work alone but on grace from on high. He commands each of the faithful who prays to do so universally, for the whole world. For he did not say 'thy will be done in me or in us', but 'on earth', the whole earth, so that error may be banished from it, truth take root in it, all vice be destroyed on it, virtue flourish on it, and earth no longer differ from heaven.[92]

Noting that 'hallowed' means 'glorified', Chrysostom says that all things should be accounted 'secondary to the work of praising' the Father and he says that 'thy kingdom come' does not account the things of this world as 'some great matter' but longs 'for the things to come'.[93] Grouping the first and second petitions together, 'Hallowed be thy name, thy kingdom come', Teresa comments:

> But since His Majesty saw that we could neither hollow, nor praise, nor extol, nor glorify this holy name of the Eternal Father in a fitting way, because of the tiny amount we ourselves are capable of doing, He provided for us by giving us here on earth His kingdom. That is why Jesus put these two petitions next to each other ... Now, then, the great good that it seems to me there will be in the kingdom of heaven, among many other blessings, is that one will no longer take any account of earthly things, but have a calmness and glory within, rejoice in the fact that all are rejoicing, experience perpetual peace and a wonderful inner satisfaction that comes from seeing that

everyone hallows and praises the Lord and blesses His name and that no one offends Him ... But there are times when, tired from our travels, we experience that the Lord calms our faculties and quiets the soul. As though by signs, He gives us a clear foretaste of what will be given to those He brings to His kingdom. And to those to whom He gives here below the kingdom we ask for, He gives pledges so that through these they may have great hope of going to enjoy perpetually what here on earth is given only in sips.[94]

Because only Jesus can say, 'I always do what is pleasing to him' (Jn 8:29), the third petition that is concerned with the Father's glory, 'Thy will be done on earth as it is in heaven',[95] asks our Father 'to unite our will to that of his Son, so as to fulfil his plan of salvation in the life of the world' (n. 2860). Chrysostom comments that we must not only long for the things of heaven but 'make the earth a heaven and do and say all things' as though we were doing and saying them in heaven.[96] Teresa recognised the spiritual struggle involved in 'not my will, but yours be done' (Lk 22:42) when she wrote:

> [T]o say that we abandon our will to another's will seems very easy until through experience we realize that this is the hardest thing one can do if one does it as it should be done.[97]

She tells us that, though her will was not yet free from self-interest, she 'had great experience of the gain that comes from' leaving it freely in God's hands.[98] It is the means by which God's kingdom comes and she recognised 'how well Jesus knows us and how much he thinks of our good':

> In this contemplation ... we don't do anything ourselves. Neither do we labor, nor do we bargain, nor is anything

else necessary – because everything else is an impediment and hindrance – than to say *fiat voluntas tua*: Your will, Lord, be done in me in every way and manner that You, my Lord, want. If You want it to be done with trials, strengthen me and let them come; if with persecutions, illnesses, dishonours, and a lack of life's necessities, here I am; I will not turn away, my Father, nor is it right that I turn my back on You. Since Your Son gave You this will of mine in the name of all, there's no reason for any lack on my part. But grant me the favour of Your kingdom that I may do Your will, since He asked for this kingdom for me, and use me as You would Your own possession, in conformity with Your will.[99]

The final four petitions of the 'Our Father' 'present our wants to him: they ask that our lives be nourished, healed of sin, and made victorious in the struggle of good over evil' (n. 2857).

The first of these petitions, 'Give us this day our daily bread',[100] asks for the 'earthly nourishment necessary to everyone for subsistence, and also to the Bread of Life: the Word of God and the Body of Christ' (n. 2861). Chrysostom comments:

It is not for riches, nor for delicate living, nor for costly raiment, nor for any other such thing, but for bread only, that He has commanded us to make our prayer. And for daily bread, so as not to take thought for the morrow.[101]

Teresa focuses on the Eucharistic dimension of this petition, presenting the Mass as the self-gift to us as food of the incarnate humanity of Jesus every day until the end of the world, the gift that makes it possible for us to do God's will on earth, as it is done in heaven:

It's as though Jesus tells the Father that He is now ours since the Father has given Him to us to die for us; and asks the Father not to take Him from us until the end of the world; that He allow Him to serve each day ... In this petition the word 'daily' seems to mean forever. Reflecting upon why after the word 'daily' the Lord said 'give us this day, Lord,' that is, be ours every day, I've come to think that it is because here on earth we possess Him and also in heaven we will possess Him if we profit well by His company. He, in fact, doesn't remain with us for any other reason than to help, encourage, and sustain us in doing this will that we have prayed might be done in us.[102]

The *Catechism* (n. 2862) describes the second of the four petitions presenting our wants to the Father, 'and forgive us our trespasses, as we forgive those who trespass against us',[103] as begging 'God's mercy for our offences, mercy which can penetrate our hearts only if we have learned to forgive our enemies, with the example and help of Christ'. Chrysostom comments that addressing God as 'Father' implies 'the duty of remitting our anger against them that have transgressed' against us[104] and of showing the same compassionate mercy to others that God shows them:

> You cannot call the God of all kindness your Father if you preserve a cruel and inhuman heart; for in this case you no longer have in you the marks of the heavenly Father's kindness.[105]

Teresa implies that the capacity to readily forgive others is normally found in those who have come to know how generously God's loving mercy has pardoned their own sins:

I cannot believe that a person who comes so close to Mercy itself, where he realizes what he is and the great deal God has pardoned him of, would fail to pardon his offender immediately, in complete ease, and with a readiness to remain on very good terms with him. Such a person is mindful of the gift and favor granted by God, by which he saw signs of great love; and he rejoices that an opportunity is offered whereby he can show the Lord some love.[106]

The third of the four petitions presenting our wants to the Father, 'and lead us not into temptation',[107] is interpreted in the *Catechism* as 'asking God not to allow us to take the path that leads to sin', imploring 'the Spirit of discernment and strength' and requesting 'the grace of vigilance and final perseverance' (n. 2863). Chrysostom comments:

As when we are dragged forth, we must stand nobly; so when we are not summoned, we should be quiet, and wait for the time of conflict; that we may show both freedom from vainglory, and nobleness of spirit.[108]

The final petition, 'but deliver us from Evil',[109] is presented as a prayer asking God to show forth 'the victory, already won by Christ, over the "ruler of this world", Satan, the angel personally opposed to God and to his plan of salvation' (n. 2864). Chrysostom comments that we are commanded to wage 'a war that knows no truce' against the wicked one, who is 'himself the cause of all our wrongs', even those that we suffer at the hands of our neighbours.[110] Teresa treats these two petitions together, identifying the 'temptation' into which we might be led as the trap laid for us by devils who are posing as angels of light. Reminding us that she 'is quite certain that those who attain perfection do not ask the Lord to deliver them from trials, temptations, persecutions and conflicts', Teresa interprets this petition as recognising that we can sometimes yield to temptation because we have been tricked by

> the devils who transfigure themselves into angels of light, who come disguised. Not until they have done much harm to the soul do they allow themselves to be recognised. They suck away our blood and destroy our virtues, and we go about in the midst of the same temptation but do not know it. With regard to these enemies, daughters, let us ask and often beg the Lord in the Our Father to free us and not let us walk into temptation, so that they will not draw us into error or hide the light and truth from us, that the poison will be discovered.[111]

Among the temptations that devils can set as traps, she lists 'making us believe that the consolations and the favours which they can counterfeit to us come from God', becoming 'in any way vainglorious', 'making us believe that we possess virtues that we do not' and thinking that the Lord who 'has given us a certain grace' would never take that grace away from us. She also adds the following two temptations: making us 'believe that we have some virtue – patience, let us say – because we have determination and make continual resolutions to suffer a great deal for God's sake', and making us 'appear very poor in spirit' when it is not, in fact, the case.

The *Catechism* describes the final 'Amen' at the end of the 'Our Father' as expressing 'our "*fiat*"' concerning the seven petitions: "So be it"' (n. 2865).

In this chapter, based on the fourth and last section of the 1992 *Catechism of the Catholic Church*, we have outlined the Church's faith in relation to prayer. The second part of the *Catechism*, 'The Celebration of the Christian Mystery', outlines the faith of the Church in relation to Liturgy and the

Sacraments. These two dimensions of the Church's faith, prayer and worship, are closely connected and the 1983 Code of Canon Law saw them as among the means by which the Church carries out the office of sanctification that it has received from Jesus, the high priest of our faith. Canon 834 §1 says:

> The Church carries out its office of sanctifying in a special way in the sacred liturgy, which is an exercise of the priestly office of Jesus Christ.

Canon 839 §1 says:

> The Church carries out its sanctifying office by other means also, that is by prayer, in which it asks God to make Christ's faithful holy in the truth, and by works of penance and charity, which play a large part in establishing and strengthening in souls the Kingdom of Christ, and so contribute to the salvation of the world.

The unity of prayer and formal worship as dimensions of the sanctifying office of the Church was highlighted by St Teresia Benedicta a Cruce (Edith Stein, 1891–1942) in her 1936 essay on the prayer of the Church. She presents the Church's prayer as a sharing in the high priestly prayer of Jesus:[112]

> The Saviour's high priestly prayer unveils the mystery of the inner life: the circumincession of the Divine Persons and the indwelling of God in the soul. In these mysterious depths the work of salvation is prepared and accomplishes itself in concealment and silence. And so it will continue until the union of all is actually accomplished at the end of time. The decision for the Redemption was conceived in the eternal silence of

the inner divine life. The power of the Holy Spirit came over the Virgin praying alone in the hidden silent room in Nazareth and brought about the Incarnation of the Saviour. Congregated around the silently praying Virgin, the emergent church awaited the promised new outpouring of the Spirit that was to quicken it into inner clarity and fruitful outer effectiveness ... The Virgin, who kept every word sent from God in her heart, is the model for such attentive souls in whom Jesus' high priestly prayer comes to life again and again.[113]

Warning about the danger of emphasising the communal dimension of formal liturgical prayer at the expense of mystical and interior prayer, she reminds us:

The mystical stream, which flows through all the centuries, is no spurious side-current that has strayed from the prayer life of the Church – it is her very life-blood. If it breaks through the traditional forms, it does so because the Spirit that blows where it listeth is living in it: He who has fashioned all the traditional forms must ever fashion new ones. Without Him there would be neither Liturgy nor Church ... All authentic prayer is prayer of the Church. Through every sincere prayer something happens in the Church, and it is the Church itself that is praying therein, for it is the Holy Spirit living in the Church that intercedes for every individual soul 'with sighs too deep for words' (Rom 8:26). That is exactly what 'authentic' prayer is, for 'no one can say "Jesus is Lord" except by the Holy Spirit' (1 Cor 12:3). What could the prayer of the church be, if not great lovers giving themselves to God who is love![114]

Notes

1. See nn. 2559, 2560, 2616, 2628, 2737, 2762, 2785, 2794, 2827 and 2837.
2. See nn. 2782, 2784, 2813, 2816, 2830 and 2845.
3. See nn. 2700, 2743, 2744, 2768, 2784 and 2825.
4. See nn. 2704 and 2709.
5. See n. 2558.
6. See Paul William Harkins, 'St John Chrysostom' in *New Catholic Encyclopedia* (Washington, DC: The Catholic University of America, 2003), 7:945–9.
7. See St John Chrysostom, *Homilies on Matthew,* 50:3–4; Jacques-Paul Migne (ed.), *Patrologia graeca* [PG], 161 vols (Paris: 1857–1866), 58:508–9.
8. St John Chrysostom, *Homilies on Prayer,* 6, in Migne (ed.), *PG,* 64, 462–6.
9. St Teresa of Avila, *The Book of Her Life,* 8.2, in Kieran Kavanaugh OCD and Otilio Rodriguez OCD (eds), *The Collected Works of Saint Teresa of Avila,* 2nd revised edition, 3 vols (Washington: ICS Publications, 1987), 1:94–5.
10. St Teresa of Avila, *The Book of Her Life,* 9.1–3, in ibid., 1:100–1.
11. St Teresa of Avila, *The Book of Her Life,* 11.6–7, in ibid., 1:113.
12. St Teresa of Avila, *The Book of Her Life,* 8:4–5, in ibid., 1:95–6.
13. St Thérèse of Lisieux, *Story of a Soul: The Autobiography of Saint Thérèse of Lisieux,* translated by John Clarke OCD (Washington, DC: ICS Publications, 1996), 17.
14. Ibid., 36.7.
15. Ibid., 65–6.
16. Ibid., 98.
17. Ibid.
18. Ibid., 99.
19. Ibid., 263.
20. Ibid., 211–4.
21. Ibid., 213.
22. See Pope John Paul II's apostolic constitution, *Divini Amoris Scientia* (1997).
23. See 'Prayer in the Christian Life' in the *Catechism,* nn. 2558–2758.
24. St Thérèse of Lisieux, *Story of a Soul,* 242.
25. St John Damascene (676–749) said that 'Prayer is the raising of one's mind and heart to God'; see *De fide orthodoxa* 3:34, in Migne (ed.), *PG,* 94:1089C.

26. St Thérèse of Lisieux, *Story of a Soul*, 36.
27. Ibid., 37.
28. Ibid., 37–8.
29. Ibid., 124–5.
30. Ibid., 125.
31. Ibid., 124–5.
32. Ibid., 99.
33. Ibid., 122.
34. Ibid., 149.
35. Ibid., 242.
36. See 'The Revelation of Prayer' in the *Catechism*, nn. 2566–2649.
37. *Catechism*, n. 2575.
38. See the *Catechism*, n. 2600.
39. See the *Catechism*, n. 2621.
40. See the *Catechism*, nn. 2623–4.
41. See the *Catechism*, nn. 2625.
42. See 'The Tradition of Prayer' in the *Catechism*, nn. 2650–96.
43. Vatican II, *Dei Verbum* 8. See the *Catechism*, n. 2650.
44. *Catechism*, n. 2652. See also n. 2662.
45. See St Thérèse of Lisieux, *Story of a Soul*, 234.
46. *Catechism*, nn. 2680–1.
47. See the *Catechism*, n. 2682.
48. Christopher O'Donnell OCarm, *Prayer: Insights from St Thérèse of Lisieux* (Dublin: Veritas, 2001), 98.
49. Quoted in Thérèse of Lisieux, *The Prayers of Saint Thérèse of Lisieux*, translated by A. Kane (Washington, DC: Institute of Carmelite Studies, 1997), 119.
50. St Thérèse of Lisieux, *Story of a Soul*, 192.
51. Ibid., 258. The saints listed by Thérèse in this passage are St Paul, St Augustine, St John of the Cross, St Thomas Aquinas, St Francis and St Dominic.
52. *Catechism*, n. 2684.
53. See the *Catechism*, n. 2694.
54. *Catechism*, n. 2691.
55. See the *Catechism*, n. 2695.
56. See 'The Life of Prayer' in the *Catechism*, nn. 2697–2758.
57. See the *Catechism*, n. 2742.
58. *Catechism*, n. 2698.
59. St John Chrysostom, *A Selection from Different Homilies on Prayer*, 2, Migne (ed.), *PG,* 63:585. Quoted in the *Catechism*, n. 2700.

60. See St Thérèse of Lisieux, *Story of a Soul*, 36.

61. Ibid., 43.

62. See ibid., 26.

63. See ibid., 41–3.

64. Ibid., 242.

65. Ibid., 243.

66. See O'Donnell OCarm, 72.

67. St Thérèse of Lisieux, *Story of a Soul*, 220.

68. Ibid., 179.

69. St Teresa of Avila, *The Book of Her Life*, 8:5, in Kavanaugh and Rodriguez (eds), 1:96. When citing this text, the *Catechism* (n. 2709) translates *'oración mental'* as 'contemplative prayer'.

70. St Thérèse of Lisieux, *The Letters of Saint Thérèse of Lisieux*, translated by J. Clarke, 2 vols (Washington, DC: Institute of Carmelite Studies, 1982, 1988), 2:801.

71. See St Thérèse of Lisieux, *Story of a Soul*, 165.

72. Ibid.

73. Ibid., 215.

74. St John Chrysostom, *Homilies on Hannah* 4:5, in Migne (ed.), *PG* 54:666. Quoted in the *Catechism*, n. 2744.

75. St John Chrysostom, *A Selection from Different Homilies on Prayer,* 2, in ibid., *PG,* 63:585. Quoted in the *Catechism*, n. 2743.

76. See the *Catechism*, nn. 2746–51.

77. St Thérèse of Lisieux, *Story of a Soul*, 255.

78. See 'The Lord's Prayer: "Our Father"' in the *Catechism*, nn. 2759–2865.

79. See the *Catechism*, n. 2773.

80. St Teresa of Avila, *The Way of Perfection*, 37, in Kavanaugh and Rodriguez (eds), 2:183.

81. St John Chrysostom, *Homilies on Matthew,* 19.4, in Migne (ed.), *PG,* 57:278. Quoted in the *Catechism*, n. 2768.

82. See St Teresa of Avila, *The Way of Perfection,* 27–38, in Kavanaugh and Rodriguez (eds), 2:137–88.

83. See 'Our Father Who Art in Heaven' in the *Catechism*, nn. 2777–2802.

84. St Teresa of Avila, *The Way of Perfection,* 27.2, in Kavanaugh and Rodriguez (eds), 1:138.

85. See the *Catechism*, n. 2798.

86. St Teresa of Avila, *The Way of Perfection,* 27.5, in Kavanaugh and Rodriguez (eds), 1:139.

87. See the *Catechism*, n. 2799.
88. See the *Catechism*, nn. 2807–15.
89. See the *Catechism*, n. 2858.
90. See the *Catechism*, nn. 2816–21.
91. See the *Catechism*, n. 2859.
92. St John Chrysostom, *Homilies on Matthew,* 19:5, in Migne (ed.), *PG,* 57:280.
93. St John Chrysostom, *Homilies on Matthew,* 19.4, in ibid., 57:279.
94. St Teresa of Avila, *The Way of Perfection,* 30.4-6, in Kavanaugh and Rodriguez (eds), 1:150–1.
95. See the *Catechism*, nn. 2822–7.
96. St John Chrysostom, *Homilies on Matthew,* 19.4, in Migne (ed.), *PG,* 57:279.
97. St Teresa of Avila, *The Way of Perfection,* 32.5, in Kavanaugh and Rodriguez (eds), 1:161.
98. See St Teresa of Avila, *The Way of Perfection,* 32.4, in ibid.
99. See St Teresa of Avila, *The Way of Perfection,* 32.10, in ibid., 1:163–4.
100. See the *Catechism*, nn. 2828–37.
101. St John Chrysostom, *Homilies on Matthew,* 19.5, in Migne (ed.), *PG,* 57:280.
102. St Teresa of Avila, *Way of Perfection,* 33.4–34.1, in Kavanaugh and Rodriguez (eds), 1:167–8.
103. See the *Catechism*, nn. 2838–45.
104. St John Chrysostom, *Homilies on Matthew,* 19.6, in Migne (ed.), *PG,* 57:281.
105. St John Chrysostom, *On the Lord's Prayer* 3, in ibid., 51:44. Quoted in the *Catechism*, n. 2784.
106. St Teresa of Avila, *Way of Perfection,* 36.12, in Kavanaugh and Rodriguez (eds), 1:182.
107. See the *Catechism*, nn. 2846–9.
108. St John Chrysostom, *Homilies on Matthew,* 19.6, in Migne (ed.), *PG,* 57:282.
109. See the *Catechism*, nn. 2850–4.
110. St John Chrysostom, *Homilies on Matthew,* 19.6, in Migne (ed.), *PG,* 57:282.
111. St Teresa of Avila, *The Way of Perfection,* 38.2, in Kavanaugh and Rodriguez (eds), 1:185.
112. We have already noted that the *Catechism* concludes its outline of the life of prayer with a section on the priestly prayer of Jesus

that is recorded for us in John 17. See the *Catechism*, nn. 2746–51.

113. Edith Stein, 'The Hidden Life: Hagiographic Essays, Meditations, Spiritual Texts', translated by Waltraut Stein, in *The Collected Works of Edith Stein*, 4, Lucy Gelber and Michael Linssen (eds) (Trivandrum: Carmel Publishing Centre, 1998), 12–13.

114. Ibid., 15.

Chapter 3

FAITH AND WORSHIP

Building on the outline of prayer in the last chapter, this chapter will present the faith of the Church concerning her own formal worship, the Liturgy and the Sacraments. As in the last chapter, we will choose three saints as witnesses and guides in our exploration of the nature of our common worship.

IGNATIUS OF ANTIOCH, AQUINAS AND EDITH STEIN AS MODELS OF WORSHIP

The most frequently cited writer in this section of the *Catechism* is the Doctor of the Church, St Thomas Aquinas, who is cited twelve times.[1] The two most frequently cited Eastern writers are St Ignatius of Antioch[2] and St John Chrysostom,[3] both cited five times. Since St John Chrysostom has already been taken as a model of prayer, and in order to include both a patristic and a medieval writer and to provide both a Western and Eastern perspective, I propose to take St Thomas and St Ignatius of Antioch as two of the models of faithful worship in this chapter. In the interests of gender balance, and in order to give a more contemporary perspective, I propose to take St Teresia Benedicta a Cruce (Edith Stein) as the third model to illustrate this dimension of the faith.

St Ignatius of Antioch (c. 35–107)[4]

Having been born about the time of the death and resurrection of Christ, Ignatius succeeded Evodius, the immediate successor of St Peter, as Bishop of Antioch. When the Emperor Trajan was passing through on an expedition against the Parthians and Armenians in the year 107, Bishop Ignatius, then in his early seventies, voluntarily presented himself before the Emperor at Antioch and professed himself to be a Christian. His public refusal to participate in the worship of the Emperor led to him being condemned to execution in the Roman amphitheatre and he wrote a number of letters during his long journey to his place of execution. In Smyrna, where Polycarp was bishop, Ignatius wrote to the Ephesians, the Magnesians, the Trallians and the Romans. From Smyrna he came to Troas, and while staying there a few days, he wrote to the Philadelphians, the Smyrnaeans and to Polycarp, whom he had met in Smyrna. He was brought overland across Macedonia, then by ship from Epirus to Italy, and finally to Rome, where he was executed in December of that same year.

Writing to the Christians at Rome, Ignatius asked them not to prevent his martyrdom, because he was impatient 'to attain to Jesus Christ' and because, 'It is better for me to die on behalf of Jesus Christ than to reign over all the ends of the earth ... Him I seek, who died for us: him I desire, who rose again for our sake ... Permit me to be an imitator of the Passion of my God!'[5] In his general audience on 14 March 2007, Pope Benedict XVI said, 'No Church Father has expressed the longing for *union* with Christ and for *life* in him with the intensity of Ignatius.'[6]

In his letters, Ignatius defends the reality of Christ's suffering against the Docetists, who claimed that the Word only seemed to have become incarnate and did not suffer in reality. Associating a refusal to recognise the Eucharist as the body and blood of Christ with the refusal of the Docetist heresy to accept the reality of the Incarnation, he describes the Eucharist as 'the medicine of immortality' and 'the antidote to death'. Ignatius emphasises the role of the bishop around whom each local church is gathered and he questions the legitimacy of any celebrations of Baptism, Eucharist or repentance that are not authorised by the bishop. The bishop is 'an image of the Father' and Ignatius also recognised the ministries of deacons and presbyters in each local Church.

St Thomas Aquinas (c. 1225–1274)

Thomas was born around 1225 in the castle of Roccasecca, south of Rome. His father was Count Landulf of Aquino and his mother, the Countess Theodora of Theate, was related to the Holy Roman emperors of the Hohenstaufen dynasty. All his brothers followed military careers but his paternal uncle, Sinibald, was abbot of the Benedictine abbey of Monte Cassino and, because it was hoped that Thomas would succeed his uncle as abbot there, the boy began his education at Monte Cassino at about the age of five.

The parents of Thomas sided with the Holy Roman Emperor Frederick II in his conflict with Pope Gregory IX, and they removed Thomas from Monte Cassino in 1239 and enrolled him at the university (*studium generale*) that Frederick had recently established in Naples. At the university, Thomas read Aristotle and he came under the influence of the Dominican preacher, John of St Julian. Thomas decided to join the Dominicans rather than the Benedictines and, in order to ensure that his mother would not prevent this, the Dominicans arranged that Thomas be sent, first to Rome and then to Paris, to study. On his way to Rome, his brothers seized him and brought him back to his parents. For two years, during which he remained in communication with the Dominicans, Thomas tutored his sisters. By 1244, recognising that all attempts to dissuade him had failed, his mother, Theodora, arranged for him to escape.

In 1245, Thomas was sent to study at the University of Paris and it was there that he met the Dominican teacher, Albert the Great, who held the Chair of Theology at the College of St James. In 1248, Thomas refused the offer by Pope Innocent IV that he become abbot of Monte Cassino as a Dominican, and when his teacher, Albert, was moved to the new *studium generale* at Cologne, Thomas found that he had been appointed the master of the Dominican students there. After he failed in his first theological disputation, Albert commented: 'We call him the dumb ox, but in his teaching he will one day produce such a bellowing that it will be heard throughout the world.'[7]

Between 1248 and 1252, Thomas lectured on the books of the Old Testament in Cologne. In 1252, he returned to Paris to study for his master's degree and to write a commentary on the *Sentences* of Peter Lombard. In 1256, Thomas was appointed regent master in theology at Paris, a position he held until 1259. During this period, he defended the Mendicant Orders against William of Saint-Amour in his *Contra impugnantes Dei cultum et religionem* (*Against Those Who Assail the Worship of God and Religion*). He also wrote his *Questiones disputatae de veritate* (*Disputed Questions on Truth*), dealing with aspects of faith and the human condition, and his *Quaestiones quodlibetales* (*Quodlibetal Questions*), a collection of his responses to various philosophical and theological questions. He also began work on one of his most famous works, the *Summa contra Gentiles*.

About 1259, Thomas returned to Naples and in 1261 he moved to Orvieto, where he was made responsible for the education of the Dominican friars who were unable to attend the *studium generale*. During his stay in Orvieto, he was able to complete his *Summa Contra Gentiles* and he also wrote the liturgy for the newly created feast of *Corpus Christi*. Between 1265 and 1268, he was engaged in the establishment of a *studium generale* for the Dominican Order at the priory of Santa Sabina in Rome. It was during his time there that he began his most famous work, the *Summa theologiae*.

At the Paris disputations of 1266–1267, the Franciscan master, William of Baglione, accused Thomas of encouraging Averroism, a radical form of Aristotelianism. In fact, Thomas was opposed to the spread of Averroism and, partly in order to oppose the growth of this movement, the Dominican Order appointed him regent master at the University of Paris for the second time. During his term as regent master from 1268 to 1272, he wrote his *De unitate intellectus, contra Averroistas* (*On the Unicity of Intellect, Against the Averroists*). In 1270, Bishop Etienne Tempier of Paris issued an edict condemning certain Aristotelian and Averroistic propositions as heretical and excommunicating those who continued to support those positions. Apparently in order to defend the philosophy of Aristotle against those who feared that it necessarily led to Averroism, Thomas conducted a series of disputations on the virtues between 1270 and 1272.

In 1272, Thomas undertook the establishment of a *studium generale* in his home province of Naples. While there he worked on the third part of his *Summa theologiae*. Towards the end of 1273, he seems to have lost confidence in logic and reason as the means towards understanding God and he told his *socius*, Reginald of Piperno, that all he had written 'seems like straw to me (*mihi videtur ut palea*)'.[8] Thomas was summoned by Pope Gregory X to attend the Second Council of Lyons in 1274, but he struck his head against an overhanging branch on his journey to the Council and retired to Monte Cassino to recover. He was taken ill again at the Cistercian abbey of Fossanova and he died there on 7 March 1274. As he received the last rites, he prayed: 'I receive Thee, ransom of my soul. For love of Thee have I studied and kept vigil, toiled, preached and taught.'[9]

In 1277, Bishop Tempier of Paris issued another decree, designed to clarify that God's absolute power transcended any of the principles of logic proposed by Aristotle or Averroes. Twenty propositions associated with Thomas were included in the list of 219 propositions condemned by this decree and, as a result, his reputation was badly damaged. The process of his rehabilitation was already evident in Dante's *The Divine Comedy*, which describes his glorified spirit as being among the other great examples of religious wisdom in heaven. Fifty years after his death, Pope John XXII declared him to be a saint and, in 1567, Pope Pius V ranked his feast alongside those of the four great Latin fathers: St Ambrose, St Augustine, St Jerome and St Gregory the Great. At the First Vatican Council (1870) he was declared a Doctor of the Church. In 1879, Pope Leo XIII described his theology as a definitive exposition of Catholic doctrine, directing the clergy to take his teachings as the basis of their theological positions. In 1880, St Thomas Aquinas was declared the patron of all Catholic education.

St Teresia Benedicta a Cruce (Edith Stein) (1891–1942)

Edith Stein was born into a devout Jewish family in what is now Wrocław (Breslau), Poland, on 12 October 1891, which was Yom Kippur, the Jewish Day of Atonement. When her father, Siegfried, died of sunstroke when she was only three years old, her mother took charge of her husband's timber business and brought up her seven children (two boys and five girls, of which Edith was the youngest) in relative prosperity. She was a vivacious and intelligent child, but inclined to criticise everything around her. At the age of thirteen, Edith was passed over for a prize on the centenary of Schiller's death and she believed that this was because she was Jewish. The event may have affected her faith in God's providential care for her, because it was not long afterwards that she 'deliberately and consciously ... gave up praying'. For health reasons, and in order to give her a change of scene, her mother withdrew Edith, then aged fourteen, from school in Breslau at Easter 1906, and for the next ten months she lived with the family of her elder sister Else in Hamburg. When she returned to Breslau, she began work on her pre-university course.

At the age of twenty, Edith decided to go to Breslau University, and between 1911 and 1913 she studied psychology, Germanic studies and History there. She moved to Göttingen University in 1913, where she studied philosophy for two years. She was deeply influenced by the lectures of Max Scheler, a convert to Roman Catholicism from Judaism, who 'was overflowing with Catholic ideas and ... pleading them with all the brilliance of his intellect and his eloquence'.[10] At Göttingen, she studied principally under Edmund Husserl – known as the father of phenomenology – whom she regarded as the greatest philosopher of the day. The First World War broke out in 1914 (Edith was then twenty-three) and the following year she completed her examinations at Göttingen and decided to do some Red Cross work as a volunteer in what is now the Czech Republic. When she returned to Göttingen, she began her doctoral thesis under Husserl.

During her time at Göttingen, Edith slowly went through the process of conversion to the Catholic Church. This was mainly thanks to the influence of one of Husserl's disciples, Professor Adolf Reinach. Reinach was born a Jew, but, along with his wife Anna, he had converted to the Lutheran Church. In 1914, however, Reinach volunteered and was killed in Flanders in 1917. Edith was asked to arrange his papers and the strength that Anna Reinach drew from her faith made a profound impression on her:

> This was my first encounter with the Cross and the divine strength that it inspires in those who bear it. For the first time I saw before my very eyes the Church, born of Christ's redemptive suffering, victorious over the sting of death. It was the moment in which my unbelief was shattered, Judaism paled, and Christ streamed out upon me: Christ in the mystery of the Cross.[11]

She was awarded a *summa cum laude* for her doctoral thesis in August 1916, afterwards accepting an appointment as Husserl's assistant at Fribourg where he was professor. She was beginning to read the New Testament and wondering about joining the

Catholic Church. While visiting a Protestant friend, she accidentally came upon the life of St Teresa of Avila:

> I picked a book at random and took out a large volume. It bore the title: 'The Life of St Teresa of Avila written by herself.' I began to read and was at once captivated and did not stop reading till I had reached the end. As I closed the book I said, 'This is the truth.'[12]

Realising that she had, at last, found the truth for which she had been searching, Edith was baptised on New Year's Day 1922, at the age of thirty-one. She took Teresia as her baptismal name and was confirmed a month later at Speyer cathedral.

After her Baptism, Edith gave up her university appointment as Husserl's assistant and accepted a teaching post in German and History at a girls' school at Speyer in the Rhineland, which was run by Third Order Dominican sisters. She became acquainted with Catholic philosophy and worked at translating the treatise, *Questions on Truth*, by St Thomas Aquinas. Edith was invited to address various Catholic audiences, especially on education and topics relating to women. She made radio broadcasts and gave talks at many centres in Germany and Switzerland. The man who had been her spiritual director, Canon Schwind of Speyer cathedral, died in 1927, so from then on her director was Abbot Raphael Walzer of the Benedictine Abbey at Beuron. He said about her:

> I seldom met a soul that united so many excellent qualities. She was simplicity and naturalness in person. She was completely a woman, gentle and even maternal, without wanting to mother anyone. Gifted with mystical graces in the true sense of the word, she never gave any sign of affectation or a sense of superiority. She was simple with simple people, learned with the learned, yet

without presumption, an enquirer with enquirers, and, I would like to add, a sinner with sinners.[13]

Early in 1928, Edith Stein wrote:

That it is possible to worship God (*Gottesdienst*) by doing scholarly research is something I learned, actually, only when I was busy with [the translation of] St Thomas [Aquinas' *Quaestiones de Veritate* from Latin into German] ... Only thereafter could I decide to resume serious scholarly research. Immediately before, and for a good while after my conversion, I was of the opinion that to lead a religious life meant one had to give up all that was secular and to live totally immersed in thoughts of the Divine. But gradually I realised that something else is asked of us in this world and that, even in the contemplative life, one may not sever the connection with the world. I even believe that the deeper one is drawn into God, the more one must 'go out of oneself,' that is, one must go to the world, in order to bring the divine life into it.[14]

In the spring of 1932, she was appointed lecturer at the Education Institute (the Collegium Marianum) at Münster in Westphalia. The Nazi campaign against the Jews was becoming more and more obvious and, on Holy Thursday that year, she made a Holy Hour at the Carmel in Cologne:

I spoke to the Saviour and told Him that I knew that it was His cross which was now being placed upon the Jewish people; that most of them did not understand this, but those who did, would have to take it up willingly in the name of all. I would do that. He should only show me how.[15]

In 1933, Edith was suspended from teaching as part of the anti-Jewish laws enforced by the Nazis. Soon afterwards, she spent some time in prayer asking Jesus to make it clear to her whether or not she should now enter Carmel. Between 16 July and mid-August of 1933, she lived as an extern to the Cologne Carmel and she entered the Carmel in Cologne in the Autumn of 1933 (she was then forty-two years old): 'In deep peace I stepped across the threshold into the house of the Lord'.

Clumsy at needlework and not particularly useful in the kitchen, she nevertheless found Carmelite life to her liking. Edith received the habit on 15 April 1934 and took the name Teresia Benedicta a Cruce (Teresa Blessed from the Cross). She made her first profession on Easter day, 21 April 1935. In Cologne, she was able to complete a philosophical-theological treatise that she had begun several years previous, *Finite Being and Eternal Being*, in which she tried to synthesise the philosophy of Aquinas with modern thought, especially with phenomenology. Her mother died in 1936, when Edith was forty-five. Soon afterwards, she heard with great joy of the conversion of her sister, Rosa, to Catholicism. She assisted at Rosa's Baptism in Cologne on Christmas Eve 1936, having been in hospital for treatment as a result of a fall. She made her final profession on 21 April 1938 and received the black veil.

Towards the end of 1938, the Nazi persecution of the Jews became increasingly more intense. Synagogues were burned and Jews and their friends were hounded down. Out of consideration for the other sisters at Cologne, Edith thought of emigrating to Palestine, but instead the Prioress, aware that Palestine had refused entry to German Jews, wrote to the Carmel at Echt in Holland asking them to receive Sr Teresia Benedicta. Following the famous assault against the Jews during *Kristallnacht* (Night of Broken Glass), Edith moved to Echt on New Year's Eve but continued to be a member of the Cologne Carmel. In Echt, she began to learn Dutch (she already spoke six other languages) and worked as assistant portress. In 1939, Hitler overran Poland and in 1940 he took over Holland. During the summer of 1940, Edith's sister Rosa escaped to Echt where she became a lay-associate of the Carmel and a member of the 'Third Order' or Secular Carmelites. During 1941, Edith began a phenomenological analysis of the life and mystical doctrine of St John of the Cross under the title *The Science of the Cross*:

> The example of the saints demonstrates ... how things should actually be: where there is genuine, lively faith, there the doctrine of faith and the 'tremendous deeds' of God are the content of life. All else steps aside for it and is determined by it. This is *holy realism*: the original inner receptivity of the soul reborn in the Holy Spirit ... Such realism, when it leads a holy soul to accept the truths of faith, becomes the *science of the saints*. If the mystery of the cross becomes its *inner form*, it turns into a *science of the cross*.[16]

On 20 July 1942, the Dutch Bishops issued a pastoral which condemned Hitler's cruel treatment of the Jews. As a reprisal, all non-Aryan members of the Dutch religious communities were arrested on 2 August 1942. Among these was Sr Teresia Benedicta a Cruce. She continued to work on her book, *The Science of the Cross*, up until the time of her arrest. At one point, she wrote: 'Why should I be spared? Is it not right that I should gain no advantage from my Baptism? If I cannot share the lot of my brothers and sisters, my life, in a certain sense is destroyed.' While she was being arrested at Echt to be taken to Auschwitz, she grasped the hand of her sister, Rosa, and, in the presence of the SS said, 'Come on, let's die for our people'.

She and Rosa were taken to the assembly camp at Westerbrook, where all Jews who had become Catholics were isolated in a hut. In a note she sent to the nuns at Echt she wrote, '*Ave Crux, spes unica* (Hail, O Cross, our only hope)'.

Soon afterwards, she was taken by train to the concentration camp at Auschwitz-Birkenau in Poland and sent immediately to the extermination camp at Birkenau. She died in the gas chamber alongside her Jewish brothers and sisters, probably on 9 August 1942. It was just a week since her arrest. She was fifty-one years old.

The cause of her beatification was introduced at Cologne in 1962 and at Rome in 1972. She was beatified as a martyr by Pope John Paul II at Cologne in 1987 and canonised by the same Pope in 1998. Among the martyrs of the Church she is probably unique in that she died a martyr for the Christian faith after having offered her death for the Jews. At her canonisation, Pope John Paul II presented 'this eminent daughter of Israel and faithful daughter of the Church as a saint to the whole world'. In his homily, he said that she says to us all: 'Do not accept anything as the truth if it lacks love. And do not accept anything as love which lacks truth! One without the other becomes a destructive lie.' In his homily at her canonisation, Pope John Paul II said that, when her feast day is celebrated, 'We must also remember the Shoah, that cruel plan to exterminate a people – a plan to which millions of our Jewish brothers and sisters fell victim. May the Lord let his face shine upon them and give them peace (see Num 6:25).' Edith Stein was made one of the patrons of Europe in 2000.

GOD SHOWS HIS POWERFUL PRESENCE AMONG US: THE SACRAMENTS[17]

St Augustine recognised the blood and water that came forth from the side of Christ as he slept the sleep of death upon the cross as prefiguring 'the sacraments by which the Church is formed'.[18] Referring to this text, Vatican II's constitution on the Liturgy, *Sacrosanctum concilium* 5.2, says:[19]

The wonderful works of God among the people of the Old Testament were but a prelude to the work of Christ the Lord in redeeming mankind and giving perfect glory to God. He accomplished this work principally by the paschal mystery of his blessed Passion, Resurrection from the dead, and glorious Ascension, whereby 'dying he destroyed our death, rising he restored our life.'

The Paschal Mystery in the Age of the Church[20]

For Edith Stein, the words 'through him, with him, and in him in the unity of the Holy Spirit, all honour and glory is yours, Almighty Father, for ever and ever' at the end of the Eucharistic Prayer 'encapsulate the prayer of the Church: honor and glory to the triune God through, with, and in Christ'.[21] The *Catechism* says that, in the liturgy of the Church:

> God the Father is blessed and adored as the source of all the blessings of creation and salvation with which he has blessed us in his Son, in order to give us the Spirit of filial adoption. (n. 1110)

For Edith:

> The liturgical unity of the heavenly with the earthly church, both of which thank God 'through Christ,' finds its most powerful expression in the preface and *Sanctus* of the Mass. However, the liturgy leaves no doubt that we are not yet full citizens of the heavenly Jerusalem, but pilgrims on the way to our eternal home.[22]

Echoing Edith, the *Catechism* says that 'through her liturgical actions the pilgrim Church already participates, as by a foretaste, in the heavenly liturgy' (n. 1111). Edith believed that, without the Holy Spirit, 'there would be no liturgy and no church'[23] and the *Catechism* says that the mission of the Holy Spirit in the liturgy of the Church is

> to prepare the assembly to encounter Christ; to recall and manifest Christ to the faith of the assembly; to make the saving work of Christ present and active by his transforming power; and to make the gift of communion bear fruit in the Church. (n. 1112)

Because the sacraments 'manifest and communicate ... the mystery of communion with the God who is love, One in three persons' (n. 1118), they enable the Church itself to function in the world 'like a sacrament (sign and instrument) in which the Holy Spirit dispenses the mystery of salvation' (n. 1111). It was for this reason that both St Augustine and St Thomas recognised that 'the sacraments make the Church'.[24] The *Catechism* describes the sacraments as 'efficacious signs of grace, instituted by Christ and entrusted to the Church, by which divine life is dispensed to us' (n. 1131). They are efficacious in the sense that they achieve what they signify by virtue of the saving work of Christ, already accomplished once for all, and 'by the very fact' of the sacramental action being performed.[25] As St Thomas put it, 'The sacrament is not wrought by the righteousness of either the celebrant or the recipient, but by the power of God.'[26] He described sacraments as signifying something that is past, something that is present and something that is yet in the future:

> A sacrament is a sign that commemorates what precedes it, Christ's Passion, demonstrates what is accomplished in us through Christ's Passion, grace, and prefigures what that Passion pledges to us, future glory.[27]

For St Thomas, the sacraments of the New Law were 'instituted by God to be employed for the purpose of conferring grace'.[28] For the *Catechism*:

The visible rites by which the sacraments are celebrated signify and make present the graces proper to each sacrament. They bear fruit in those who receive them with the required dispositions. (n. 1131)

Recognising that, during his earthly ministry, Christ himself explained the hidden meaning of the mysteries of the kingdom of heaven (see Mt 13:11) to his disciples, as he did on the road to Emmaus, Edith Stein points out that 'only when the Holy Ghost had been sent were the apostles able to do this exegetical work themselves'.[29] Making a similar point, the *Catechism* says:

The Holy Spirit prepares the faithful for the sacraments by the Word of God and the faith which welcomes that word in well-disposed hearts. (n. 1133)

The Sacramental Celebration of the Paschal Mystery[30]

In her Pentecost poem, Edith Stein describes the wonderful harmony that the Holy Spirit produces as different individuals allow their own 'pure tone' to become lost in the polyphony of the communion of saints, the praise poured forth 'with gladness' as each member of Christ's Mystical Body finds the 'secret meaning' of their particular voice in its contribution to the choral symphony of the saints in heaven:

Are you the sweet song of love and of holy awe resounding ever round God's throne triune, which unifies the pure tone of all beings within itself? The harmony fits the limbs to the Head, so that each blissfully finds the secret meaning of his being, and exudes it with gladness freely dissolved in your streams: Holy Spirit – Eternal Jubilation![31]

The *Catechism* also recognises the harmonious diversity of different roles and activities in the Church's liturgy:

The liturgy is the work of the whole Christ, head and body. Our high priest celebrates it unceasingly in the heavenly liturgy, with the holy Mother of God, the apostles, all the saints and the multitude of those who have already entered the kingdom. In a liturgical celebration, the whole assembly is '*leitourgos*', each member according to his own function. The baptismal priesthood is that of the whole Body of Christ. But some of the faithful are ordained through the sacrament of Holy Orders to represent Christ as head of the Body. (nn. 1187–8)

St Thomas held that, 'Since the sacred things which are signified by the sacraments are the spiritual and intelligible goods by means of which man is sanctified, it follows that the sacramental signs consist in sensible things.'[32] The *Catechism* formulates this general principle in the following way:

The liturgical celebration involves signs and symbols relating to creation (candles, water, fire), human life (washing, anointing, breaking bread) and the history of salvation (the rites of the Passover). Integrated into the world of faith and taken up by the power of the Holy Spirit, these cosmic elements, human rituals, and gestures of remembrance of God become bearers of the saving and sanctifying action of Christ. (n. 1189)

Since the Eucharist is 'a mystery of faith', St Thomas believed that the readings during Mass were necessary for the 'instruction of the faithful' and he distinguished between the Gospel and the other readings, because 'the people are instructed "perfectly" by Christ's teaching contained in the Gospel'.[33] According to the *Catechism*:

The Liturgy of the Word is an integral part of the celebration. The meaning of the celebration is expressed by the Word of God which is proclaimed and by the response of faith to it. (n. 1190)

In his letter to the Colossians (3:16), St Paul encourages them: '[A]nd with gratitude in your hearts sing psalms, hymns, and spiritual songs to God.' The *Catechism* quotes St Augustine, who tells us that he had been deeply moved by singing he had heard in the Church:

> How I wept, deeply moved by your hymns, songs, and the voices that echoed through your Church! What emotion I experienced in them! Those sounds flowed into my ears, distilling the truth in my heart. A feeling of devotion surged within me, and tears streamed down my face – tears that did me good. (n. 1157)[34]

Presumably on the basis of his own experience, Augustine believed that 'He who sings prays twice'[35] and, noting that 'song and music are closely connected with the liturgical action', the *Catechism* points out that the criteria for their proper use 'are the beauty expressive of prayer, the unanimous participation of the assembly, and the sacred character of the celebration' (n. 1191).

When Edith Stein was being driven from Cologne to the greater safety of the Carmel at Echt on New Year's Eve 1938, she made a short stop at the Carmelite church of Mary of Peace in the centre of Cologne, where she prayed at the statue of Our Lady, Queen of Peace.[36] While she was at Echt, Edith once said to Johannes Hirschmann SJ:

> You don't know what it means to me when I come into the chapel in the morning and, seeing the tabernacle and the picture of Mary, say to myself: they were of our blood.[37]

The *Catechism* recognises the importance of such images when it says:

> Sacred images in our churches and homes are intended to awaken and nourish our faith in the mystery of Christ. Through the icon of Christ and his works of salvation it is he whom we adore. Through sacred images of the holy Mother of God, of the angels and of the saints, we venerate the persons represented. (n. 1192)

Edith followed the yearly cycle of the Church's liturgy and its feasts and, in a reflection she wrote for the Epiphany in 1941, she describes the 'saints whom the church shows us' during that season (St Stephen, the Holy Innocents and St John the Evangelist) as 'the court of the new-born King of Kings'.[38] Quoting Vatican II's *Sacrosanctum Concilium* 102.2, the *Catechism* says that, in the course of the year, the Church

> [U]nfolds the whole mystery of Christ from his Incarnation and Nativity through his Ascension, to Pentecost and the expectation of the blessed hope of the coming of the Lord. (n. 1194)

It adds:

> By keeping the memorials of the saints – first of all the holy Mother of God, then the apostles, the martyrs and other saints – on fixed days of the liturgical year, the Church on earth shows that she is united with the liturgy of heaven. She gives glory to Christ for having accomplished his salvation in his glorified members; their example encourages her on her way to the Father. (n. 1195)

For Edith Stein, the purpose of the 'Divine Office' is to see that whatever arises from hearts filled with the Holy Spirit 'continues to resound from generation to generation'.[39] The *Catechism* says:

> The faithful who celebrate the Liturgy of the Hours are united to Christ our high priest, by the prayer of the Psalms, meditation on the Word of God, and canticles and blessings, in order to be joined with his unceasing and universal prayer that gives glory to the Father and implores the gift of the Holy Spirit on the whole world. (n. 1196)

Edith says that, in place of Solomon's temple:

> Christ has built a temple of living stones, the communion of saints. At its center, he stands as the eternal high priest; on its altar he is himself the perpetual sacrifice.[40]

The *Catechism* says:

> Christ is the true temple of God, 'the place where his glory dwells'; by the grace of God, Christians also become temples of the Holy Spirit, living stones out of which the Church is built. (n. 1197)

In 1916, long before her conversion to Christianity, Edith visited Frankfurt as a tourist and her experience in the cathedral there made a deep impression:

> We stopped in at the cathedral for a few minutes; and, while we looked around in respectful silence, a woman carrying a market basket came in and knelt down in one of the pews to pray briefly. This was something entirely

new to me. To the synagogues or to the Protestant churches which I had visited, one went only for services. But here was someone interrupting her everyday shopping errands to come into this church, although no other person was in it, as though she were here for an intimate conversation. I could never forget that.[41]

Recognising that, in her earthly state, 'the Church needs places where the community can gather together' and that churches are 'holy places, images of the holy city, the earthly Jerusalem' (n. 1198), the *Catechism* also recognises that 'churches are also places of recollection and personal prayer' (n. 1199).

The word 'Catholic' comes from the Greek word '*kath'olou*' (meaning 'according to the whole' or 'in general') and it was first used to describe the church in the writings of St Ignatius of Antioch: 'Where the bishop is to be seen, let all the people be; just as where Jesus Christ is, there is the catholic church'.[42] Recognising that 'the liturgy itself generates cultures and shapes them', the *Catechism* recognises that 'liturgical celebration tends to express itself in the culture of the people where the Church finds itself' (n. 1207). The various legitimate liturgical traditions or rites 'manifest the catholicity of the Church, because they signify and communicate the same mystery of Christ' (n. 1208). Echoing St Ignatius, the *Catechism* says:

> The criterion that assures unity amid the diversity of liturgical traditions is fidelity to apostolic Tradition, i.e., the communion in the faith and the sacraments received from the apostles, a communion that is both signified and guaranteed by apostolic succession. (n. 1209)

THE SEVEN SACRAMENTS OF THE CHURCH[43]

For St Thomas, the seven sacraments touch all the significant moments of Christian life.[44] Baptism is the first step in the

Christian walk of life and the Sacrament of the Sick is the last sacrament, because it 'completes in a certain sense the whole spiritual care' provided for us by all seven sacraments.[45] St Teresia Benedicta a Cruce held that:

> The union of the soul with Christ ... is a rooting and growing in Him (so we are told by the parable of the vine and the branches) which begins in baptism, and which is constantly strengthened and formed through the sacraments in diverse ways.[46]

The *Catechism* recognises that, within the organic whole of the seven sacraments, 'the Eucharist occupies a unique place as the "Sacrament of sacraments"' (n. 1211). It quotes St Thomas, who regarded the Eucharist as the 'most important (*potissimum*)' of the sacraments, and who held that 'all the other sacraments are ordered to it as to their end'.[47]

The Sacraments of Christian Initiation: Baptism, Confirmation and Eucharist[48]

The *Catechism* sums up the roles of Baptism, Confirmation and Eucharist in the process of being initiated into Christianity when it says:

> Christian initiation is accomplished by three sacraments together: Baptism which is the beginning of new life; Confirmation which is its strengthening; and the Eucharist which nourishes the disciple with Christ's Body and Blood for his transformation in Christ. (n. 1275)

In order to cultivate an appreciation of the way in which these three Sacraments are closely associated with one another, the links between them are highlighted by the way in which they are celebrated:

When Confirmation is celebrated separately from Baptism, its connection with Baptism is expressed, among other ways, by the renewal of baptismal promises. The celebration of Confirmation during the Eucharist helps underline the unity of the sacraments of Christian initiation. (n. 1321)

In this section, I will outline what the Catholic Church believes about the sacraments of Baptism, Confirmation and Eucharist.

Jesus began his public life after being baptised by John the Baptist in the Jordan (see Mt 3:13) and, after his resurrection, he gave the following mission to his disciples (n. 1276):

Go therefore and make disciples of all nations, baptizing them in the name of the Father and of the Son and of the Holy Spirit, and teaching them to obey everything that I have commanded you (Mt 28:19-20).

But what is the essential rite of the sacrament of Baptism? For St Thomas, the rite lay not in the water as such, but rather in the application of water to the person being baptised, i.e. in the washing (*ablutio*) accompanied with the form of words.[49] According to the *Catechism*, the essential rite 'consists in immersing the candidate in water or pouring water on his head, while pronouncing the invocation of the Most Holy Trinity: the Father, the Son, and the Holy Spirit' (n. 1278).

What changes does Baptism bring about? For St Ignatius of Antioch, it enables the Incarnate Word to dwell in our souls, providing us with the protection of belonging to the community of the Church in our spiritual battle with the powers of evil: 'Let your baptism serve as a shield, faith as a helmet, love as a spear, endurance as full armour'.[50] The specific effects of baptism mentioned by St Thomas Aquinas include absolution from all guilt and punishment, giving grace, increasing virtue, incorporating a person into Christ, and opening up the way into the reign of God.[51] The *Catechism* summarises the faith of the Church on this question:

> The grace or fruit of baptism is a rich reality that includes forgiveness of original sin and all personal sins, birth into the new life by which man becomes an adoptive son of the Father, a member of Christ and a temple of the Holy Spirit. By this very fact the person baptised is incorporated into the Church, the Body of Christ, and made a sharer in the priesthood of Christ. (nn. 1279–80)

The *Catechism* also says:

> Baptism imprints on the soul an indelible spiritual sign, the character, which consecrates the baptized person for Christian worship. Because of the character Baptism cannot be repeated.[52] (n. 1280)

For St Thomas Aquinas, Baptism is 'necessary for salvation inasmuch as humanity's salvation is not possible without possession of baptism at least in will'.[53] Based on the position adopted in Vatican II's Dogmatic Constitution on the Church (*Lumen gentium* 16), the *Catechism* says:

> Those who die for the faith, those who are catechumens, and all those who, without knowing of the Church but acting under the inspiration of grace, seek God sincerely and strive to fulfil his will, are saved even if they have not been baptized. (n. 1281)

St Thomas also held that the gratuitous character of salvation and the communal nature of the Church justified the baptism of those incapable of personal faith.[54] If infants could contract original sin from Adam, then they could 'far sooner receive grace through Christ'.[55] For St Thomas, the (natural) faith and intention required of an adult are substituted – in the case of a child or of those lacking the use of reason – by the faith and intention of those requesting baptism on its behalf or by the faith and intention of the Church as such.[56] The *Catechism* sums up the faith of the Church on infant baptism as follows:

> Since the earliest times, Baptism has been administered to children, for it is a grace and a gift of God that does not presuppose any human merit; children are baptized in the faith of the Church. Entry into Christian life gives access to true freedom. (n. 1282)

For Aquinas, infants could, perhaps, receive grace from God as a special privilege and, as a result, they might enjoy a certain natural happiness ('Limbo'), even though they were denied the fullness of beatitude since they were not, as such, baptised.[57] Recent official teaching documents of the Church tend to omit any reference to Limbo in favour of a position that emphasises God's mercy and our ignorance about how unbaptised children might find salvation. In 1980, the *Instruction on Infant Baptism* said:

> The Church has ... shown by her teaching and practice that she knows no other way apart from baptism for ensuring children's entry into eternal happiness ...As for children who die without baptism, the Church can only entrust them to God's mercy, as she does in the funeral rite provided for them. (n. 13)

The *Catechism* repeated this position: 'With respect to children who have died without Baptism, the liturgy of the Church invites us to trust in God's mercy and to pray for their salvation' (n. 1283).

For St Ignatius of Antioch, the term 'Baptism' referred to the process of Christian initiation as a whole, including the three sacraments that are now known as Baptism, Confirmation and First Eucharist. Recognising the role of the bishop in this process, he insisted that it was not permitted to celebrate baptism 'without the bishop'.[58] For St Thomas, the usual minister was a presbyter, but anybody could baptise in an emergency 'so that no one may be deprived of their salvation because they have not come to baptism'.[59] The *Catechism* adopts the same position, specifying the minimum requirements:

> In case of necessity, any person can baptize provided that he have the intention of doing that which the Church does and provided that he pours water on the candidate's head while saying: 'I baptize you in the name of the Father, and of the Son, and of the Holy Spirit.' (n. 1284)

The Catholic Church believes that the process of Christian initiation is begun, rather than completed, in Baptism and that the gift of new life in Christ that we receive in Baptism is sealed and strengthened in Confirmation. Aquinas held that Christ did not institute the sacrament of Confirmation directly (*non exhibendo*), but by means of a promise (see Jn 16:7) in view of the fact that the Spirit could not be given before the Lord's resurrection and ascension.[60] On the basis of chapter eight of the Acts of the Apostles, he argued that Confirmation was the prerogative of bishops who were the successors of the Apostles.[61] Like Aquinas, the principal New Testament text quoted by the *Catechism* (see n. 1315) in relation to the sacrament of Confirmation is Acts 8:14–17:

> Now when the apostles at Jerusalem heard that Samaria had accepted the word of God, they sent Peter and John to them. The two went down and prayed for them that they might receive the Holy Spirit (for as yet the Spirit

had not come upon any of them; they had only been baptized in the name of the Lord Jesus). Then Peter and John laid their hands on them and they received the Holy Spirit.

St Augustine interpreted 1 John 2:20, 'You have been anointed by the Holy One', as a reference to the anointing with chrism by the bishop that took place immediately after Baptism with water and before the Eucharist during the all night liturgy of Christian initiation: 'The spiritual anointing is the Holy Spirit himself, the mystery of whose coming is in a visible anointing'.[62] For St Thomas, Baptism is sealed, perfected and brought to full Christian maturity (*aetas perfecta*) by Confirmation.[63] It brings about 'the increase and defence of righteousness'[64] and it is the Pentecost in the life of a Christian because it gives the baptised the fullness of the Spirit to strengthen them (*ad robur*)[65] and enable them to 'carry out what belongs to the spiritual struggle against the enemies of faith'.[66] The *Catechism's* debt to St Thomas can be seen in its description of the fruits of Confirmation:

> Confirmation perfects Baptismal grace; it is the sacrament which gives the Holy Spirit in order to root us more deeply in the divine filiation, incorporate us more firmly into Christ, strengthen our bond with the Church, associate us more closely with her mission, and help us bear witness to the Christian faith in words accompanied by deeds. (n. 1316)

Like Baptism, Confirmation imprints an indelible character on the Christian's soul, 'the sign that Jesus Christ has marked a Christian with the seal of his Spirit' (n. 1304), and 'for this reason, one can receive this sacrament only once in one's life' (n. 1317). Quoting St Thomas, who said, 'The confirmed person receives the power to profess faith in Christ publicly and as it were officially (*quasi ex officio*)',[67] the *Catechism* describes the 'character' of Confirmation as perfecting 'the common priesthood of the faithful, received in Baptism' (n. 1305).

In the Eastern tradition, which highlights 'the unity of the three sacraments of Christian initiation', Confirmation 'is administered immediately after Baptism and is followed by participation in the Eucharist' (n. 1318). St Thomas was more familiar with the traditions of the Latin Church, where:

> [Confirmation] is administered when the age of reason has been reached, and its celebration is ordinarily reserved to the bishop, thus signifying that this sacrament strengthens the ecclesial bond. (n. 1319)

He recognised, however, that Confirmation has enabled many children to attain spiritual maturity:

> Age of body does not determine age of soul. Even in childhood man can attain spiritual maturity: as the book of Wisdom says: 'For old age is not honoured for length of time, or measured by number of years' (Wis 4:8). Many children, through the strength of the Holy Spirit they have received, have bravely fought for Christ even to the shedding of their blood.[68]

By the Middle Ages, anointing with chrism was the usual way of conferring this sacrament and St Thomas believed that the reference to laying on of hands in chapter eight of the Acts of the Apostles was an earlier symbolic form of this anointing.[69] In order to retain the direct association between the rite of Confirmation and the laying on of hands, both anointing and laying on of hands form part of the present rite:

> The essential rite of Confirmation is anointing the forehead of the baptized with sacred chrism (in the East

other sense-organs as well), together with the laying on of the minister's hand and the words: *Accipe signaculum doni Spiritus Sancti* [Be sealed with the Gift of the Holy Spirit] in the Roman rite, or 'The seal of the gift that is the Holy Spirit' in the Byzantine rite. (n. 1320)

We believe that the Eucharist continually nourishes the gift of new life that we have received in Baptism, and the sealing and strengthening of that gift of new life in Confirmation. It is the Eucharist that completes the process of our Christian initiation[70] by enabling us to abide in Christ and Christ to abide in us:

Jesus said: 'I am the living bread that came down from heaven; if any one eats of this bread, he will live for ever ... he who eats my flesh and drinks my blood has eternal life and ... abides in me, and I in him' (Jn 6:51, 54, 56). (n. 1406)

St Teresia Benedicta a Cruce wrote:

Whoever wants to preserve this [divine] life continually within herself must nourish it constantly from the source whence it flows without end – from the holy sacraments, above all from the sacrament of love.[71]

The *Catechism* presents the Eucharist as enabling the Church to be associated with, and to receive the graces that flow from, Christ's saving death on the Cross:

The Eucharist is the heart and the summit of the Church's life, for in it Christ associates his Church and all her members with his sacrifice of praise and thanksgiving offered once for all on the cross to his Father; by this sacrifice he pours out the graces of salvation on his Body which is the Church. (n. 1407)

The essential elements of the Eucharist, which constitute 'one single act of worship', are outlined in the *Catechism* as:

> The proclamation of the Word of God; thanksgiving to God the Father for all his benefits, above all the gift of his Son; the consecration of bread and wine; and participation in the liturgical banquet by receiving the Lord's body and blood. (n. 1408)

St Teresia Benedicta described participation in the Holy Sacrifice of the Mass as consummating 'the holy sacrifice *as* an offering in union with the Eucharistic Lord'.[72]

Since the words of consecration are those of Christ, and since it was only to the Twelve that he said 'Do this in memory of me', St Thomas argued that only ordained presbyters/priests, who can act 'in the person of Christ (*in persona Christi*)', can validly celebrate the Eucharist.[73] Following the teaching of the Council of Trent,[74] the *Catechism* teaches us:

> By the consecration the transubstantiation of the bread and wine into the Body and Blood of Christ is brought about. Under the consecrated species of bread and wine Christ himself, living and glorious, is present in a true, real and substantial manner: his Body and his Blood, with his soul and his divinity. (n. 1413)

St Ignatius of Antioch associated a refusal to recognise the Eucharist as the body and blood of Christ with the refusal of the Docetist heresy to accept the reality of the Incarnation:

> [F]or these there will be judgment, if they do not believe in the blood of Christ. Take note of those who hold heterodox opinions on the grace of Jesus Christ which has come to us, and see how contrary their opinions are to the mind of God. For love they have no care, nor for

the widow, nor for the orphan, nor for the distressed, nor for those in prison or freed from prison, nor for the hungry and thirsty. They abstain from the Eucharist and from prayer, because they do not confess that the Eucharist is the flesh of our Saviour Jesus Christ, flesh which suffered for our sins and which the Father, in his goodness, raised up again. They who deny the gift of God (see Jn 4:10) are perishing in their disputes. It would be better for them to have love, for that they might rise again. It is right to shun such people, and not even to speak to them, either in public or in private.[75]

Recognising 'transubstantiation' as a suitable name for the change of substance that takes place during the Eucharist, St Thomas Aquinas insisted that the substance of bread and wine are no longer present because they have been changed into the substance of Christ's body and blood.[76] He believed that the change in substance 'cannot be apprehended by the senses but *only by faith*, which relies on divine authority'.[77] Gerard Manley Hopkins translates the meditation on this truth in the *Adoro te*, which is attributed to St Thomas, as follows:

> Seeing, touching, tasting, are in thee deceived;
> How says trusty hearing? that shall be believed;
> What God's Son has told me, take for truth I do;
> Truth himself speaks truly or there's nothing true.[78]

From the earliest centuries, the sacrifice of the Mass has been offered for the faithful departed. The *Catechism* (n. 1371) notes that, when she was dying, St Augustine's mother, St Monica, told her sons: 'Put this body anywhere! Don't trouble yourselves about it! I simply ask you to remember me at the Lord's altar wherever you are.'[79] The *Catechism* says:

As sacrifice, the Eucharist is also offered in reparation for the sins of the living and the dead, and to obtain spiritual or temporal benefits from God. (n. 1414)

Noting that it 'moves us to an ever more complete participation in our Redeemer's sacrifice which we celebrate in the Eucharist', the *Catechism* also says (n. 1372) that St Augustine admirably summed up the doctrine about offering the sacrifice of Mass when he wrote:

This wholly redeemed city, the assembly and society of the saints, is offered to God as a universal sacrifice by the high priest who in the form of a slave went so far as to offer himself for us in his Passion, to make us the Body of so great a head ... Such is the sacrifice of Christians: 'we who are many are one Body in Christ' (Rom 12:5). The Church continues to reproduce this sacrifice in the sacrament of the altar so well-known to believers wherein it is evident to them that in what she offers she herself is offered.[80]

St Thomas held that sin is an obstacle to the fruitful reception of the sacrament[81] and the *Catechism* says:

Anyone who desires to receive Christ in Eucharistic communion must be in the state of grace. Anyone aware of having sinned mortally must not receive communion without having received absolution in the sacrament of Penance. (n. 1415)

The *Catechism* states: 'Communion with the Body and Blood of Christ increases the communicant's union with the Lord, forgives his venial sins and preserves him from grave sins' (n. 1416). It also adds: 'Since receiving this sacrament strengthens the bonds of charity between the communicant and Christ, it also reinforces the unity of the church as the Mystical Body of Christ.' St Teresia Benedicta held that 'guidance towards frequent communion, ideally daily reception', was a necessary part of religious education if 'the strongest realities of nature' were to be 'confronted with the even stronger realities of the supernatural'.[82] Pointing out that the Eucharistic Communion of the whole Church is the 'first meaning of the phrase "communion of saints" in the Apostolic Creed', the *Catechism* says that, every time we celebrate the mystery of the Eucharist, 'the work of our redemption is carried on' (n. 1331). As St Ignatius of Antioch put it:

> [We] break the one bread that provides the medicine of immortality, the antidote to death, and the food that makes us live for ever in Jesus Christ.[83]

Eucharistic Communion presumes communion with the Pope and the bishops, and the *Catechism* quotes St Ignatius of Antioch when it points out that the bishop of the place 'is always responsible for the Eucharist, even when a priest presides' (n. 1369):

> Let only that Eucharist be regarded as legitimate, which is celebrated under [the presidency of] the bishop or him to whom he has entrusted it.[84]

St Ignatius of Antioch emphasised the unity of the local church under its bishop and he associated this unity with the unity of the diocese as expressed in the way it celebrated the Eucharist:

> Make certain therefore, that you all observe one common Eucharist, for there is but one body of our Lord Jesus Christ, and but one cup of union with his blood, and one single altar of sacrifice even as also there

is but one *episcopos* with his clergy and my own fellow servitors the deacons.[85]

St Thomas recognised that Christ continues to be present in the Eucharist that is reserved in the church for adoration or for those who may not have been present when the Eucharist was celebrated (due to illness, for example), but who may want to receive it later.[86] St Teresia Benedicta wrote:

> Whoever is imbued with a lively faith in Christ present in the tabernacle, whoever knows that a friend awaits here constantly – always with the time, patience, and sympathy to listen to complaints, petitions, and problems, with counsel and help in all things – this person cannot remain desolate and forsaken even under the greatest difficulties. He always has a refuge where quietude and peace can again be found.[87]

For St Thomas, the Eucharist leads us ultimately to the glory of heaven, 'the society of the saints where there will be peace and full and perfect unity':

> The sacrament does not immediately lead us into glory, but it gives us the power to reach glory.[88]

St Teresia Benedicta wrote that 'life with the Eucharistic Savior induces the soul to be lifted out of the narrowness of its individual, personal orbit'.[89] The *Catechism* outlines this dimension of the Eucharist in the following terms:

> Having passed from this world to the Father, Christ gives us in the Eucharist the pledge of glory with him. Participation in the Holy Sacrifice identifies us with his Heart, sustains our strength along the pilgrimage of this life, makes us long for eternal life and unites us even now

to the Church in heaven, the Blessed Virgin Mary and all the saints. (n. 1419)

Having outlined the teaching of the *Catechism* on the three sacraments of Christian initiation, we now turn to the two sacraments of healing.

The Sacraments of Healing: Penance/Reconciliation and the Sacrament of the Sick[90]

The principal New Testament text quoted by the *Catechism* (n. 1485) in relation to the sacrament of Penance and Reconciliation is John 20:19-23, where Jesus gives his apostles his divine power to forgive sin 'to exercise in his name' (n. 1441):

> When it was evening on that day, the first day of the week ... Jesus showed himself to his apostles ... He breathed on them and said to them, 'Receive the Holy Spirit. If you forgive the sins of any, they are forgiven them; if you retain the sins of any, they are retained' (Jn 20:19, 22-23).

The effects of sin are described by the *Catechism* in the following terms:

> The sinner wounds God's honour and love, his own human dignity as a man called to be a son of God, and the spiritual well-being of the Church, of which each Christian ought to be a living stone. (n. 1487)

St Ignatius of Antioch held that the Lord 'forgives all who repent, if their repentance leads to the unity of God and to the council of the bishop'.[91] According to the *Catechism*:

> The movement of return to God, called conversion and repentance, entails sorrow for and abhorrence of sins

committed, and the firm purpose of sinning no more in the future. Conversion touches the past and the future, and is nourished by hope in God's mercy. (n. 1490)

For Aquinas, the penitent's contrition, confession of sin and intention to make reparation function as the essential 'matter' of the sacrament of penance and the action of the priest granting absolution provides the required 'form'.[92] St Teresia Benedicta a Cruce highlights the aspect of inner restoration in this sacrament:

> In all instances where sin was committed through one's own fault and the danger of being cut off from the stream of grace exists, there comes the possibility of an inner restoration through the sacrament of penance: one can be freed always from the burden of the past and, as one newborn, face the future.[93]

Aquinas held that venial sin did not rupture a person's relationship either with God or with the Church, while mortal sin ruptured both these relationships.[94] The sacrament was the external symbolic expression of the interior virtue of repentance and genuine contrition. Perfect contrition, the repentance that arises from love of charity for God,[95] already obtains the forgiveness of sins and reconciliation with the Church. It did so, however, as an 'anticipated effect' of the actual celebration of the sacrament which such contrition necessarily desires. Imperfect contrition was perfected by the sacrament. After mortal sin, therefore, the sacrament of Penance was a normative and necessary part of restoring the relationship between the sinner and the Church so that the individual could express their communion with God and with the Church by receiving the Eucharist:

> [T]hey should not, nevertheless, be admitted to the sacraments of the Church, unless they are reconciled to

the Church, unless they are absolved beforehand by a priest, so that those who have been baptised, once [that] baptism is in flames, are not admitted to the Eucharist.[96]

According to the *Catechism* (n. 1496), the spiritual effects of the sacrament of Penance are:

- reconciliation with God by which the penitent recovers grace;
- reconciliation with the Church;
- remission of the eternal punishment incurred by mortal sins;
- remission, at least in part, of temporal punishments resulting from sin;
- peace and serenity of conscience, and spiritual consolation;
- an increase of spiritual strength for the Christian battle.

St Thomas understood the forgiveness of sin in the sacrament of Penance as an act of jurisdiction by which the priest, in the name of the Church, authoritatively made the fruits of the Church's intercession for sinners available to a particular individual. He understood indulgences in the same way, as the application to a particular individual of the fruits of the Church's intercession for those who were in need of such purification.[97] The *Catechism* sums up the faith of the Church in relation to indulgences in this way:

> Through indulgences the faithful can obtain the remission of temporal punishment resulting from sin for themselves and also for the souls in Purgatory. (n. 1498)

The idea of the sacrament of Penance and Reconciliation as a sacrament of 'healing', in the broad sense of that term, has become relatively commonplace. The same cannot be said for the sacrament of the Sick, unfortunately, and many people continue to regard it as a sure sign that all hope has been lost, that death is imminent and that no 'healing' is either likely or possible. Writing at a time when this sacrament was the final sacrament that a person received before dying, St Thomas Aquinas saw it as primarily intended to prepare the dying for future glory, but he accepted that it could help the dying person to recover:

> By means of it, the person is prepared, so to say, to enter into glory; and for this reason it is called Extreme Unction. And it is therefore evident that this sacrament is not conferred on every sick person, but on those who, because of their sickness, are near to death. Nevertheless, if they recover, the sacrament may be conferred on them again, whenever they find themselves in the same situation.[98]

The text of James 5:14-15 describes the anointing of the sick by the presbyters as the Church's normal response to serious sickness:

> Are any among you sick? They should call for the elders of the Church and have them pray over them, anointing them with oil in the name of the Lord. The prayer of faith will save the sick, and the Lord will raise them up; and anyone who has committed sins will be forgiven. (n. 1526)

The *Catechism* presents this sacrament as providing a special grace for those experiencing grave illness or old age, something that should be received as soon as death becomes a threat, rather than when the person is already on their deathbed. It may be repeated each time someone falls into serious illness:

The sacrament of Anointing of the Sick has as its purpose the conferral of a special grace on the Christian experiencing the difficulties inherent in the condition of grave illness or old age. The proper time for receiving this holy anointing has certainly arrived when the believer begins to be in danger of death because of illness or old age. Each time a Christian falls seriously ill, he may receive the Anointing of the Sick, and also when, after he has received it, the illness returns. (nn. 1527–9)

Because of the fact that it also forgave sins under certain circumstances, St Thomas recognised the close association between the sacrament of the Sick and the sacrament of Penance. He recognised, however, that:

This sacrament is not given against the sins which take life, i.e. original and mortal sin, but against the shortcomings which spiritually weaken a person by taking away the needed strength for the activities of the life of grace and of glory. These shortcomings are nothing other than a certain weakness and ineptitude remaining in us after actual sin or after original sin. It is against this weakness that a person is fortified by this sacrament ... But since this fortifying effect is produced by a grace which, as such, is incompatible with sin, it follows that, if there is some mortal or venial sin, the sacrament [of anointing] takes it away as a consequence in so far as there is blame ... The healing of the body is not always derived from this sacrament, but only that which is useful to spiritual healing.[99]

According to the *Catechism* (n. 1532), the special grace of the sacrament of the Anointing of the Sick has as its effects:

- the uniting of the sick person to the Passion of Christ, for his own good and that of the whole Church;
- the strengthening, peace and courage to endure in a Christian manner the sufferings of illness or old age;
- the forgiveness of sins, if the sick person was not able to obtain it through the sacrament of Penance;
- the restoration of health, if it is conducive to the salvation of his soul;
- the preparation for passing over to eternal life.

St Thomas held that only ordained priests could validly administer this sacrament[100] and that is also the position of the *Catechism*:

> Only priests (presbyters and bishops) can give the sacrament of the Anointing of the Sick, using oil blessed by the bishop, or if necessary by the celebrating presbyter himself. (n. 1530)

Having outlined the three sacraments of Christian initiation and the two sacraments of healing, we now turn to the two sacraments at the service of communion.

The Sacraments at the Service of Communion: Holy Orders and Matrimony[101]

The *Catechism* refers to the New Testament letters of St Paul to Timothy and Titus when it indicates the nature of the sacrament of Holy Orders as a gift received through the laying on of hands and as the task of providing leadership in each local community:

> St Paul said to his disciple Timothy: 'I remind you to rekindle the gift of God that is within you through the laying on of my hands' (2 Tim 1:6) and 'If any one aspires to the office of bishop, he desires a noble task' (1

Tim 3:1). To Titus he said: 'This is why I left you in Crete, that you amend what was defective, and appoint presbyters in every town, as I directed you' (Titus 1:5). (n. 1590)

In addition to the deacons, priests and bishops of the Church, St Ignatius of Antioch recognised the role played by 'prophets' who speak God's word to the people and instruct them about Jesus through the Gospel:

> [G]ive heed to the prophets, and above all, to the Gospel, in which the passion (of Christ) has been revealed to us, and the resurrection has been fully proved.[102]

In his commentary on the Letter to the Hebrews (8:4), St Thomas Aquinas recognised that there is only one true priest, Jesus Christ, and that it is as his ministers that others have received a share in his priesthood: 'Only Christ is the true priest, the others being only his ministers'.[103] The *Catechism* describes the way in which Baptism and Holy Orders enable people to share in Christ's priesthood in two different ways:

> The whole Church is a priestly people. Through Baptism all the faithful share in the priesthood of Christ. This participation is called the 'common priesthood of the faithful.' Based on this common priesthood and ordered to its service, there exists another participation in the mission of Christ: the ministry conferred by the sacrament of Holy Orders, where the task is to serve in the name and in the person of Christ the Head in the midst of the community. (n. 1591)

The ministerial priesthood of the ordained differs in essence from the common priesthood of the faithful 'because it confers a sacred power for the service of the faithful' that is exercised 'by teaching (*munus docendi*), divine worship (*munus liturgicum*) and pastoral governance (*munus regendi*)' (n. 1592). Unlike the Old Testament priests who prefigured Christ, the sacrament of Holy Orders enables the ministerial priest to act in the person of Christ, the Head of the Church. The *Catechism* refers to 'the beautiful expression of St Ignatius of Antioch' who described the bishop as being 'an image of the Father (*typos tou Patris*)' (n. 1549).[104] Developing a similar understanding of the ministerial priesthood, St Thomas wrote:

> Christ is the source of all priesthood: the priest of the old law was a figure of Christ, and the priest of the new law acts in the person of Christ (*in persona Christi*, see 2 Cor 2:10).[105]

St Ignatius of Antioch recognised the ministry of deacons, presbyters (priests) and bishops as essential elements of the Church:

> In like manner let everyone respect the deacons as they would respect Jesus Christ, and just as they respect the bishop as a type of the Father, and the presbyters as the council of God and college of the apostles. Without these, it cannot be called a Church.[106]

Ignatius described a kind of ascending hierarchy of deacons, presbyters and bishops, and he insisted that the laity should be subject to this hierarchy:

> Let all be subject to the bishop, just as Jesus Christ is subject to his Father, and to the presbyterium just as to the apostles; as to the deacons, respect them just as you respect the law of God.[107]

119

St Thomas originally regarded episcopal orders as a special honour given to some priests, rather than as a sacrament, but he later changed his mind.[108] The *Catechism* says:

> The bishop receives the fullness of the sacrament of Holy Orders, which integrates him into the episcopal college and makes him the visible head of the particular Church entrusted to him. As successors of the apostles and members of the college, the bishops share in the apostolic responsibility and mission of the whole Church under the authority of the Pope, successor of St Peter. (n. 1594)

The role of presbyters (priests) is described in the *Catechism* as follows:

> Priests are united with the bishops in sacerdotal dignity and at the same time depend on them in the exercise of their pastoral functions; they are called to be the bishops' prudent co-workers. They form around their bishop the presbyterium which bears responsibility with him for the particular Church. They receive from the bishop the charge of a parish community or a determinate ecclesial office. (n. 1595)

The ministry of deacons is summarised in the *Catechism* in the following words:

> Deacons are ministers ordained for tasks of service of the Church; they do not receive the ministerial priesthood, but ordination confers on them important functions in the ministry of the word, divine worship, pastoral governance and the service of charity, tasks which they must carry out under the pastoral authority of their bishop. (n. 1596)

St Thomas held that a priest consecrates the Eucharist 'not by his own power, but as Christ's minister in whose person he acts'.[109] In a similar way, the *Catechism* recognises that it is God, and not the ordaining minister, who is the source of the graces of ordination when it says that the sacrament of Holy Orders

> is conferred by the laying on of hands followed by a solemn prayer of consecration asking God to grant the ordinand the graces of the Holy Spirit required for his ministry. (n. 1597)

St Thomas Aquinas held that, 'in its principle signification, namely the intellectual nature', the image of God 'is found both in man and in woman'.[110] Since 'it is Christ who principally baptises', he held that 'a man and a woman can, in the same way, baptise in the case of necessity'.[111] He also seems to have accepted that a woman could represent the whole human race, for he regarded the Blessed Virgin Mary at the Annunciation as giving consent 'in lieu of that of the entire human nature' to its spiritual wedlock with the Son of God.[112] He accepted that the priest consecrates the Eucharist 'not by his own power, but as Christ's minister in whose person he acts',[113] but he insisted that all 'sacramental signs signify by reason of their natural likeness'. Since the priest acts in Christ's 'person' when the Eucharist is consecrated, he seems to have held that only a male could validly receive the sacrament of Holy Orders.[114] St Teresia Benedicta a Cruce gave her view of 'the difficult and much debated question of priesthood for women' in the following, rather lengthy, text:

> If we consider the attitude of the Lord himself, we understand that he accepted the free loving services of women for himself and his Apostles and that women were among his disciples and most intimate confidantes. Yet he did not grant them the priesthood,

not even to his mother, Queen of Apostles, who was exalted above all humanity in human perfection and fullness of grace. In the early Church, women played an active part in the various congregational charities, and their intense apostolate as confessors and martyrs had a profound effect. Virginal purity was celebrated in the liturgy, and for women there was also a consecrated ecclesiastical office – the diaconate with its special ordination – but the church did not go so far as to admit them to the priesthood as well. And in later historical developments, women were displaced from these posts; also, it seems that under the influence of the Hebraic and Roman judicial concepts, there was a gradual decline in their canonical status. We are witnessing a decided change here in recent times: feminine energies are now strongly demanded as help in church charities and pastoral work. In recent militant movements, the women are demanding that their ministries be recognized once more as an ordained church ministry, and it may well be that one day attention will be given to their demands. Whether this will be the first step then, finally, on the path leading to women in the priesthood is the question. It seems to me that such an implementation by the church, until now unheard of, cannot be forbidden by dogma. However, the practicality of such a recommendation brings into play various arguments both pro and con. The whole tradition speaks *against* it from the beginning. But in my opinion, even more significant is the mysterious fact emphasized earlier – that Christ came on earth as the *Son* of Man. The first creature on earth fashioned in an unrivalled sense as God's image was therefore a man; that seems to indicate to me that He wished to institute only men as His official representatives on earth.[115]

The *Catechism* sums up the teaching of the Church on this question as follows:

> The Church confers the sacrament of Holy Orders only on baptized men (*viri*) whose suitability for the exercise of the ministry has been duly recognized. Church authority alone has the responsibility and right to call someone to receive the sacrament of Holy Orders. (n. 1598)

St Thomas understood the discipline of priestly celibacy as a matter of Church rather than divine law.[116] The *Catechism* says:

> In the Latin Church the sacrament of Holy Orders for the presbyterate is normally conferred only on candidates who are ready to embrace celibacy freely and who publicly manifest their intention of staying celibate for the love of God's kingdom and the service of men. (n. 1599)

The New Testament text chosen by the *Catechism* (n. 1659) to sum up the meaning of the sacrament of Matrimony comes from chapter five of Ephesians, where the union of Christ and the Church seems to be seen as the model of the 'becoming one flesh' of husband and wife (see Gen 2:24):

> St Paul said: 'Husbands, love your wives, as Christ loved the Church ... This is a great mystery, and I mean in reference to Christ and the Church' (Eph 5:25, 32).

Based on Vatican II's Pastoral Constitution on the Church in the Modern World (*Gaudium et spes* 48.1) and on the theological outline of Matrimony in the 1983 Code of Canon Law (canon 1055.1), the *Catechism* presents the sacrament of Matrimony as a covenant that has been founded and endowed with its own special laws by the Creator:

The marriage covenant, by which a man and woman form with each other an intimate communion of life and love, has been founded and endowed with its own special laws by the Creator. By its very nature it is ordered to the good of the couple, as well as to the generation and education of children. Christ the Lord raised marriage between the baptized to the dignity of a sacrament. (n. 1660)

St Ignatius of Antioch says that marriage is something that honours God when it is undertaken with the consent of the bishop and not for the sake of lust:

It is proper for men and women who wish to marry to be united with the consent of the bishop, so that their marriage will be acceptable to the Lord, and not entered into for the sake of lust. Let all things be done for the honour of God.[117]

St Thomas Aquinas held that, unlike the marriage of those who had not been baptised, the marriage of two Christians was grace-giving.[118] St Teresia Benedicta a Cruce described the sacrament of marriage as 'an additional source of grace for the wife and mother':

When the bride gives her consent at the wedding before the witnessing priest, she becomes a special organ in the Mystical Body of Christ.[119]

The *Catechism* outlines the way in which Matrimony graces the lives of spouses as follows:

The sacrament of matrimony signifies the union of Christ and the Church. It gives spouses the grace to love each other with the love with which Christ has loved his Church; the grace of the sacrament thus perfects the human love of the spouses, strengthens their indissoluble unity and sanctifies them on the way to eternal life.[120] (n. 1661)

St Thomas Aquinas regarded the partners' mutual consent as the essential element in marriage[121] and he recognised that, in certain respects, marriage 'becomes an obligation in those matters that are contractible'.[122] The *Catechism* also recognises these aspects of Matrimony when it says:

Marriage is based on the consent of the contracting parties, that is, on their will to give themselves, each to the other, mutually and definitively, in order to live a covenant of faithful and fruitful love. (n. 1662)

St Teresia Benedicta a Cruce recognises that Catholic dogma 'views marriage as a sacrament and the begetting and upbringing of progeny as its essential purpose'.[123] The *Catechism* teaches:

Unity, indissolubility and openness to fertility are essential to marriage. Polygamy is incompatible with the unity of marriage; divorce separates what God has joined together; the refusal of fertility turns married life away from its 'supreme gift', the child.[124] (n. 1664)

The *Catechism* repeats the teaching of Jesus on divorce, while recognising that those who are divorced are not separated from the Church:

The remarriage of persons divorced from a living, lawful spouse contravenes the plan and law of God as taught by Christ. They are not separated from the Church, but they cannot receive Eucharistic communion. They will lead Christian lives especially by educating their children in the faith. (n. 1665)

The *Catechism* concludes its teaching on matrimony by recognising the Christian home and family as a community of grace and prayer:

> The Christian home is the place where children receive the first proclamation of the faith. For this reason the family home is rightly called 'the domestic church', a community of grace and prayer, a school of human virtues and of Christian charity. (n. 1666)

Notes

1. See the *Catechism*, nn. 1118, 1128, 1130, 1210, 1211, 1305, 1308, 1374, 1381 (twice), 1545 and 1548. St Augustine of Hippo (354–430) is cited eleven times, see *Catechism*, nn. 1067, 1118, 1156, 1157, 1228, 1274, 1372, 1396, 1398, 1458 and 1584. St Augustine's mother, St Monica, is quoted in n. 1371.
2. See nn. 1331, 1369, 1405, 1549 and 1554.
3. See nn. 1137, 1375, 1397, 1551 and 1620.
4. See Francis Xavier Murphy, 'St. Ignatius of Antioch' in *New Catholic Encyclopedia* (Washington, DC: The Catholic University of America, 2003), 7:310–2.
5. St Ignatius of Antioch, 'Letter to the Romans', 5–6, in P. Th. Camelot (ed.), *Ignace d'Antioche: Lettres* (*Sources Chrétiennes*, 10, edited by H. de Lubac and J. Daniélou) (Paris: Cerf, 1958), 133–5.
6. See the Vatican website, consulted on 6/12/2009: http://www.vatican.va/holy_father/benedict_xvi/audiences/2007/documents/hf_ben-xvi_aud_20070314_en.html.
7. Cited in Eleonore Stump, *Aquinas* (London & New York: Routledge, 2003), 3.
8. See Brian Davies, *The Thought of Thomas Aquinas* (Oxford: University Press, 1993), 9.
9. *An Aquinas Reader: Selections from the Writings of Thomas Aquinas*, Mary T. Clark (ed.) (New York: Fordham University Press, 2000), 12.

10. Teresia Renata de Spiritu Sancto Posselt OCD, *Edith Stein: The Life of a Philosopher and Carmelite. Authorized and Revised Biography by Her Prioress Sister Teresia Renata Posselt, O.C.D. (Text, Commentary and Explanatory Notes)*, Susanne M. Batzdorff, Josephine Koeppel and John Sullivan (eds) (Washington, DC: ICS Publications, 2005), 44.

11. Ibid., 59–60.

12. Quoted in ibid., 63.

13. Ibid., 80.

14. Letter 45: Edith Stein, 'Self Portrait in Letters, 1916–1942', translated by Josephine Koeppel OCD, in *Collected Works of Edith Stein* (Washington, DC: ICS Publications, 1993), 5:54–5.

15. Edith Stein, 'How I Came to the Cologne Carmel' in *Edith Stein: Selected Writings*, Suzanne M. Batzdorff (ed.) (Springfield Illinois: Templegate, 1990), 13–30, 17.

16. Edith Stein, 'The Science of the Cross', translated by Josephine Koeppel OCD, in *The Collected Works of Edith Stein*, 6, Dr L. Gelber and Romaeus Leuven OCD (eds) (Washington, DC: ICS Publications, 2002), 9–11.

17. See the *Catechism*, nn. 1066–76.

18. St Augustine, *Explanations of the Psalms,* 138.2, in Jacques-Paul Migne (ed.), *Patrologia latina [PL]*, 221 vols (Paris: 1844–1864), 37:1784–5.

19. See the *Catechism*, n. 1067.

20. See the *Catechism*, nn. 1077–1134.

21. Stein, *The Hidden Life* (1998), 7.

22. Ibid., 10.

23. Ibid., 15.

24. St Augustine, *City of God,* 22.17, in Migne (ed.), *PL*, 41:779. See also St Thomas Aquinas, *Summa theologiae* III, 64.2 and 3.

25. *Catechism*, n. 1128.

26. St Thomas Aquinas, *Summa theologiae* III, 68.8, quoted in the *Catechism*, n. 1128.

27. Ibid., 60.3, quoted in the *Catechism*, n. 1130.

28. Ibid., 62.1.

29. Quoted in Hilda C. Graef (ed.), *Writings of Edith Stein, selected, translated and introduced by Hilda Graef* (London: Peter Owen Ltd., 1956), 93–4.

30. See the *Catechism*, nn. 1135–1209.

31. Batzdorff (ed.), *Edith Stein: Selected Writings*, 99.

32. St Thomas Aquinas, *Summa theologiae* III, 60.4.
33. St Thomas Aquinas, *Summa theologiae* III, 83.4.
34. St Augustine, *Confessions,* 9.6.14, in Migne (ed.), *PL*, 32:769–70.
35. St Augustine, *Explanations of the Psalms,* 72.1, in ibid., 36:914. Quoted in the *Catechism*, n. 1156.
36. See Joanne Mosley, *Edith Stein – Woman of Prayer: Her Life and Ideals* (Leominster: Herefordshire: Gracewing, 2004), 39.
37. Waltraud Herbstrith (Teresia a Matre Dei OCD), *Edith Stein: Ein Lebensbild in Zeugnissen und Selbstzeugnissen* (Mainz: Matthias-Grünewald-Verlag (Topos Taschenbücher), 1998), 134.
38. Stein, *The Hidden Life* (1998), 113.
39. Ibid., 15.
40. Ibid., 9.
41. Edith Stein, 'Life in a Jewish Family: Her Unfinished Autobiographical Account', translated by Josephine Koeppel, in *The Collected Works of Edith Stein*, 1, Lucy Gelber and Romaeus Leuven (eds) (Trivandrum: Carmel Publishing Centre, 1998), 401.
42. St Ignatius of Antioch, *Letter to the Smyrnaeans,* 8.2, in Camelot (ed.), 162.
43. See the *Catechism*, nn. 1210–11.
44. St Thomas Aquinas, *Summa theologiae* III, 65.1. See the *Catechism*, n. 1210.
45. St Thomas Aquinas, *Summa Contra Gentiles,* 4.73.
46. Edith Stein, 'Woman', translated by Freda Mary Oben, in *The Collected Works of Edith Stein*, 2, Lucy Gelber and Romaeus Leuven OCD (eds) (Trivandrum: Carmel Publishing Centre, 1998), 238.
47. St Thomas Aquinas, *Summa theologiae* III, 65.3. See also *Summa theologiae* III, 73.3, which is quoted in the *Catechism*, n. 1374.
48. See the *Catechism*, nn. 1212–1419.
49. See St Thomas Aquinas, *Summa theologiae* III, 66.8.
50. St Ignatius of Antioch, *Letter to Polycarp*, 6.2, in Camelot (ed.), 176.
51. See St Thomas Aquinas, *Liber Sententiarum* IV, 4.2.2 qc 1–6; *Summa theologiae* III, 68.2 ad 2.
52. See H. Denzinger and A. Schönmetzer SJ (eds), *Enchiridion symbolorum definitionum et declarationum de rebus fidei et morum*, 36 (Rome: Herder, 1976), nn. 1609 and 1624.
53. St Thomas Aquinas, *Summa theologiae* III, 68.2 ad 3.

54. See St Thomas Aquinas, *Summa theologiae* III, 68.9 ad 1–2; 68.10 ad 3.
55. St Thomas Aquinas, *Summa theologiae* III, 68.9.
56. Ibid.
57. For Aquinas, there were four levels in 'hell'. The lowest was for the damned, the next lowest for unbaptised infants (who experienced a double darkness as they lacked divine grace and the beatific vision), the next Purgatory and the uppermost for the Fathers of the Old Testament, who awaited the coming of Christ.
58. See St Ignatius of Antioch, *Letter to the Smyrnaeans,* 8.1, in Camelot (ed.), 162.
59. St Thomas Aquinas, *Summa theologiae* III, 67.3, see 67.5 ad 1.
60. See St Thomas Aquinas, *Summa theologiae* III, 72.1 ad 1.
61. See St Thomas Aquinas, *De articulis fidei et Ecclesiae sacramentis.*
62. St Augustine, *Homilies on 1 John,* 3.5, in Migne (ed.), *PL,* 35:2000.
63. See St Thomas Aquinas, *Summa theologiae* III, 72.7.
64. St Thomas Aquinas, *Summa theologiae* III, 72.7 ad 1.
65. See ibid.
66. St Thomas Aquinas, *Summa theologiae* III, 72.5.
67. St Thomas Aquinas, *Summa theologiae* III, 72.5 ad 2.
68. St Thomas Aquinas, *Summa theologiae* III, 72.8 ad 2. Quoted in the *Catechism*, n. 1308.
69. See St Thomas Aquinas, *De articulis fidei et Ecclesiae sacramentis.*
70. See St Thomas Aquinas, *Summa theologiae* III, 72.12 ad 3.
71. Stein, *Woman*, 56.
72. Ibid., 138–9.
73. See St Thomas Aquinas, *Summa theologiae* III, 82.3.
74. See Denzinger and Schönmetzer SJ (eds), nn. 1640 and 1651.
75. St Ignatius of Antioch, *Letter to the Smyrnaeans,* 6:1–2; 7:1–2, in Camelot (ed.), 160, 2.
76. St Thomas Aquinas, *Summa theologiae* III, 75.2.
77. St Thomas Aquinas, *Summa theologiae* III, 75.1. Quoted in the *Catechism*, n. 1381.
78. Quoted in the *Catechism*, n. 1381.
79. St Augustine, *Confessions,* 9.11.27, in Migne (ed.), *PL,* 32:775.
80. St Augustine, *City of God,* 10.6, in ibid., 41:283.
81. See St Thomas Aquinas, *Summa theologiae* III, 80.1 ad 3.
82. Stein, *Woman*, 243.
83. St Ignatius of Antioch, *Letter to the Ephesians,* 20.2, in Camelot (ed.), 76. See the *Catechism*, n. 1405.

84. St Ignatius of Antioch, *Letter to the Smyrnaeans,* 8.1, in ibid., 162.
85. St Ignatius of Antioch, *Letter to the Philadelphians,* 4, in ibid., 142, 4.
86. See St Thomas Aquinas, *Summa theologiae* III, 78.1; 80.12 ad 3.
87. Stein, *Woman,* 120.
88. St Thomas Aquinas, *Summa theologiae* III, 79.2 ad 1.
89. Stein, *Woman,* 125.
90. See the *Catechism,* nn. 1420–1532.
91. St Ignatius of Antioch, *Letter to the Philadelphians,* 8.1, in Camelot (ed.), 148.
92. See St Thomas Aquinas, *Summa theologiae* III, 84.1 ad 1, 2.
93. Stein, *Woman,* 121.
94. See St Thomas Aquinas, *Liber Sententiarum* IV, 17.3.1; 17.3.3 qla. ad 3.
95. See the *Catechism,* n. 1492.
96. See St Thomas Aquinas, *Liber Sententiarum* IV, 17.3.3 qla. ad 3.
97. St Thomas Aquinas, *Liber Sententiarum* IV, 45.2.2 sol 2.
98. St Thomas Aquinas, *Summa Contra Gentiles,* 4.73.
99. St Thomas Aquinas, *Liber Sententiarum* IV, 23.1.2.
100. See St Thomas Aquinas, *Summa Contra Gentiles,* 4.73.
101. See the *Catechism,* nn. 1533–1666.
102. St Ignatius of Antioch, *Letter to Symrnaeans,* 7.2, Camelot (ed.), 162.
103. This text is quoted in the *Catechism,* n. 1545.
104. St Ignatius of Antioch, *Letter to the Trallians,* 3.1, in Camelot (ed.), 112.
105. St Thomas Aquinas, *Summa theologiae* III, 22.4. Quoted in the *Catechism,* n. 1548.
106. St Ignatius of Antioch, *Letter to the Trallians,* 3.1, in Camelot (ed.), 112. Cited in the *Catechism,* n. 1554.
107. St Ignatius of Antioch, *Letter to the Smyrnaeans,* 8.1, in ibid., 162.
108. St Thomas Aquinas, *Summa Contra Gentiles,* 4.75.
109. St Thomas Aquinas, *Summa Theologiae* III, 82.5.
110. St Thomas Aquinas, *Summa Theologiae* I, 93.5 ad 1.
111. St Thomas Aquinas, *Summa Theologiae* III, 67.4 R. and ad 3.
112. St Thomas Aquinas, *Summa Theologiae* III, 30.1 ad 4.
113. St Thomas Aquinas, *Summa Theologiae* III, 82.5.
114. See St Thomas Aquinas, *Summa Theologiae Supplementum,* 39.1.
115. Edith Stein, *Woman,* 81–4.
116. St Thomas Aquinas, *Summa Theologiae* II–IIa, 88.11.

117. St Ignatius of Antioch, *Letter to Polycarp*, 5.2, in Camelot (ed.), 176.

118. See St Thomas Aquinas, *Liber Sententiarum* IV, 26.2.3; 2.1.1 sol. 2.

119. Stein, *Woman*, 121.

120. See the Council of Trent: Denzinger and Schönmetzer SJ (eds), n. 1799.

121. See St Thomas Aquinas, *Liber Sententiarum* IV, 25.2.1 ad 2; *Summa Contra Gentiles*, 4.78.

122. St Thomas Aquinas, *Liber Sententiarum* IV, 27.1.2 sol. 2. See also 31.1.2 ad 2.

123. Stein, *Woman*, 150.

124. See Vatican II's Pastoral Constitution on the Church in the Modern World, *Gaudium et spes*, 50.1.

Chapter 4

FAITH AND RIGHTEOUSNESS

Having outlined the Church's faith in relation to prayer and worship in the last two chapters, which correspond to the fourth and second section of the Catechism, we turn now to the third section, 'Life in Christ', which outlines the faith of the Church in relation to righteousness. The sections on prayer and worship are both concerned with the way in which Christ's priestly office continues in the life of the Church and, in a similar way, the Church's faith in relation to righteousness is concerned with the way in which Christ's kingly or royal office, his service of the coming Kingdom of God, continues in the life of the Church.

As before, we will take three of the Church's saints, one from the patristic, the medieval and the modern period, as our guides and witnesses as we explore this aspect of faith.

AUGUSTINE, CATHERINE OF SIENA AND JOHN XXIII AS MODELS OF RIGHTEOUSNESS

The most frequently cited writer in this section of the *Catechism* is the Doctor of the Church, St Augustine of Hippo, cited thirty-four times.[1] The next most cited writers are St Thomas Aquinas, cited nineteen times,[2] and Popes Pius XII (1876–1958) and John Paul II (1920–2005), both cited eight times.[3] Four writers are cited five times: St Irenaeus (*c.* 130– *c.* 200),[4] St John Chrysostom,[5] Pope Leo XIII (1810–1903)[6]

.and Blessed Pope John XXIII.[7] Five women, St Joan of Arc
(c. 1412–1431), St Catherine of Siena, St Teresa of Avila, St
Thérèse of Lisieux and St Rose of Lima (1586–1617), are each
cited once in this section.[8] Since I have already taken St Teresa
and St Thérèse as models of prayer, I propose taking the other
Doctor of the Church, St Catherine of Siena, as one of the
models of righteousness in this chapter. As the most frequently
cited writer, I propose taking St Augustine as another model.
With the patristic and medieval periods already represented, I
propose to take Pope Blessed John XXIII as the third, more
contemporary, witness to righteousness.

St Augustine of Hippo (354–430)[9]

Aurelius Augustinus was born of a Christian mother, St
Monica, and a pagan father, Patricius, in Tagaste, Numidia (now
Souk Ahras, Algeria), a modest Roman community in North
Africa, in AD 355. Although he had not been formally
baptised, he was enrolled as a catechumen in his youth and
reared as a Christian.[10] When he was sixteen, his studies were
interrupted for a year because his family had insufficient funds
to pay for them and, when he returned to his studies the
following year at Carthage, he had a liaison with a concubine,
whose name is unknown, and she bore him a son, Adeodatus.[11]

After reading Cicero's *Hortensius*, he became enthralled
with the ideal of wisdom and, from then on, he recognised a
personal call from Christ.[12] When he tried to read the Sacred
Scriptures, however, he was repelled by the lack of literary style
and gave up the attempt.[13] At the age of nineteen, he joined a
dualistic sect known as the Manichees because of their claim
to provide him with an understanding of all that exists. After
spending a year teaching in Tagaste, he spent eight years
teaching rhetoric at Carthage, and throughout this period he
was an active member of the Manichees. He abandoned the
sect, however, after a meeting with the Manichaean Bishop
Faustus, who failed to answer Augustine's questions in a

satisfactory manner.[14] In 383, at the age of twenty-eight, he left Africa for Rome, where he taught for a year. Thanks to some influential Manichees, he was appointed as imperial professor of rhetoric and he spent two years in Milan, where the Emperor of the Western Roman Empire then lived.

During this time, Augustine was converted to Christianity, thanks to the eloquent preaching of Bishop Ambrose of Milan. He enrolled in the catechumenate of the Catholic Church and began to prepare for Baptism.[15] Thanks to the spiritual interpretation of Scripture proposed by St Ambrose, Augustine came to recognise that it was in our spiritual nature and in our capacity for worship that human beings were created in the image of God.[16] When his mother, St Monica, joined him in Milan, she insisted that he send the mother of his son, Adeodatus, back to Africa and prepare for marriage with a suitable woman of her choosing. The woman in question was not of legal age, however, and, faced with a two-year delay, Augustine took another concubine.[17] As he wrestled with the obligations to chastity implicit in Baptism, Augustine read what he describes as 'certain Platonic books' that had been translated into Latin by Marius Victorinus. These books helped him to recognise both his own innate capacity for spiritual experience and the way in which God transcended all such experience.[18] Up to this point, he had not yet understood the role of the Incarnation in human salvation but, through reading the letters of St Paul, he gradually came to understand how the grace of Christ enlightens our darkness, liberating us from the bonds of habit and slavery to sin, and showing us the way to our spiritual homeland in heaven.[19] During his famous conversion experience, he was filled 'with a light of certainty, and all shadow of doubt disappeared' after he heard a voice telling him to take and read the text of Romans 13:13-14:

> Let us live honorably as in the day, not in revelling and
> drunkenness, not in debauchery and licentiousness, not

in quarrelling and jealousy. Instead, put on the Lord Jesus Christ, and make no provision for the flesh, to gratify its desires.

Abandoning his teaching career and his proposed marriage in August 386, he retired to an estate at Cassiciacum, near Milan, to live a life of prayer and study that was supported by his mother. Along with Adeodatus, his son, he inscribed his name among those intending to be baptised at the beginning of Lent the following year. They were baptised by St Ambrose during the Paschal Vigil that Easter (24 April, AD 387) in the octagonal font in the Baptistery of San Giovanni alle Fonti.[20] When Augustine's mother, St Monica, died at Ostia on their journey back to Africa in search of a suitable place to live a life of prayer and retreat, Augustine remained in Rome for a year before eventually returning to Tagaste with Adeodatus in 388. Selling his property and giving the money to the poor, he retired with some friends to a monastic way of life. Adeodatus died shortly afterwards at the age of sixteen and Augustine became a junior clergyman in the coastal city of Hippo Regius (now Annaba, Algeria), the second most important ecclesiastical city in Africa at that time. He became a presbyter in Hippo in 391 and, from 395 until the end of his life in 430, he was Bishop of Hippo.

More than a hundred of the treatises written by St Augustine have survived, including works on Baptism, Original Sin and Christian marriage. He also treats of various aspects of the Church's liturgy in his other works, especially in his commentaries on Scripture. He drew a clear distinction between the mere reception of a Sacrament and the full fruitfulness of receiving that Sacrament in the life of an individual.[21] Insisting that Jesus is himself the true minister of all the Sacraments, St Augustine also rejected the view that a Sacrament could be ineffective simply because the minister was unworthy, in heresy or in schism.[22] His thought had a significant influence on later writers, notably Pope Leo I and Gregory I, and, through his influence on the writers of the Middle Ages and during the time of the Protestant Reformation, he remains a significant influence on Christian thought right through to our own time.

St Catherine of Siena (1347–1380)[23]

Born the last of the twenty-five children of Giacomo di Benincasa, a prosperous wool dyer, and his wife, Lapa, Catherine was given the pet name of Euphrosyne, which is Greek for 'joy', by her family. At the age of six, she had a vision of Christ seated in glory with the Apostles Peter, Paul and John and, a year later, she made a secret vow to give her whole life to God. Under pressure to prepare for marriage by her mother, she began to pay more attention to her appearance but, repenting of this vanity, she cut off her hair and told her family that she would never marry. Punished by being forced to do menial work in the household and by being prevented from having any time on her own, she later wrote that God had shown her how to build in her soul a private cell where no tribulation could enter. When her father realised that any further pressure on her to marry was useless, Catherine found that she was free to live a life of prayer and fasting in her room and, despite considerable opposition from her family, she became a Third Order Dominican at the age of sixteen. These years were a time of temptation and trial for Catherine and she later recalled that, at one point, when she asked God where he had been when her heart 'was so sorely vexed with foul and hateful temptations', she heard a voice saying, 'Daughter, I was in your heart, fortifying you by grace'.

During the Spring of 1366, she experienced what Catherine describes as a 'mystical marriage' with Jesus. She was praying in her room when she had a vision of Christ, his mother and the heavenly host. Taking Catherine's hand, Our Lady held it up to Christ, who placed a ring upon it and espoused her to Himself, bidding her to be of good courage, for now she was armed with a faith that could overcome all temptations. Afterwards, the ring was always visible to Catherine, though invisible to everyone else. Following this experience, she dedicated herself to the care of the sick and the poor of Siena, and attracted a group of followers, both men and women. They included her two Dominican confessors, Thomas della Fonte and Bartholomew Dominici, the artist Vanni, who left us a famous portrait of Catherine, her sister-in-law Lisa and a noble young widow, Alessia Saracini.

During the summer of 1370, she received a series of mystical revelations, which culminated in a prolonged trance during which she had a vision of hell, purgatory and heaven, and heard a divine command to leave her cell and enter the public life of the world. She responded to this command by informing herself about the social and religious circumstances of the time and by writing letters, more than three hundred of which have survived, to members of her immediate circle and to many of the significant figures in public life, including the kings of France and Hungary. By means of these letters she sought to bring about peace between the warring city republics and principalities in Italy and to reform the Church. In her letters to Pope Gregory XI, she refers to him affectionately as 'Daddy' (*Babbo* in Italian) and she encourages him to reform the clergy and ensure that the Papal States in central Italy were administered properly.

In 1374, the Dominican Order called her to Florence to respond to a charge of possible heresy, but she was exonerated and the new lector for the order in Siena, Raymund de Capua, was appointed as her confessor. He later became her biographer. While at Pisa, during the fourth Sunday of Lent in 1375, she received the Stigmata – the marks and sufferings of Christ's crucifixion – on her body. She tells us that, when she prayed that the marks would not be visible on her body while she lived, her prayer was answered and, from then on, she suffered from them but the marks were invisible to others.

In 1376, she went to Avignon as the ambassador of Florence in an unsuccessful attempt to make peace between Florence and the Papal States. She was, however, successful in persuading the Pope to return to Rome and, against the advice of the French king and almost all of the College of Cardinals, Pope Gregory XI moved his administration back to Rome in 1377. Her major work, *The Dialogue of Divine Providence,* was recorded by members of her circle between 1377 and 1378. It is a dialogue between a soul who 'rises up' to God, represented by Catherine herself, and the Eternal Father. Early in 1378, Catherine was sent by Pope Gregory to Florence in a fresh effort to make peace between Florence and the Papal States. During her time there, she became involved in the local politics of the city and an attempt was made on her life. During the Western Schism following Pope Gregory's death in 1378, she supported Urban VI, the Roman claimant to the papacy, and she tried to convince various nobles and cardinals that he was the legitimate successor of St Peter. She died of a stroke in Rome in 1380 at the age of thirty-three.

Following her death, her body was buried in the basilica of Santa Maria supra Minerva in Rome. Her head was brought to Siena and placed in the basilica of San Domenico, where it remains to this day. Her confessor, Fra Raymund de Capua, who later became General of the Dominicans, published a biography of Catherine, known as the 'Legend', in 1395. A second biography, known as the 'Supplement', was written by Tomaso Caffarini in the early years of the fifteenth century. Between 1411 and 1413, the depositions of the surviving witnesses of her life and work were collected at Venice to form the famous 'Process' for her canonisation.

St Catherine was canonised in 1461, eighty years after her death. In 1940, Pope Pius XII named her joint patron saint of Italy along with St Francis of Assisi. In 1970, she and St Teresa of Avila were the first women to be named as Doctors of the Church by Pope Paul VI. Pope John Paul II named her as one of the patron saints of Europe in 2000.

Blessed John XXIII (1881–1963)

Angelo Giuseppe Roncalli was born in Sotto il Monte, a small country village in the Province of Bergamo in the north of Italy, the fourth of a family of fourteen. His father, Giovanni Battista Roncalli, worked as a sharecropper. John was ordained a priest at the age of twenty-three in 1904, the year he had finished his doctoral studies in Church history. Roncalli was sympathetic to the advances that had been made by the historical movement during the twentieth century and he taught Church history in the diocesan seminary during the period that he worked as secretary to the Bishop of Bergamo from 1905 until 1914. During this period, he unambiguously held himself aloof from Modernism, but insisted on the benefits of a greater emphasis on 'positive' historical theology. During World War I, he served in the medical corps of the Royal Italian Army and, in 1921, he was appointed as the Italian president of the Society for the Propagation of the Faith. In 1925, when Pope Pius XI consecrated him as titular bishop of Areopolis and made him Apostolic Visitor to Bulgaria, Roncalli chose *Obedientia et Pax* ('Obedience and Peace') as his episcopal motto. In 1935, he was made Apostolic Delegate to Turkey and Greece and used this office to help the Jewish underground in saving thousands of European refugees. In 1944, Pope Pius XII named him Apostolic Nuncio to France.

In 1953, Pope Pius XII appointed him as the Patriarch and Archbishop of Venice and raised him to the rank of cardinal. Following the death of Pope Pius XII in 1958, to his great surprise (he had bought a return train ticket to Venice), Roncalli was elected Pope at the age of seventy-seven. On Christmas Day in 1958, he became the first pope since 1870 to make pastoral visits in his diocese of Rome, when he visited children infected with polio at the Bambin Gesù Hospital and the Santo Spirito Hospital. The following day he visited Rome's Regina Coeli prison, where he told the inmates: 'You could not come to me, so I came to you'.

John XXIII was convinced that the Church needed to adapt its preaching, organisation and pastoral methods to the fundamentally changed world of the second part of the twentieth century and he coined the Italian world *aggiornamento* (literally 'bringing things up to date', but including also the notion of inner renewal) to sum up what he had in mind. As he has explained, it was not the result of any well-thought-out plan, but the following of a 'divine challenge' (*divinum incitamentum*). In order to achieve this '*aggiornamento*', he announced his intention to summon an Ecumenical Council on 25 January 1959, three months after his election as Pope. He composed a special prayer for the forthcoming Council, asking the Holy Spirit to renew the wonders of Pentecost:

O Divine Spirit, who, sent by the Father in the name of Jesus, infallibly assists and guides the Church, pour out on the Ecumenical Council the fullness of your gifts. O gentle Master and Consoler, illumine the minds of our prelates who, solicitous about the invitation of the Supreme Roman Pontiff, will gather in the solemn meeting. Let abundant fruit mature from this Council: may the light and the power of the Gospel be ever more diffused in human society; may the Catholic religion and its missionary endeavour acquire new vigour; may a deeper knowledge of the doctrine of the Church and a salutary growth of Christian customs be reached. O sweet Guest of souls, confirm our minds in the truth and make our hearts obedient so that the deliberations of the Council may find in us generous assent and prompt execution. We pray to you also for the sheep who no longer belong to the one fold of Jesus Christ, so that they also, who enjoy the name of Christian, may finally find unity again under one Shepherd. Renew in our time the wonders as in a new Pentecost; and bring it about that the holy Church, gathered in unanimous, more intense prayer around Mary, the Mother of Jesus, and guided by Peter, may spread the kingdom of the divine Saviour, which is a kingdom of truth, of justice, of love and of peace. Amen.[24]

In his encyclical letter on the missions, *Princeps pastorum* (1959), John XXIII highlighted the need for the cooperation of properly prepared laity in the Church's mission, particularly in public life. His encyclical, *Mater et magistra* (1961), responded to the new socio-economic conditions resulting from social legislation, the influence of independent bodies such as insurance societies, and the disparity in working conditions between urban and rural areas and between prosperous and developing countries. While defending the principle of private ownership, the encyclical emphasised the need, not only for a subsistence wage, but also for the exercise of personal responsibility.

John XXIII was first diagnosed with cancer in September 1962, shortly before the opening of the Second Vatican Council on October 11, 1962. In his opening speech, the Pope criticised some of his own advisers who,

> though burning with zeal, are not endowed with much sense of discretion or measure. In these modern times they can see nothing but prevarication and ruin.

He described them as the 'prophets of doom, who are always forecasting disaster, as though the end of the world were at hand'. In contrast, his own attitude was fundamentally optimistic. He insisted that the preservation of doctrine would not be the principal aim of the Council, which would concern itself with how doctrine was presented rather than with the substance of doctrine itself, and he suggested that the Church counteracts errors by 'demonstrating the validity of her teaching rather than by condemnations.'[25]

Pope John XXIII issued his final encyclical, *Pacem in terris* (Peace on earth), in April 1963. The first part of the encyclical is concerned with the rights and duties of the human person, and the remaining sections are concerned with the relationship between people and the State, between States, and between States and the world community. John XXIII made his last public appearance in May that year, when the Italian president awarded him the Balzan prize for his engagement with peace. As he lay dying at the age of eighty-one, having been Pope for only four years and seven months, his last words were:

> I had the great grace to be born into a Christian family, modest and poor, but with the fear of the Lord … My time on earth is drawing to a close. But Christ lives on and continues his work in the Church. Souls, souls, *Ut omnes unum sint* (That all may be one).[26]

From his early teens, John kept a diary of spiritual reflections that was subsequently published as *Journal of a Soul*. The collection of writings charts his efforts both as a young man and during his papacy to 'grow in holiness'. Known affectionately as 'Good Pope John', he was declared Blessed by Pope John Paul II in 2000. At a Mass in honour of the fiftieth anniversary of Blessed Pope John XXIII's election as Pope in 2008, Pope Benedict XVI described the Seocnd Vatican Council, which had been 'called, prepared and begun' by John XXIII, as 'a truly special gift for the Church'.[27]

Since the Second Vatican Council can, in many respects, be regarded as Blessed Pope John XXIII's legacy to the Church, I will draw on its documents, as well as on the Pope's own writings, in what follows.

LIFE IN THE SPIRIT AS OUR COMMON HUMAN VOCATION[28]

The *Catechism* presents the faith of the Church on righteousness in two sections, first 'Life in the Spirit as Our Common Human Vocation' and then 'The Ten Commandments'. In this first section, the *Catechism* identifies our being created in God's image as the source of our common human vocation and dignity, and it presents the gift of life in the Holy Spirit as the fulfilment of our common divine calling and as the means of our salvation. Living in the Holy Spirit means loving God wholeheartedly and our neighbour as ourselves, and it fulfils all the requirements of the Ten Commandments, which are considered individually in the second section.

The Dignity of the Human Person[29]

Blessed John XXIII suggests that the true dignity of the human person emerges only when considered in the light of the divinely revealed truth:

> If we look upon the dignity of the human person in the light of the divinely revealed truth, we cannot help but esteem it far more highly. For human beings are redeemed by the blood of Jesus Christ; they are by grace the children and friends of God and heirs of eternal glory.[30]

The *Catechism* outlines its teaching on the dignity of the human person using Vatican II's Pastoral Constitution on the Church in the Modern World, *Gaudium et spes*. It begins by outlining how the exalted vocation of humanity is revealed in Christ:

> Christ ... in the very revelation of the mystery of the Father and of his love, makes man fully manifest to man himself and brings to light his exalted vocation.[31]

Having been created in the image and likeness of the Creator, but having disfigured the divine image by our sin, the original beauty of the divine image in us is restored in Christ:

> It is in Christ, 'the image of the invisible of God' (Col 1:15), that man has been created 'in the image and likeness' of the Creator. It is in Christ, Redeemer and Saviour, that the divine image, disfigured in man by the first sin, has been restored to its original beauty and ennobled by the grace of God.[32]

Describing human beings as 'endowed with a spiritual soul,[33] with intellect and free will', the *Catechism* presents the common vocation of humanity as 'seeking and loving what is true and good' (n. 1711).[34] Blessed John XXIII recognised that the Creator 'has imprinted in the heart of human beings an order which their conscience reveals to them and strongly enjoins them to obey'.[35] Quoting *Gaudium et spes* 17, the *Catechism* describes humanity's 'true freedom' as an 'outstanding manifestation of the divine image' (n. 1712) and it reminds us that conscience obliges humanity 'to follow the moral law, which urges him "to do what is good and avoid what is evil"' (n. 1713).[36] According to *Gaudium et spes*:

> Man is divided in himself. As a result, the whole life of men, both individual and social, shows itself to be a struggle, and a dramatic one, between good and evil, between light and darkness. (13.2)

Quoting this text, the *Catechism* says that Man 'still desires the good, but his nature bears the wound of original sin. He is now inclined to evil and subject to error' (n. 1707). By his Passion, Christ has 'delivered us from Satan and from sin' and has 'merited for us the new life in the Holy Spirit', the gracious gift to those who believe in Christ that 'restores what sin has damaged in us' (n. 1708). This gift of life in the Spirit makes us 'capable of acting rightly and doing good' and such moral living 'blossoms into eternal life in the glory of heaven' (n. 1709).

The human heart longs for the fullness of life in the Spirit, eternal life in the glory of heaven. Quoting St Augustine, who recognised that 'we all want to live happily',[37] and that, in seeking God, we 'seek a happy life',[38] the *Catechism* describes the Beatitudes (Mt 5:3-12), which are 'at the heart of Jesus' preaching',[39] as responding 'to the natural desire for happiness' (n. 1718), which God has placed in the human heart in order to draw it 'to the One who alone can fulfil it'.[40] The *Catechism*[41] also quotes St Augustine when it describes the beatitude to which we are all called by God as eternal rest in the Kingdom of God:

> There we shall rest and see, we shall see and love, we shall love and praise. Behold what will be at the end without end. For what other end do we have, if not to reach the kingdom which has no end.[42]

This state of blessedness 'comes from an entirely free gift of God' (n. 1722) and, like the grace that leads us there, it is supernatural (see n. 1727). This gift of grace confronts us 'with decisive choices concerning earthly goods' that 'purify our hearts in order to teach us to love God above all things' (n. 1728). True happiness 'is not found in riches or well-being, in human fame or power, or in any human achievement – however beneficial it may be ... or indeed in any creature' (n. 1723).

Quoting *Gaudium et spes* 17.1, the *Catechism* outlines the nature of the gift of free will that God has given us:

> God willed that man should be left in the hand of his own counsel (see Sir 15:14), so that he might of his own

accord seek his creator and freely attain his full and blessed perfection by cleaving to him. (n. 1743)

St Augustine recognised that, while every good is from God, 'the movement of turning away from God ... is a defective movement' and 'because it is voluntary, this very defect lies within our power'.[43] The *Catechism* says that 'The choice to disobey and do evil is an abuse of freedom and leads to "the slavery of sin" (see Rom 6:17)' (n. 1733). It also points out that freedom 'makes the human being responsible for acts of which he is the voluntary agent. His deliberate acts properly belong to him' (n. 1745). An individual's responsibility for a particular action can, however, 'be diminished or nullified by ignorance, duress, fear and other psychological or social factors' (n. 1746).

Citing Vatican II's Declaration on Religious Liberty, *Dignitatis humanae* 2.7, the *Catechism* points out:

> The *right to the exercise of freedom*, especially in moral and religious matters, is an inalienable requirement of the dignity of the human person. This right must be recognized and protected by civil authority within the limits of the common good and public order. (n. 1738)

The *Catechism* (n. 1750) recognises that the morality of human acts depends on the object chosen (the good towards which the will deliberately directs itself), the intention (the purpose pursued in the action) and the circumstances. We are influenced by whether our reason recognises and judges the object chosen to be good or evil.[44] There are 'some concrete acts – such as fornication – that it is always wrong to choose, because choosing them entails a disorder of the will, that is, a moral evil' (n. 1755). Our intention aims at the good anticipated from the action undertaken, but the end does not justify the means and 'the condemnation of an innocent person cannot be justified as a legitimate means of saving the nation'

(n. 1753). The circumstances of our actions can increase or diminish both their moral goodness (the amount of a theft, for example) and our responsibility for those actions (acting out of a fear of death, for example).[45] 'A morally good act requires the goodness of its object, of its end, and of its circumstances together' (n. 1760).

The *Catechism* (nn. 1771–2) identifies our passions with our affections or feelings of love and hatred, desire and fear, joy, sadness and anger. Following St Augustine,[46] it says (n. 1766) that feelings have their source in the way the human heart responds to the good, which alone can be loved. In themselves, 'passions are neither good nor evil' (n. 1767) but, 'insofar as they engage reason and will, there is moral good or evil in them' (n. 1773). St Augustine held that the passions 'are evil if love is evil and good if it is good'[47] and, recognising that they 'can be taken up into the virtues or perverted by the vices' (n. 1774), the *Catechism* teaches that the passions 'are morally good when they contribute to a good action, evil in the opposite case' (n. 1768).

The *Catechism* quotes *Gaudium et spes* 16 when it describes moral conscience as 'our most secret core and sanctuary' where we are 'alone with God whose voice echoes' in our depths (n. 1795). Recognising conscience as a judgement of human reason on the moral quality of our acts (n. 1796), it quotes St Augustine on the need to be 'sufficiently present' to ourselves 'to hear and follow the voice' of conscience (n. 1779): 'Return to your conscience, question it ... Turn inward, brethren, and in everything you do, see God as your witness'.[48] The *Catechism* insists that 'A human being must always obey the certain judgement of his conscience' (n. 1800) and it recognises that, for those who have committed evil, the verdict of their consciences 'remains a pledge of conversion and of hope' (n. 1797). Our moral conscience is not infallible, however:

> Faced with a moral choice, conscience can make either
> a right judgement in accordance with reason and the

divine law or, on the contrary, an erroneous judgement that departs from them. (n. 1799)

The *Catechism* points out that, while conscience 'can remain in ignorance, or make erroneous judgements', such 'ignorance and errors are not always free of guilt' (n. 1801). Learning to hear and follow the voice of conscience is a matter of using the available means, which include the Word of God (having been assimilated in faith and prayer and put into practice), the gifts of the Holy Spirit, the witness and advice of others, and the authoritative teaching of the Church:[49]

A well-formed conscience is upright and truthful. It formulates its judgements according to reason, in conformity with the true good willed by the wisdom of the Creator.[50]

St Augustine held that a virtue is to be distinguished from a vice by its end or purpose, 'that on account of which it is to be done'.[51] The *Catechism* describes a virtue as 'a habitual and firm disposition to do good' (n. 1833) and it understands the various human virtues as 'stable dispositions of the intellect and the will that govern our acts, order our passions and guide our conduct in accordance with reason and faith' (n. 1834). It notes, too, that they 'can be grouped around the four cardinal virtues: prudence, justice, fortitude and temperance' (see Wis 8:7). The *Catechism* describes prudence as disposing the practical reason to discern 'our true good and to choose the right means for achieving it', justice as 'the firm and constant will to give God and neighbour their due', fortitude as ensuring 'firmness in difficulties and constancy in the pursuit of the good' and temperance as the virtue that 'moderates the attraction of the pleasures of the senses and provides balance in the use of created goods' (nn. 1836–8). St Augustine describes these four moral virtues as being rooted in love of God:

> To live well is nothing other than to love God with all one's heart, with all one's soul and with all one's efforts; from this it comes about that love is kept whole and uncorrupted (through temperance). No misfortune can disturb it (and this is fortitude). It obeys only [God] (and this is justice), and is careful in discerning things, so as not to be surprised by deceit or trickery (and this is prudence).[52]

The *Catechism* says that, having been 'acquired by education, by deliberate acts and by a perseverance ever-renewed in repeated efforts', the various human virtues 'are purified and elevated by divine grace' (n. 1810).

These human virtues are 'rooted' in the theological virtues of faith, hope and love (see 1 Cor 13:13), which 'have God for their origin, their motive and their object – God known by faith, God hoped in and loved for his own sake'. Faith, hope and love adapt our human faculties 'for participation in the divine nature' (see 2 Pet 1:4) by disposing Christians 'to live in a relationship with the Holy Trinity'.[53] Vatican II's Dogmatic Constitution on Divine Revelation, *Dei Verbum* 5,[54] outlines the relationship between faith and revelation in these words:

> To God who reveals himself must be given 'the obedience of faith' (Rom 16:26), by which one freely commits one's whole self to God, offering 'the full submission of intellect and will to God who reveals himself'[55] and freely assenting to the revelation granted by him.

The *Catechism* says that, by faith, 'we believe in God and believe all that he has revealed to us and that Holy Church proposes for our belief' (n. 1842). The Letter to Titus 3:6-7 describes the Holy Spirit as having been 'poured out upon us richly through Jesus Christ our Saviour, so that we might be justified by his grace and become heirs in hope of eternal life'. Quoting this text (n. 1817), the *Catechism* says that, by hope, 'we desire, and with steadfast trust await from God, eternal life and the graces to merit it' (n. 1843). For the *Catechism*, it is thanks to charity that 'we love God above all things and our neighbour as ourselves for love of God' (n. 1844). Recognising that it binds everything together 'in perfect harmony' (Col 3:14) because it is the 'form of all the virtues', the *Catechism* (n. 1829) quotes St Augustine who presents charity as our goal:

> Love is itself the fulfilment of all our works. There is the goal; that is why we run: we run towards it, and once we reach it, in it we shall find rest.[56]

The *Catechism* recognises that the moral life of Christians 'is sustained by' the gifts of the Holy Spirit (wisdom, understanding, counsel, fortitude, knowledge, piety and fear of the Lord, see Isa 11:1–2), which it describes as 'permanent dispositions' that make us 'docile in following the promptings of the Holy Spirit' (n. 1830).

Quoting St Augustine, for whom sin is 'an utterance, a deed, or a desire contrary to the eternal law',[57] the *Catechism* says that sin 'is an offence against reason, truth, and right conscience' (n. 1849) that 'wounds the nature of man and injures human solidarity'.[58] It recognises, however, that human sin does not ultimately frustrate God's purpose: 'God has consigned all men to disobedience, that he may have mercy upon all' (Rom 11:32) (n. 1870). The *Catechism* quotes St Augustine, 'God created us without us: but he did not will to save us without us',[59] when it insists that 'we must admit our faults' in order to receive his mercy (n. 1847). We need to recognise that the root of all sins lies in our own hearts,[60] our love for ourselves 'even to contempt of God'.[61] Our sins are mortal when they destroy 'the charity without which eternal beatitude is impossible' and, unrepented, such sins bring 'eternal death' (n. 1874). Describing venial sin as being 'reparable by charity, which it allows to subsist in us' (n. 1875), the *Catechism* again quotes St Augustine:

> Venial sin does not deprive the sinner of sanctifying grace, friendship with God, charity, and consequently eternal happiness.[62]

Sins have a tendency to proliferate and the *Catechism* recognises that the 'repetition of sins – even venial sins – engenders vices' (n. 1876). 'Vices can be classified according to the virtues they oppose', and they include the seven capital sins (pride, avarice, envy, wrath, lust, gluttony and sloth), which 'engender other sins, other vices' (n. 1866).

The Human Community[63]

Citing *Gaudium et spes* 24.3, the *Catechism* says that there is 'a certain resemblance between the union of the divine persons and the fraternity that men are to establish among themselves in truth and love' (n. 1878). It also cites *Gaudium et spes* 25.1 when it describes the human person as needing life in society in order to develop in accordance with his nature (n. 1891) and when it highlights the human person as the primary value to be considered in any social organisation: 'The human person ... is and ought to be the principle, the subject and the object of every social organization' (n. 1892). Quoting Blessed John XXIII, it says that, in order to promote the participation of the greatest number in the life of a society on both national and international levels, people should encourage the creation of voluntary associations and institutions 'which relate to economic and social goals, to cultural and recreational activities, to sport, to various professions, and to political affairs' (n. 1882).[64] Noting that the promotion of increased productivity by public authority with a view to social progress is 'based on the principle of subsidiarity', Blessed John XXIII affirmed:

> [I]n the economy the first place must be given to the personal initiative of private citizens, working as individuals or in various associations for the pursuit of common interests.[65]

The *Catechism* echoes this position when it says:

> In accordance with the principle of subsidiarity, neither the state nor any larger society should substitute itself for the initiative and responsibility of individuals and intermediary bodies. (n. 1894)

Quoting the words of Blessed John XXIII, the *Catechism* says that, 'animated by a just hierarchy of values', society 'ought to promote the exercise of virtue, not obstruct it' (n. 1895):

> Human society must primarily be considered something pertaining to the spiritual. Through it, in the bright light of truth, men should share their knowledge, be able to exercise their rights and fulfil their obligations, be inspired to seek spiritual values; mutually derive genuine pleasure from the beautiful, of whatever order it be; always be readily disposed to pass on to others the best of their own cultural heritage; and eagerly strive to make their own the spiritual achievements of others.[66]

Citing Vatican II's Dogmatic Constitution on the Church, *Lumen gentium* 36, the *Catechism* points out that appealing

> to the spiritual and moral capacities of the human person and to the permanent need for his inner conversion ...

in no way eliminates but on the contrary imposes the obligation of bringing the appropriate remedies to institutions and living conditions when they are an inducement to sin, so that they conform to the norms of justice and advance the good rather than hinder it. (n. 1888)

Citing St Paul (see Rom 13:1), the *Catechism* insists that there 'is no authority except from God, and those authorities that exist have been instituted by God' (n. 1918). It quotes Blessed John XXIII when it points out that every human community 'needs an authority in order to endure and develop' (n. 1919):

Human society can be neither well-ordered nor prosperous unless it has some people invested with legitimate authority to preserve its institutions and to devote themselves as far as is necessary to work and care for the good of all.[67]

Quoting *Gaudium et spes* 74.3, the *Catechism* says:

The political community and public authority are based on human nature and therefore ... belong to an order established by God.

If authority is not exercised legitimately, however, its arrangements might not be morally binding, because if rulers

were to enact unjust laws or take measures contrary to the moral order, such arrangements would not be binding in conscience.

In such cases, as Blessed John XXIII put it, 'authority breaks down completely and results in shameful abuse'.[68] Noting that, according to *Gaudium et spes* 74.3, 'the choice of the political regime and the appointment of rulers are left to the free decision of the citizens', the *Catechism* recognises:

> The diversity of political regimes is morally acceptable, provided they serve the legitimate good of the communities that adopt them. (n. 1901)

Citing *Gaudium et spes* 74.2 (see n. 1902), the *Catechism* insists that political authority 'must be exercised within the limits of the moral order and must guarantee the conditions for the exercise of freedom' (n. 1923).

The *Catechism* recognises that the dignity of the human person 'requires the pursuit of the common good' (n. 1926), which, quoting *Gaudium et spes* 26.1, is described as comprising

> the sum total of social conditions which allow people, either in groups or as individuals, to reach their fulfilment more fully and more easily. (n. 1924)

Citing *Gaudium et spes* 26.2 (see nn. 1907–9), it lists the 'three essential elements' of the common good as:

> [R]espect for and promotion of the fundamental rights of the person; prosperity, or the development of the spiritual and temporal goods of society; the peace and security of the group and of its members. (n. 1925)

The *Catechism* recognises that it is the role of the political community, the state, 'to defend and promote the common good of civil society' (n. 1910). Citing *Gaudium et spes* 84.2, it also recognises that the universal common good calls for an organisation of society on the international level (n. 1911).

Blessed John XXIII taught: 'Justice is to be observed not only in the distribution of wealth by production but also with respect to the conditions under which production is achieved.'[69] The *Catechism* teaches:

> Society ensures social justice by providing the conditions that allow associations and individuals to obtain their due. (n. 1943)

John XXIII recognised that the dignity of the human person means that 'each one has rights and duties' that are 'universal, inviolable and inalienable' and he listed those natural human rights in his encyclical, *Pacem in terris* 11–27. Citing his recognition that a refusal to recognise such rights could undermine the moral authority of a society,[70] the *Catechism* reminds us:

> Respect for the human person considers the other 'another self'. It presupposes respect for the fundamental rights that flow from the intrinsic dignity of the person. (n. 1944)

Citing the words spoken by God to St Catherine of Siena, the *Catechism* notes that the differences among persons 'belong to God's plan, who wills that we should need one another' (n. 1946):

> It is true that all the virtues are bound together, and it is impossible to have one without having them all. But I give them in different ways so that one virtue might be, as it were, the source of all the others. So to one person I give charity as the primary virtue, to another justice, to another humility, to another a lively faith or prudence or temperance or patience, and to still another courage … I have distributed them all in such a way that no one has all of them. Thus have I given you reason — necessity, in fact — to practice mutual charity. For I could well have

'supplied each of you with all your needs, both spiritual and material. But I wanted to make you dependent on one another so that each of you would be my minister, dispensing the graces and gifts you have received from me.[71]

John XXIII believed that the natural rights that flow from the dignity of the human person are 'inseparably connected, in the person who is their subject, with just as many respective duties'. Rights as well as duties 'find their source, their sustenance and their inviolability in the natural law which grants or enjoins them'.[72] He also argued:

> The nations which enjoy an abundance of goods should not ignore the grave internal difficulties of others, where hunger and want grind people down and deny them the enjoyment of even elementary human rights.[73]

The *Catechism* makes a similar point, highlighting its basis in equal human dignity and extending it to spiritual as well as material goods:

> The equal dignity of human persons requires the effort to reduce excessive social and economic inequalities. It gives urgency to the elimination of sinful inequalities. Solidarity is an eminently Christian virtue. It practices the sharing of spiritual goods even more than material ones. (nn. 1947–8)

God's Salvation: Law and Grace[74]

Having outlined the way in which our being created in God's image is the basis of our common human vocation and dignity, and of our solidarity with all our brothers and sisters, the *Catechism* reminds us that, both individually and collectively, we have been 'wounded by sin' and that we stand 'in need of salvation from God' (n. 1949). It is in Christ, and through his law and his grace, that salvation comes to us.

The *Catechism* says that the moral law 'is the work of divine Wisdom' (n. 1950) and that its biblical meaning can be defined as 'fatherly instruction by God which prescribes for man the ways that lead to the promised beatitude, and proscribes the ways of evil' (n. 1975). Following St Thomas Aquinas, who understood law as 'an ordinance of reason for the common good, promulgated by the one who is in charge of the community',[75] the *Catechism* recognises that the moral law 'finds its fullness and its unity in Christ' (n. 1953) (see Rom 10:4). Quoting St Augustine, the *Catechism* says that the moral law is called 'natural' because the reason that decrees it 'properly belongs to human nature' (n. 1955):

> Where then are these rules written, if not in the book of that light we call the truth: In it is written every just law; from it the law passes into the heart of the man who does justice, not that it migrates into it, but that it places its imprint on it, like a seal on a ring that passes onto wax, without leaving the ring.[76]

This natural law, humanity's participation 'in the wisdom and goodness of the Creator' who gives us the ability to govern ourselves 'with a view to the true and the good',[77] is an expression of 'the dignity of the human person' and it forms the basis of his or her 'fundamental rights and duties' (n. 1978). It is '*immutable* and permanent through the variations of history'[78] for, as St Augustine put it, it is 'written in the human heart':

> Theft is surely punished by your law, O Lord, and by the law that is written in the human heart, the law that iniquity itself does not efface.[79]

The Old Law, summed up in the Ten Commandments, was the first stage of divinely revealed law[80] for, as St Augustine put it, 'God wrote on the tables of the Law what men did not read in their hearts',[81] even though those truths were 'naturally accessible to reason' (n. 1981). This Old Law was a preparation for the New Law of the Gospel, the 'grace of the Holy Spirit received by faith in Christ', which works through charity and 'finds expression above all in the Lord's Sermon on the Mount and uses the sacraments to communicate grace to us':[82]

> If anyone should meditate with devotion and perspicacity on the sermon our Lord gave on the mount, as we read in the Gospel of Saint Matthew, he will doubtless find there ... the perfect way of the Christian life ... This sermon contains ... all the precepts needed to shape one's life.[83]

The entire Law of the Gospel (n. 1970) is contained in the 'new commandment' of Jesus, to love one another as he has loved us (see Jn 15:12; 13:34). The Law of the Gospel 'fulfils and surpasses the Old Law and brings it to perfection' (see Mt 5:17-19). In the Beatitudes, it fulfils the divine promises by elevating and orienting them towards the kingdom of heaven, and by reforming the heart, the root of human acts, it fulfils the commandments of the Old Law.[84] The New Law is a law of love, making it possible for us to act out of the love poured into our hearts by the Holy Spirit (see Rom 5:5). It is a law of grace, conferring on us, by means of faith and the sacraments, 'the strength of grace to act'. It is a law of freedom, setting us free from the juridical observances of the Old Law and inclining us 'to act spontaneously by the prompting of charity' so that we become, not merely the servants, but the friends of Christ (see Jn 15:15).[85]

St Catherine of Siena recognised that, among Christ's disciples, some commit themselves to following Christ's teaching by observing the evangelical counsels as well as by following the commandments:

> And why did he say, 'Come to me and drink?' Because you can follow his teaching and come to him by either of two ways: by living the commandments in the spirit of the counsels (the way of ordinary charity), or by actually living the counsels as well as the commandments. Along either way you will find the fruit of the blood to drink and enjoy, thanks to the union of the divine nature with the human.[86]

In addition to the commandments and precepts that 'are intended to remove whatever is incompatible with charity', the *Catechism* says that the New Law also includes evangelical counsels whose aim is 'to remove whatever might hinder the development of charity, even if it is not contrary to it'.[87] Quoting Vatican II's Dogmatic Constitution on the Church, *Lumen gentium* 42.2, the *Catechism* says that the Church's holiness 'is fostered in a special way by the manifold counsels which the Lord proposes to his disciples in the Gospel' (n. 1986).

The *Catechism* recognises that the grace of the Holy Spirit 'has the power to justify us, that is, to cleanse us from our sins and to communicate to us "the righteousness of God through faith in Jesus Christ" (Rom 3:22)' through Baptism, by means of which we are 'dead to sin and alive to God in Christ Jesus' (n. 1987) (see Rom 6:11). This justification is brought about through conversion, the 'first work of the grace of the Holy Spirit', as, moved by grace, Man 'turns toward God and away from sin, thus accepting forgiveness and righteousness from on high' (n. 1989). Quoting the Council of Trent (n. 1989), the *Catechism* points out that justification 'is not only the remission of sins, but also the sanctification and renewal of the interior man'.[88] The *Catechism* says that the justification that has 'been merited for us by the Passion of Christ' and that is 'granted to us through Baptism' has 'for its goal the glory of God and of Christ, and the gift of eternal life' (n. 2020). It quotes St Augustine who held that 'the sanctification of the wicked is a greater work than the creation of heaven and earth' because 'heaven and earth will pass away but the salvation and justification of the elect ... will not pass away'.[89] The *Catechism* describes grace as 'the help God gives us to respond to our vocation of becoming his adopted sons' and daughters (n. 2021). It is God who takes the initiative in the work of grace, however, since, as St Augustine pointed out, 'he who completes his work by cooperating with our will began by working so that we might will it'.[90] Our work is a collaboration with divine grace:

> Indeed we also work, but we are only collaborating with God who works, for his mercy has gone before us. It has gone before us so that we may be healed, and follows us so that once healed, we may be given life; it goes before us so that we may be called, and follows us so that we may be glorified; it goes before us so that we may live devoutly, and follows us so that we may always live with God: for without him we can do nothing.[91]

God's grace 'responds to the deepest yearnings of human freedom, calls freedom to co-operate with it and perfects freedom' (n. 2022). As St Augustine points out, it is only by cooperating with God's grace that our yearning for eternal truth and goodness can be satisfied:[92]

> If at the end of your very good works ... you rested on the seventh day, it was to foretell by the voice of your book that at the end of our works, which are indeed 'very good' (Gen 1:31) since you have given them to us, we shall also rest on the sabbath of eternal life.[93]

The *Catechism* describes sanctifying or deifying grace,[94] which is 'infused by the Holy Spirit into the soul to heal it of sin and to sanctify it', as 'the gratuitous gift of his life that God makes to us' (n. 2023). The special graces of the Holy Spirit, which are known as charisms, 'are oriented to sanctifying grace and are intended for the common good of the Church'. God 'also acts through many actual graces, to be distinguished from habitual grace which is permanent in us' (n. 2024). Recognising that, with regard to God, 'there is no strict right to any merit' on our part because of the 'immeasurable inequality' between us and our Creator (n. 2007), the *Catechism* teaches that:

> We can have merit in God's sight only because of God's free plan to associate man with the work of his grace. Merit is to be ascribed in the first place to the grace of God, and secondly to man's collaboration. (n. 2025)

Our merit 'is due to God' because our 'good actions proceed in Christ, from the predispositions and assistance given by the Holy Spirit' (n. 2008) for, as St Augustine recognised, 'Our merits are God's gifts'[95] and, in crowning the merits of his saints, it is his own gifts that God crowns.[96] The *Catechism* insists that the initiative in the order of Grace belongs to God (n. 2010), that 'no one can merit the initial grace which is at the origin of conversion' (n. 2027), and that it is the charity of Christ that 'is the source in us of all our merits before God' (n. 2011). Having become partakers by grace in the divine nature (see 2 Pet 1:4), however, it recognises that the grace of the Holy Spirit 'can confer true merit on us … in accordance with God's gratuitous justice' (nn. 2026–7). Moved by the Holy Spirit, we can merit for ourselves and for others all the graces needed to attain eternal life, as well as necessary temporal goods.

Jesus tells his disciples, 'Be perfect, therefore, as your heavenly Father is perfect' (Mt 5:48) and, quoting Vatican II's *Lumen gentium* 40.2, the *Catechism* recognises that 'All Christians ... are called to the fullness of Christian life and to the perfection of charity' (n. 2028). There is 'no holiness without renunciation and spiritual battle', however, and our spiritual journey towards perfection necessarily 'passes by way of the Cross':[97] 'If any man would come after me, let him deny himself and take up his cross and follow me' (Mt 16:24).[98] The Church plays a crucial role in enabling us to reach the perfection of charity. It is from the Church that we receive the Word of God and its teachings concerning 'the law of Christ' (Gal 6:2). It is from the Church that we receive the grace of the sacraments that sustain us on our spiritual journey. It is from the Church that we learn to recognise the all-holy Virgin Mary as the outstanding model of holiness in the Church.[99] It is within the Body of Christ that we present our bodies 'as a living sacrifice, holy and acceptable to God' (Rom 12:1) and that our activity 'finds its nourishment in the liturgy and the celebration of the sacraments'.[100] Vatican II's *Lumen gentium* 17 describes the Church, 'the pillar and bulwark of the truth' (1 Tim 3:15), as having received the 'solemn command of Christ from the apostles to announce the saving truth'. Quoting this text (n. 2032), the *Catechism* points out that the Church

> has the right always and everywhere to announce moral principles, including those pertaining to the social order, and to make judgments on any human affairs to the extent that they are required by the fundamental rights of the human person or the salvation of souls.[101]

The authoritative teaching of the Roman pontiff and of the bishops of the Church in moral matters, which is based on the universally valid principles of the Ten Commandments, 'is ordinarily exercised in catechesis and preaching, with the help of the works of theologians and spiritual authors'.[102] Quoting *Lumen gentium* 25, the *Catechism* describes the bishops as preaching 'the faith to the people entrusted to them, the faith to be believed and put into practice' (n. 2034). It is also 'incumbent on them to pronounce on moral questions that fall within the natural law and reason' (n. 2050). Thanks to the charism that they have received from the Holy Spirit,[103] the infallibility of the teaching authority of the Pastors of the Church 'extends to all the elements of doctrine, including moral doctrine, without which the saving truths of the faith cannot be preserved, expounded or observed' (n. 2051).

THE TEN COMMANDMENTS[104]

In the first section of its presentation of the faith of the Church on righteousness, 'Life in the Spirit as Our Common Human Vocation', the *Catechism* presents our being created in God's image as the basis of our common human vocation and the gift of life in the Holy Spirit, loving God wholeheartedly and our neighbour as ourselves, as the fulfilment of that vocation. This second section, 'The Ten Commandments', outlines the way in which the gift of life in the Holy Spirit fulfils the requirements of each of the Ten Commandments.

By his life and his preaching, Jesus 'attested to the permanent validity' of the Ten Commandments: 'What good deed must I do, to have eternal life? … If you would enter into life, keep the commandments' (Mt 19:16-17).[105] In her *Dialogue*, the following words addressed to St Catherine of Siena by God are recorded:

> And because I loved you without being loved by you, even before you existed (in fact it was love that moved me to create you in my own image and likeness) you

cannot repay me. But you must give this love to other people, loving them without being loved by them. You must love them without any concern for your own spiritual or material profit, but only for the glory and praise of my name, because I love them. In this way you will fulfil the whole commandment of the Law, which is to love me above all things and your neighbour as your very self (see Mt 22:37–40).[106]

It was in the context of the Exodus, 'God's great liberating event at the centre of the Old Covenant', that God spoke the 'ten words' that 'contain the terms of the covenant' that he concluded with his people.[107] It is only 'in and through this covenant' that the commandments 'take on their true meaning', for 'they express the implications of belonging to God through the establishment of the covenant'.[108] They show that our morality is 'a worship of thanksgiving' in response to 'the Lord's loving initiative' in establishing the covenant with us.[109]

Noting that since the time of St Augustine, 'the Ten Commandments have occupied a predominant place in the catechesis of baptismal candidates and the faithful' (n. 2065), the *Catechism* quotes *Lumen gentium* 29, which says that salvation is attained 'through faith, Baptism, and the observance of the Commandments' (n. 2068). St Catherine of Siena held that the other commandments are so bound up with the commandment to love God and neighbour that those who observe the commandments to love God and neighbour 'necessarily observe them all, and those who let go of this one let go of them all'.[110] Echoing her, the *Catechism* says that the Commandments form 'a coherent whole' in which 'they reciprocally condition one another' in such a way that to transgress one 'is to infringe all the others' (n. 2069) (see Jas 2:10–11). They are 'a privileged expression of the natural law' but they also 'belong to God's revelation' and 'sinful humanity needed this revelation' in order to arrive at 'a complete and certain understanding of the requirements of the natural law'.[111] In their fundamental content, they state 'grave obligations' that apply always and everywhere but which God makes possible by his grace.[112] They also imply 'obligations in matter which is, of itself, light', such as the prohibition on abusive language, which would only be a grave offence in certain circumstances.[113]

You Shall Love the Lord Your God with All Your Heart, Soul and Mind[114]

Quoting St Augustine (n. 2067), the *Catechism* describes the first three of the Ten Commandments as being concerned with love of God and the other seven as being concerned with love of neighbour:

> As charity comprises the two commandments to which the Lord related the whole Law and the prophets ... so the Ten Commandments were themselves given on two tablets. Three were written on one tablet and seven on the other.[115]

In this subsection, we will outline the teaching of the *Catechism* on the first three commandments.

As presented in Exodus 20:2-5 and Deuteronomy 5:6-9, the first commandment summons us 'to believe in God, to hope in him and to love him above all else' (n. 2134). Quoting Matthew 4:10, 'You shall worship the Lord your God', and St Augustine, 'Every action done so as to cling to God in communion of holiness, and thus achieve blessedness, is a true sacrifice',[116] the *Catechism* says:

> Adoring God, praying to him, offering him the worship that belongs to him, fulfilling the promises and vows made to him, are acts of the virtue of religion which fall under obedience to the first commandment. (n. 2135)

Recognising that the duty of offering God authentic worship 'concerns man both as an individual and as a social being' (n. 2136), the *Catechism* quotes Vatican II's Decree on Religious Liberty, *Dignitatis humanae* 15, when it says that our contemporaries 'want to profess their religion freely in private and in public' (n. 2137).

Proscribing superstition, idolatry, divination and magic,[117] the first commandment 'forbids honouring gods other than the one Lord who has revealed himself to his people' (n. 2110). It also 'condemns the main sins of irreligion: tempting God, in words or deeds, sacrilege, and simony' (n. 2118). The term 'atheism' covers many very different phenomena (n. 2124) but, insofar as it 'rejects or denies the existence of God', atheism is a sin against the first commandment (n. 2140). Despite prohibiting every representation of God by the hand of man (see Deut 4:15-16), the Old Law 'permitted the making of images that pointed symbolically towards salvation by the incarnate Word: so it was with the bronze serpent, the ark of the covenant, and the cherubim' (n. 2130).[118] Recognising that, by becoming incarnate, 'the Son of God introduced a new "economy" of images', the seventh ecumenical council at Nicaea (787) accepted that the veneration of sacred images 'is not contrary to the first commandment' (n. 2141).

As presented in Exodus 20:7 and Deuteronomy 5:11, the second commandment 'forbids every improper use of God's name' (n. 2162). For St Augustine:

> [God's] name is great when spoken with respect for the greatness of his majesty. God's name is holy when said with veneration and fear of offending him.[119]

The *Catechism* describes blasphemy as 'the use of the name of God, of Jesus Christ, of the Virgin Mary, and of the saints in an offensive way' (n. 2162). Describing false oaths as calling on God 'to be witness to a lie', it describes perjury as 'a grave offence against the Lord who is always faithful to his promises' (n. 2163).

Noting that 'the Lord's name sanctifies' us in Baptism and that Christians receive their names 'in the Church', the *Catechism* says that the name given in Baptism should not be 'foreign to Christian sentiment' (n. 2156).[120] God calls each one by name (see Isa 43:1) and the name one receives 'is a name for eternity'.[121] The *Catechism* also notes that, by beginning their activities with the Sign of the Cross, those who have been baptised call 'on the Saviour's grace' that allows them to 'act in the Spirit as a child of the Father' (n. 2157).

As presented in Exodus 20:8-10 and Deuteronomy 5:12-15, the third commandment 'recalls the holiness of the sabbath: "The seventh day is a sabbath of solemn rest, holy to the Lord" (Exod 31:15)' (n. 2168). The resurrection of Jesus, which symbolises the new creation, took place 'on the first day of the week' (See Mt 28:1; Mk 16:2; Lk 24:1; Jn 20:1), sometimes known as the 'eighth day' because it was the day after the Jewish sabbath (see Mk 16:1; Mt 28:1).[122] As a result, the sabbath, 'which represented the completion of the first creation', has been replaced in the New Law 'by Sunday, which recalls the new creation inaugurated by the Resurrection of Christ' (n. 2190). Citing Vatican II's Constitution on the Sacred Liturgy, *Sacrosanctum concilium* 106, which describes the Lord's Day as 'the original feast day', the *Catechism* says that the Church 'celebrates the day of Christ's Resurrection on the "eighth day", Sunday, which is rightly called the Lord's Day' (n. 2191).

Recognising Sunday as 'the foremost holy day of obligation in the universal Church',[123] the *Catechism* says that on Sundays and other holy days of obligation, the faithful are bound to 'participate in the Mass' and to 'abstain from those labours and business concerns which impede the worship to be rendered to God, the joy which is proper to the Lord's Day, or the proper relaxation of mind and body'.[124] St Augustine recognised that certain needs and services warranted some exceptions to the 'holy leisure' of Sunday: 'The charity of truth seeks holy leisure; the necessity of charity accepts just work.'[125] Insisting that every Christian 'should avoid making unnecessary demands on others that would hinder them from observing the Lord's Day',[126] it describes the observance of Sunday as helping us all 'to be allowed sufficient rest and leisure to cultivate their familial, cultural, social and religious lives'.[127]

You Shall Love Your Neighbour as Yourself[128]

Having presented the teaching of the *Catechism* on the first three commandments, which are concerned with loving God, the remaining seven commandments, which are concerned with loving our neighbour, are outlined here.

As presented in Exodus 20:12 and Deuteronomy 5:16, the fourth commandment is: 'Honour your father and your mother' (n. 2247) (see Mk 7:10). The *Catechism* interprets this commandment in terms of God wishing that 'after him, we should honour our parents and those whom he has vested with authority for our good' (n. 2248).

The Christian family 'is a communion of persons, a sign and image of the communion of the Father and the Son in the Holy Spirit' (n. 2204). It is ordered to the good of the spouses, whose 'conjugal community' is established upon their covenant and consent, and to the procreation and education of the children (n. 2249). Quoting Vatican II's *Gaudium et spes* 47.1, the *Catechism* recognised that the well-being of the individual person and of both human and Christian society 'is closely bound up with the healthy state of conjugal and family life' (n. 2250). The *Catechism* describes all the members of the family as 'persons equal in dignity' and it notes that, for the common good of its members and of society, 'the family necessarily has manifold responsibilities, rights, and duties' (n. 2203). Writing to her brother, Benincasa, St Catherine of Siena reminded him that he was 'obligated by God's commandment' to the duty he owed his mother.[129] The *Catechism* says that children 'owe their parents respect, gratitude, just obedience and assistance', whereas parents have 'the first responsibility for the education of their children in the faith, prayer and all the virtues' as well as 'the duty to provide as far as possible for the physical and spiritual needs of their children'.[130] Children 'have the right and duty to choose their profession and state in life' and parents 'should respect and encourage their children's vocations', remembering and teaching 'that the first calling of the Christian is to follow Jesus'.[131]

Public authorities 'are obliged to respect the fundamental rights of the human person and the conditions for the exercise of his freedom', especially those 'of families and the disadvantaged'.[132] Citizens are obliged 'to work with civil authority for building up society in a spirit of truth, solidarity and freedom', but, since we 'must obey God rather than men' (Acts 5:29), they 'are obliged in conscience not to follow the directives of civil authorities when they are contrary to the demands of the moral order'.[133] Quoting *Gaudium et spes* 76.5, the *Catechism* says that it is part of the Church's mission 'to pass moral judgements even in matters related to politics, whenever the fundamental rights of man or the salvation of souls requires it'.

As presented in Exodus 20:13 and Deuteronomy 5:17, the fifth commandment teaches us that 'the life of every living thing and the breath of all mankind' (n. 2318) is in God's hand (see Job 12:10). On this basis, the *Catechism* teaches:

> Every human life, from the moment of conception until death, is sacred because the human person has been willed for its own sake in the image and likeness of the living and holy God. (n. 2319)

As the account of the murder of Abel by Cain makes clear (see Gen 4:8–12), 'the murder of a human being is gravely contrary to the dignity of the person and the holiness of the Creator' (n. 2320). Recognising that legitimate defence 'is a grave duty for whoever is responsible for the lives of others or the common good', the *Catechism* says that the prohibition of murder 'does not abrogate the right to render an unjust aggressor unable to inflict harm' (n. 2321).

Quoting *Gaudium et spes* 27.3, which describes 'abortion willed as an end or as a means' as a 'criminal' practice that is gravely contrary to the moral law, the *Catechism* insists that the child has the right to life 'from its conception' and that 'the embryo must be defended in its integrity, cared for and healed like every other human being'.[134] Because it is 'gravely contrary to the dignity of the human person and to the respect due to the living God, his Creator', intentional euthanasia is murder 'whatever its forms or motives' (n. 2324). Suicide, which is 'seriously contrary to justice, hope and charity' (n. 2325), is also forbidden by the fifth commandment. We should 'not despair of the eternal salvation of persons who have taken their own lives' (n. 2283), however, and the Church prays for them. Recognising that scandal 'is a grave offence when by deed or omission it deliberately leads others into sin', the *Catechism* also recognises that the person who gives scandal can 'draw his brother into spiritual death'.[135]

Because of 'the evils and injustices that all war brings with it, we must do everything reasonably possible to avoid it' (n. 2327). Quoting *Gaudium et spes* 79.4, however, the *Catechism* acknowledges that 'governments cannot be denied the right to lawful self-defence, once all peace efforts have failed' (n. 2308). Even during armed conflicts, the moral law does not lose its 'permanent validity' and practices 'deliberately contrary to the law of nations and to its universal principles are crimes' (n. 2328). Quoting *Gaudium et spes* 81.3, the *Catechism* describes the arms race as 'one of the greatest curses on the human race', adding that 'the harm it inflicts on the poor is more than can be endured' (n. 2329). Citing St Augustine, who described peace as 'the tranquillity of order',[136] the *Catechism* presents peace on earth as 'the image and fruit of *the peace of Christ*' (n. 2304–5), the peace of the one who 'is our peace' (Eph 2:14) and who said, 'Blessed are the peacemakers, for they shall be called sons of God' (Mt 5:9).

The sixth commandment is, 'You shall not commit adultery' (Exod 20:14; Deut 5:18). Recognising that both men and women are created in God's image and that God blessed their fruitful union and procreation (see Gen 1:27-28), the *Catechism* describes love as 'the fundamental and innate vocation of every human being'.[137] Every man and woman should 'acknowledge and accept' their sexual identity, recognising that the physical, moral and spiritual difference and complementarity of men and women 'are oriented towards the goods of marriage and the flourishing of family life' (n. 2333).

The *Catechism* presents Christ as the model of chastity and it insists that, according to their particular state in life, every baptised person 'is called to lead a chaste life' (n. 2394). The 'integration of sexuality within the person' is a gradual process (n. 2395), as St Augustine recognised:

> Indeed it is through chastity that we are gathered together and led back to the unity from which we were fragmented into multiplicity.[138]

Having freely entered into an indissoluble covenant that 'entails faithful love', married people 'are called to live conjugal chastity', recognising that adultery, divorce, polygamy and free union are 'grave offences against the dignity of marriage'.[139] All others are called to practise chastity 'in continence', recognising that 'masturbation, fornication, pornography and homosexual practices' are among 'the sins gravely contrary to chastity'.[140] Within marriage, sexuality 'is a source of joy and pleasure' and the fruitfulness of the union of husband and wife 'is a good, a gift and an end of marriage' that enables the spouses to 'participate in God's fatherhood'.[141] Recognising that the regulation of births 'represents one of the aspects of responsible fatherhood and motherhood', the *Catechism* insists that the legitimate intentions to regulate births on the part of the spouses 'do not justify recourse to morally unacceptable means (for example, direct sterilization or contraception)' (n. 2399).

The *Catechism* says that the seventh commandment, 'You shall not steal' (Exod 20:15; Deut 5:19), 'enjoins the practice of justice and charity in the administration of earthly goods and the fruits of men's labour' (n. 2451). In the beginning, 'God entrusted the earth and its resources to the common stewardship of mankind' (see Gen 1:26-29), but, because human life was 'endangered by poverty and threatened by violence', people legitimately appropriated property in order 'to assure the security of their lives', to guarantee their 'freedom and dignity' and to help them meet their 'basic needs' and the needs of those in their charge.[142] Noting that *Gaudium et spes* 69.1 recognises that privately owned goods 'can benefit others as well' (n. 2404), the *Catechism* defines theft, not as the usurpation of another's goods as such, but as their usurpation 'against the reasonable will of the owner' (n. 2453). Whenever another person's property is taken and used unjustly, restitution must be made.[143]

Disregarding the personal dignity of human beings by acts that, for whatever reason, lead to their enslavement, or to their 'being bought, sold or exchanged like merchandise', is forbidden by the moral law.[144] The dominion that humanity has been given 'over the mineral, vegetable and animal resources of the universe' (see Gen 1:28-31) includes certain 'moral obligations ... towards generations to come' and, while

173

they may be used to serve the just satisfaction of our needs, we must also show kindness to the animals that have been entrusted to our stewardship.[145]

Gaudium et spes 76.5 recognises that, when 'the fundamental rights of the person or the salvation of souls requires it', the Church can make judgements about economic and social matters.[146] Since humanity itself is the 'author, centre and goal of all economic and social life', theories are morally unacceptable if they make profit 'the exclusive norm and ultimate end of economic activity' or if they prevent the goods created by God for everyone reaching everyone 'in accordance with justice and with the help of charity'.[147] Humanity is called to 'prolong the work of creation by subduing the earth' (see Gen 1:28) and, as well as honouring the Creator's gifts and benefiting others, human work can also be a collaboration in the redemptive work of Christ.[148] People should be able to draw from work the means of providing for their life and that of their family, and of serving the human community.[149] The Gospel obliges us to recognise the hungry beggar, Lazarus (see Lk 17:19–31), 'in the multitude of human beings without bread, a roof or a place to stay' for, as well as being 'a witness to fraternal charity', giving alms to the poor is 'a work of justice pleasing to God'.[150] Rich nations have 'a grave moral responsibility towards those which are unable to ensure the means of their development by themselves' and they should cultivate the kind of development that would be 'concerned with increasing each person's ability to respond to his vocation and hence to God's call'.[151]

The *Catechism* says that the eighth commandment, 'You shall not bear false witness against your neighbour' (Exod 20:16; Deut 5:20), 'forbids misrepresenting the truth in our relations with others' (n. 2464). 'Full of grace and truth' (Jn 1:14), Jesus Christ came as the 'light of the world' (Jn 8:12) and his disciples, 'putting away falsehood' (Eph 4:25), are to rid themselves of 'all malice, and all guile, insincerity, envy and all slander' (1 Pet 2:1).[152] Before Pilate, Christ proclaims that he has come 'to testify to the truth' (Jn 18:37) and his disciples are not to 'be ashamed of the testimony about our Lord' (2 Tim 1:8), the 'supreme witness given to the truth of the faith' being martyrdom.[153]

For St Augustine, a lie 'consists in speaking a falsehood with the intention of deceiving'[154] and it contradicts the virtue of truthfulness,

> which consists in showing oneself true in deeds and truthful in words, and guarding against duplicity, dissimulation and hypocrisy.[155]

Among the offences against truth, the *Catechism* lists false witness and perjury, rash judgement, detraction (disclosing another's faults and failings to those who do not know them without objectively valid reason), calumny (harming the reputation of others by remarks contrary to the truth), boasting and maliciously caricaturing some aspect of another person's behaviour.[156] The *Catechism* insists that any offence committed against the truth 'requires reparation' (n. 2509), but it also recognises that the good and safety of others, respect for privacy and the common good are 'sufficient reasons for being silent about what ought not to be known or for making use of discreet language' (n. 2489). Describing the seal of confession as 'inviolable',[157] the *Catechism* says that professional secrets 'must be kept' and that confidences prejudicial to another 'are not to be divulged' (n. 2511). Citing Vatican II's Decree on the Means of Social Communication, *Inter mirifica* 11, the *Catechism* says that the information provided by social communications media 'is at the service of the common good' and that society has 'a right to information based on truth, freedom, justice, and solidarity' (n. 2494). Quoting Vatican II's Constitution on the Sacred Liturgy, *Sacrosanctum Concilium* 122, the *Catechism* says that, of their nature, the fine arts, but above all sacred art, are directed toward expressing in some way the infinite beauty of God in works made by human hands. Their dedication to the increase of God's praise and of his glory is more complete, the more exclusively they are devoted to turning men's minds devoutly toward God. (n. 2513)

In the Catholic exegetical tradition, the ninth commandment, 'Thou shalt not covet your neighbour's wife, or his manservant, or his maidservant' (Exod 20:17), is associated with the prohibition, 'Every one who looks at a woman lustfully has already committed adultery with her in his heart' (Mt 5:28).[158] It warns us against carnal lust and invites us to purity of heart and the practice of temperance.[159] Noting the connection between purity of heart, of body and of faith, the *Catechism* quotes St Augustine (n. 2518), who held that the faithful must believe the articles of the Creed

so that by believing they may obey God, by obeying may live well, by living well may purify their hearts, and with pure hearts may understand what they believe.[160]

The purity of heart that will enable us to see God 'enables us even now to see things according to God',[161] and it demands modesty, which 'protects the intimate centre of the person' (n. 2533), as well as the practice of chastity, purity of intention and of vision, and prayer.[162] Reflecting on his struggle to attain continence, St Augustine wrote:

I thought that continence arose from one's own powers, which I did not recognise in myself. I was foolish enough not to know ... that no one can be continent unless you grant it. For you would surely have granted it if my inner groaning had reached your ears and I with firm faith had cast my cares on you.[163]

Quoting the Lord's words, 'Where your treasure is, there will your heart be also' (Mt 6:21), the *Catechism* says that the tenth commandment 'forbids avarice arising from a passion for riches and their attendant power'.[164] The *Catechism* describes envy as 'sadness at the sight of another's goods and the immoderate desire to have them for oneself' (n. 2553). It is one of the capital sins that engender other sins and vices[165] and St Augustine describes it as 'the diabolical sin'.[166] According to the *Catechism*, the means to combat envy are 'good will, humility and abandonment to the providence of God' (n. 2554). Thanks to Baptism, 'the flesh with its passions and desires' has been crucified in us (see Gal 5:24) and we have committed ourselves to being led by the Spirit and following what he desires.[167] The story of the rich young man (Mk 19:16–22) warns us that our attachment to riches can prevent us entering the kingdom of heaven,[168] and St Augustine highlights the contrast between the proud and poor in spirit on this point:

> Let the proud seek and love earthly kingdoms, but blessed are the poor in spirit for theirs is the Kingdom of heaven.[169]

It is our desire for true happiness that frees us from our 'immoderate attachment to the goods of this world' so that we can find our fulfilment 'in the vision and beatitude of God' (n. 2548). This desire, this thirst for God, helps us to mortify our cravings and, by God's grace, to 'prevail over the seductions of pleasure and power' (n. 2549), and it will be 'quenched by the water of eternal life' (n. 2557) (see Jn 4:14), which St Augustine describes as the common possession of all the blessed:

> God himself will be the goal of our desires; we shall contemplate him without end, love him without surfeit, praise him without weariness. This gift, this state, this act, like eternal life itself, will assuredly be common to all.[170]

Having outlined the teaching of the *Catechism* on prayer, worship and righteousness, we now turn to the profession of what we believe in the Creed.

Notes

1. See the *Catechism*, nn. 1718 (twice), 1720, 1766 (twice), 1779, 1809, 1829, 1847, 1849, 1850, 1863, 1955, 1958, 1962, 1966, 1994, 2001 (twice), 2002, 2006, 2009, 2067, 2099, 2149, 2185, 2304, 2340, 2482, 2518, 2520, 2539, 2547 and 2550.
2. See the *Catechism*, nn. 1718, 1766, 1767 (twice), 1806, 1849, 1856, 1902, 1951, 1955, 1964, 1973, 2132, 2176, 2263, 2264, 2302 and 2469 (twice).
3. Pope Pius XII is cited in nn. 1887, 1939, 1942, 1960, 2108, 2286, 2362 and 2501. Pope John Paul II is cited nn. 1697, 1848, 1863, 1864, 1869, 1929, 1939 and 2516.
4. See nn. 1722, 1730, 1964, 2063 and 2070.
5. See nn. 2179, 2365, 2446, 2538 and 2540.
6. See nn. 1898, 1951, 1954, 2105 and 2108.
7. See nn. 1882, 1886, 1897, 1903 and 1930.
8. In the order in which they are cited in the *Catechism*: St Teresa of Avila (n. 1821), St Thérèse of Lisieux (n. 2011), St Joan of Arc (n. 2005), St Catherine of Siena (n. 1937) and St Rose of Lima (n. 2449).
9. See Roland J. Teske, 'St. Augustine' in *New Catholic Encyclopedia* (Washington, DC: The Catholic University of America, 2003), 1:850–68.
10. See St Augustine, *Confessions,* 1.11.17; 3.4.8, in Migne (ed.), *PL*, 32:669, 686.
11. See *Confessions,* 9.6.14, in ibid., 32:769.
12. See *Confessions,* 3.4.7–8, in ibid., 32:685–6.
13. See *Confessions,* 3.5.9, in ibid., 32:686.
14. See *Confessions,* 5.6.11–5.7.13, in ibid., 32:710–11.
15. See *Confessions,* 5.14.24–5, in ibid., 32:717–18.
16. See *Confessions,* 6.3.4, in ibid., 32:721.
17. See *Confessions,* 6.13.23–6.15.25, in ibid., 32:730–2.
18. See *Confessions,* 7.9.13–7.10.16, in ibid., 32:740–2.
19. See *Confessions,* 8.11.27, in ibid., 32:761.
20. The ruins of this font, including the elaborate plumbing system associated with it, were discovered in 1899 under Milan Cathedral.

21. See, for example, St Augustine, *Against Cresconius the Grammarian,* 1.29.34, in Migne (ed.), *PL,* 43:463–4.

22. See, for example, St Augustine, *Against the Letter of Petilian,* 1.9.10, in ibid., 43:250.

23. See Kenelm Francis Foster, 'St Catherine of Siena' in *New Catholic Encyclopedia* (Washington, DC: The Catholic University of America, 2003), 3, 272–4.

24. See G. Caprile (ed.), *Il Concilio Vaticano II: Cronache del Concilio Vaticano II,* 5 vols (Rome: La Civiltà Cattolica, 1966–1969), 1/1:128–9, 303.

25. See *Acta synodalia sacrosancti Concilii Vaticani II,* 4 vols of 4, 6, 8 and 7 parts respectively (Vatican City: Archivum Concilii Oecumenici Vaticani II, 1970–1978), 1/1:96–7.

26. Quoted in Peter Hebblethwaite, *John XXIII, Pope of the Council,* revised edition (Glasgow: HarperCollins, 1994), 502.

27. See the Vatican website, accessed on 14/11/2009: http://vatican.va/holy_father/benedict_xvi/speeches/2008/october/documents/hf_ben-xvi_spe_20081028_giovanni-xxiii_en.html.

28. See the *Catechism,* nn. 1699–2051.

29. See the *Catechism,* nn. 1700–1876.

30. Blessed John XXIII, *Pacem in terris,* 10, in Jacques Dupuis (ed.), *The Christian Faith in the Doctrinal Documents of the Catholic Church,* 7th and enlarged edition (New York: Alba House, 2001), n. 2027.

31. *Gaudium et spes* 22.1.

32. *Catechism,* n. 1701, see *Gaudium et spes* 22.

33. *Gaudium et spes* 14.2.

34. *Gaudium et spes* 15.2.

35. Blessed John XXIII, *Pacem in terris,* 5, in Dupuis (ed.), *The Christian Faith,* n. 2026.

36. *Gaudium et spes* 16.

37. St Augustine, *The Morality of the Catholic Church,* 1.3.4, in Migne (ed.), *PL,* 32:1312.

38. St Augustine, *Confessions,* 10.20, in ibid., 32:791.

39. *Catechism,* n. 1716.

40. See the *Catechism,* n. 1725.

41. See the *Catechism,* n. 1720. See also n. 1726.

42. St Augustine, *City of God,* 22.30.5, in Migne (ed.), *PL,* 41:804.

43. St Augustine, *Free Choice,* 2.20.54, in ibid., 32:1269–70.

44. See the *Catechism,* n. 1751.

45. See the *Catechism*, n. 1754.
46. See St Augustine, *The Trinity*, 8.3.4, in Migne (ed.), *PL*, 42:949–50.
47. St Augustine, *City of God*, 14.7.2, in ibid., 41:410.
48. St Augustine, *Homilies on the Letter of John*, 8.9, in ibid., 35:2041.
49. See the *Catechism*, n. 1785.
50. *Catechism*, n. 1798.
51. St Augustine, *Against Julian*, 4.3.21, in Migne (ed.), *PL*, 44:749.
52. St Augustine, *The Morality of the Catholic Church*, 1.25.46, in ibid., 32:1330–1. See the *Catechism*, n. 1809.
53. See the *Catechism*, nn. 1812, 1840.
54. See Dupuis (ed.), *The Christian Faith*, n. 152.
55. Vatican I, *Dei Filius*, chapter 3, in ibid., n. 118.
56. St Augustine, *Homilies on the Letter of John*, 10.4, in Migne (ed.), *PL*, 35:2057.
57. St Augustine, *Against Faustus the Manichean*, 22, in ibid., 42:418.
58. See the *Catechism*, nn. 1871–2.
59. St Augustine, *Sermons*, 169.11.13, in Migne (ed.), *PL*, 38:923.
60. See the *Catechism*, n. 1873.
61. St Augustine, *City of God*, 14.28, in Migne (ed.), *PL*, 41:436. See the *Catechism*, n. 1850.
62. St Augustine, *Homilies on the Letter of John*, 1.6, in ibid., 35:1982. Quoted in the *Catechism*, n. 1863.
63. See the *Catechism*, nn. 1877–1948.
64. Blessed John XXIII, *Mater et magistra*, 60. See the *Catechism*, n. 1893.
65. Blessed John XXIII, *Mater et magistra*, 51.
66. Blessed John XXIII, *Pacem in terris*, 36, see the *Catechism*, n. 1886.
67. Blessed John XXIII, *Pacem in terris*, 46, see the *Catechism*, n. 1897.
68. Blessed John XXIII, *Pacem in terris*, 51, see the *Catechism*, n. 1903.
69. Blessed John XXIII, *Mater et magistra*, 82.
70. See Blessed John XXIII, *Pacem in terris*, 65. See also the *Catechism*, n. 1930.
71. St Catherine of Siena, 'The Dialogue', 7, in Suzanne Noffke (ed.), *Catherine of Siena: The Dialogue (Classics of Western*

Spirituality, edited by Richard J. Payne) (New York - Mahwah: Paulist Press, 1980), 37–8.

72. Blessed John XXIII, *Pacem in terris*, 28.
73. Blessed John XXIII, *Mater et magistra*, 157.
74. See the *Catechism*, nn. 1949–2051.
75. St Thomas Aquinas, *Summa theologiae* I-II, 90.4. See the *Catechism*, n. 1976.
76. St Augustine, *The Trinity*, 14.15.21, in Migne (ed.), *PL*, 42:1052.
77. See the *Catechism*, n. 1954.
78. *Catechism*, n. 1979.
79. St Augustine, *Confessions*, 2.4.9, in Migne (ed.), *PL*, 32:678. See the *Catechism*, n. 1958.
80. See the *Catechism*, n. 1980.
81. St Augustine, *Explanations of the Psalms*, 57.1, in Migne (ed.), *PL*, 36:673. See the *Catechism*, n. 1962.
82. See the *Catechism*, nn. 1982–3.
83. St Augustine, *The Lord's Sermon on the Mount in Matthew*, 1.1, in Migne (ed.), *PL*, 34:1229–30. See the *Catechism*, n. 1966.
84. See the *Catechism*, nn. 1967–8, 1984.
85. See the *Catechism*, n. 1972.
86. St Catherine of Siena, *The Dialogue*, 53, in Noffke (ed.), 106.
87. *Catechism*, n. 1974. See St Thomas Aquinas, *Summa theologiae* II-II, 184.3.
88. Council of Trent (1547), in Dupuis (ed.), *The Christian Faith*, 1932.
89. St Augustine, *Homilies on the Gospel of John*, 72.3, in Migne (ed.), *PL*, 35:1823. See the *Catechism*, n. 1994.
90. St Augustine, *Grace and Free Choice*, 17, in ibid., 44:901. See the *Catechism*, n. 2001.
91. St Augustine, *Nature and Grace*, 31, in ibid., 44:264. See the *Catechism*, n. 2001.
92. See the *Catechism*, n. 2002.
93. St Augustine, *Confessions*, 13.36.51, in Migne (ed.), *PL*, 32:868. See the *Catechism*, n. 2002.
94. See the *Catechism*, n. 1999.
95. St Augustine, *Sermons*, 298.4–5, in Migne (ed.), *PL*, 38:1367. See the *Catechism*, n. 2009.
96. St Augustine, *Explanations of the Psalms*, 102.7, in ibid., 37:1321–2. See the *Catechism*, n. 2006.

97. See the *Catechism*, n. 2015.
98. *Catechism*, n. 2029.
99. See the *Catechism*, n. 2030.
100. *Catechism*, nn. 2031, 2047.
101. Code of Canon Law, canon 747.2.
102. *Catechism*, nn. 2033, 2049.
103. See the *Catechism*, n. 2035.
104. See the *Catechism*, nn. 2052–2557.
105. *Catechism*, nn. 2075–6.
106. St Catherine of Siena, *The Dialogue*, 89, in Noffke (ed.), 165.
107. *Catechism*, n. 2056–8.
108. *Catechism*, nn. 2077, 2062.
109. See the *Catechism*, n. 2062.
110. St Catherine of Siena, *The Dialogue*, 155, in Noffke (ed.), 330.
111. *Catechism*, nn. 2070–1.
112. See the *Catechism*, nn. 2072, 2082.
113. See the *Catechism*, n. 2072.
114. See the *Catechism*, nn. 2083–2195.
115. St Augustine, *Sermons,* 33.2.2, in Migne (ed.), *PL*, 38:208.
116. St Augustine, *City of God,* 10.6, in ibid., 41:283. See the *Catechism*, n. 2099.
117. See the *Catechism*, nn. 2112–17.
118. See Num 21:4-9; Wis 16:5-14; Jn 3:14-15; Exod 25:10-22; 1 Kings 6:23-28, 7:23-26.
119. St Augustine, *The Lord's Sermon on the Mount in Matthew,* 2.3.19, in Migne (ed.), *PL*, 34:1278. See the *Catechism*, nn. 2149, 2161.
120. See the Code of Canon Law, canon 855.
121. See the *Catechism*, nn. 2158–9.
122. See the *Catechism*, n. 2174.
123. Code of Canon Law, canon 1246.1.
124. Code of Canon Law, canon 1247, see the *Catechism*, n. 2192–3.
125. St Augustine, *City of God,* 19.19, in Migne (ed.), *PL*, 41:547. See the *Catechism*, n. 2185.
126. *Catechism*, n. 2195.
127. Vatican II's Pastoral Constitution on the Church in the Modern World, *Gaudium et spes* 67.3, see the *Catechism*, n. 2194.
128. See the *Catechism*, nn. 2196–2557.
129. See Suzanne Noffke (ed.), *The Letters of St. Catherine of Siena* (*Medieval & Renaissance Texts & Studies*, 52) (New York: Medieval & Renaissance Texts & Studies), 1988, 64.

130. *Catechism*, nn. 2251–2.

131. *Catechism*, nn. 2230, 2253.

132. *Catechism*, nn. 2237, 2254.

133. See the *Catechism*, nn. 2255–6.

134. *Catechism*, nn. 2322–3.

135. *Catechism*, nn. 2284, 2326.

136. St Augustine, *City of God*, 19.13.1, in Migne (ed.), *PL*, 41:640. See the *Catechism*, n. 2304.

137. *Catechism*, nn. 2331, 2392.

138. St Augustine, *Confessions*, 10.29.40, in Migne (ed.), *PL*, 32:796. See the *Catechism*, n. 2340.

139. *Catechism*, nn. 2349, 2397.

140. *Catechism*, nn. 2349, 2396, 2400.

141. *Catechism*, nn. 2362, 2398.

142. See the *Catechism*, n. 2402.

143. See the *Catechism*, n. 2454.

144. See the *Catechism*, nn. 2414, 2455.

145. See the *Catechism*, nn. 2456–7.

146. See the *Catechism*, nn. 2420, 2458.

147. See the *Catechism*, nn. 2424, 2459.

148. See the *Catechism*, n. 2427.

149. See the *Catechism*, n. 2428.

150. See the *Catechism*, nn. 2462–3.

151. See the *Catechism*, nn. 2439, 2461.

152. *Catechism*, nn. 2466, 2475.

153. See the *Catechism*, n. 2506.

154. St Augustine, *Lying*, 4.5, Migne (ed.), in *PL*, 40:491. See the *Catechism*, nn. 2482, 2508.

155. *Catechism*, n. 2505.

156. See the *Catechism*, nn. 2476–7, 2481.

157. Code of Canon Law, canon 983.1.

158. See the *Catechism*, nn. 2514, 2528.

159. See the *Catechism*, nn. 2529–30.

160. St Augustine, *Faith and the Creed*, 10.25, in Migne (ed.), *PL*, 40:196.

161. *Catechism*, n. 2531.

162. See the *Catechism*, n. 2532.

163. St Augustine, *Confessions*, 6.11.20, in Migne (ed.), *PL*, 32:729–30. See the *Catechism*, n. 2520.

164. See the *Catechism*, nn. 2551–2.

165. See the *Catechism*, nn. 1866, 2553.
166. St Augustine, *Rudimentary Catechesis,* 4.8, in Migne (ed.), *PL*, 40:315–6. See the *Catechism*, n. 2539.
167. See the *Catechism*, n. 2555.
168. See the *Catechism*, n. 2556.
169. St Augustine, *The Lord's Sermon on the Mount in Matthew,* 1.1.3, in Migne (ed.), *PL*, 34:1232. See the *Catechism*, n. 2547.
170. St Augustine, *City of God,* 22.30, in ibid., 41:801–2. See the *Catechism*, n. 2550.

Chapter 5

FAITH AND BELIEF

The previous chapters correspond to the fourth, second and third parts of the Catechism. In this chapter, we turn to the first part, 'The Profession of Faith', which outlines the faith of the Church in relation to the elements of belief in the Creed. Just as the chapters on prayer and worship are concerned with Christ's priestly office, and the chapter on righteousness is concerned with Christ's kingly office, this chapter on belief is concerned with the way in which Christ's prophetic office continues in the life of the Church.

As before, we will take three of the Church's saints, one from the patristic, the medieval and the modern period, as our models as we explore this aspect of faith.

IRENAEUS, JOAN OF ARC AND ELIZABETH OF THE TRINITY AS MODELS OF BELIEF

The most frequently cited writers in this section of the *Catechism* are St Augustine, cited twenty-eight times,[1] St Thomas Aquinas, cited twenty-three times,[2] and St Irenaeus, who is cited twenty-one times.[3] St Thérèse of the Child Jesus is cited four times,[4] St Joan of Arc[5] and St Catherine of Siena[6] twice, and there are also references to St Caesaria the Younger (*d. c.* 559), Egeria (*fl. c.* 384), St Teresa of Jesus, St Rose of Lima (1586–1617), and Bl. Elizabeth of the Trinity.[7] Having already taken St Thérèse as a model of prayer, St Thomas as a model of worship and Sts Augustine and Catherine as models of righteousness, I propose to take St Irenaeus as one of the models of belief in this chapter. In order to balance the gender representation, I propose to take St Joan of Arc and Bl. Elizabeth of the Trinity as the other two models.

St Irenaeus (c. 130–c. 200)[8]

In later life, St Irenaeus recalled having both seen and heard Bishop Polycarp of Smyrna (d. AD 155) and he was probably born in Polycarp's hometown of Smyrna, now Izmir in Turkey. Raised in a Christian family, he moved to Rome, where he attended the school of Justin Martyr.[9] He was a priest in Lyons, France (then Lugdunum in Gaul), during the twenty-year persecution of the Roman Emperor, Marcus Aurelius, from 161–180. In 177 or 178, the clergy of Lyons sent him to Rome with a letter to Pope Eleuterus concerning the Montanist heresy. When he returned, he succeeded the martyred St Pothinus as bishop.

Towards the end of the persecution of Marcus Aurelius, between 175 and 185, Irenaeus wrote his best-known work, the five-volume *On the Detection and Overthrow of the So-Called Gnosis*, normally known as *Against Heresies*. Irenaeus also wrote an instruction for recent Christian converts, *The Demonstration of the Apostolic Preaching*. Against the various Gnostic sects, who claimed to possess a secret knowledge based on oral tradition coming from Jesus himself, Irenaeus emphasised the roles of the books of the Old and New Testament, of the common tradition and of the bishops of the Church, in determining the authentic Christian teaching. Although they were widely read at that time and claimed scriptural authority, Irenaeus refused to accept that the writings of the Gnostics should be regarded as among the books of the Bible.

Irenaeus did not forget his origins in Asia Minor and, about the year 190, he interceded on behalf of the Christian communities there when Pope St Victor I excommunicated them because they refused to accept the Roman date for the celebration of Easter. Although he was later named as a martyr, we know nothing certain about his death. He was buried in the church of Saint John in Lyons, which was later renamed in his honour. His tomb was destroyed in 1562 by the Huguenots.

St Joan of Arc (c. 1412–1431)[10]

In the period between 1337 and 1430, the so-called Hundred Years' War was a protracted dispute between the English and the French about the rightful successor to the French throne. Although there were some long periods of peace, the scorched earth policy of the English had devastated the French economy and it seemed that the English were on the verge of achieving their goal of a dual monarchy of England and France under English control. King Charles VI of France suffered from bouts of insanity and the role of regent was disputed between the king's brother, Duke Louis of Orléans, the leader of the Armagnacs, and the king's cousin, Duke John of Burgundy, who was the leader of the Burgundians. In 1407, the Duke of Burgundy ordered the assassination of the Duke of Orléans, but the opposition between the Armagnacs and the Burgundians continued.

Jeanne d'Arc was born in Domrémy, in eastern France, around 1412. Her father, Jacques d'Arc, was a small landowner who was responsible for collecting taxes in the area and loyal to the Armagnacs. His land was surrounded by Burgundian lands and, on one occasion, the village of Domrémy was sacked and burned by the Burgundians. Taking advantage of the disputed leadership of France at the time, King Henry V of England invaded France and won a dramatic victory over the French at Agincourt in 1415. In 1417, Charles, who was the eldest surviving son of Charles VI, assumed the title of Dauphin, the heir to the French throne. In 1419, the Dauphin signed a peace treaty with Burgundy but, at a meeting organised under the Dauphin's protection, the Duke of Burgundy was murdered by the Armagnacs. The new duke of Burgundy, Philip the Good, blamed the Dauphin and entered into an alliance with the English. In 1420, the Dauphin's mother, Queen Isabeau, who was acting on behalf of her husband, King Charles VI of France, concluded the Treaty of Troyes, by means of which her daughter, Catherine, would marry King Henry V of England, and the French royal succession would pass to Henry V and his heirs rather than to the Dauphin. When both Henry V of England and Charles VI of France died within months of each other in 1422, the infant King Henry VI of England became the nominal monarch of both kingdoms, and his father's brother, John of Lancaster, became regent.

When Joan was about thirteen years old, she experienced a vision and heard voices telling her that she would raise the siege of Orléans.[11] A few years later, at the age of sixteen, she persuaded a kinsman to bring her to nearby Vaucouleurs where she asked the local garrison commander for permission to visit the royal French court at Chinon. Undeterred by his sarcastic response, she was able to organise a second interview with the commander, during which she predicted that there would be a significant military victory for the French at Orléans. When this prediction was confirmed, she was brought to the court at Chinon. Although she impressed the Dauphin during a private interview with her prediction that the siege of Orléans would be lifted, he was worried that she might be considered a sorceress and he ordered a commission of enquiry to examine her theological orthodoxy. In April 1429, the commission of inquiry 'declared her to be of irreproachable life, a good Christian, possessed of the virtues of humility, honesty and simplicity'.[12] The commission did not pronounce on the legitimacy of her visions, arguing that their authenticity would be proven if the siege of Orléans, then under siege by the combined forces of the English and Burgundians, was lifted. Soon afterwards, the Dauphin approved her request to don the armour of a knight and form part of a relief mission to the city of Orléans. Despite the dismissive attitude of some veteran commanders and her initial exclusion from the councils of war, her inspiration led to the siege being lifted in only nine days. Following this unexpected victory, she persuaded the Dauphin to grant her co-command of the army with Duke John II of Alençon. The Dauphin approved her plan to recapture nearby bridges along the Loire and then to advance on Reims, then deep in enemy territory, where she proposed that he be crowned as King of France.[13]

A number of other victories eventually led to the coronation of the Dauphin as King Charles VII at Reims, with the result that the long-disputed succession to the French throne eventually came to an end. Defending the town of Compiègne, which was under siege by the English and Burgundians, Joan was captured by the Burgundians on 23 May 1430. When her family were unable to pay the ransom and her various attempts to escape proved unsuccessful, the Burgundians sold their prisoner to the English government. Apparently motivated by a desire to undermine the legitimacy of the coronation of Charles VII, rather than by genuinely religious concerns, Joan was accused of heresy and her trial in an ecclesiastical court at Rouen began in January 1431. During her interrogation, she was asked if she was in God's grace. Had she answered yes, she would have convicted herself of heresy, since Church doctrine held that no one could be certain of being in God's grace. Had she answered no, she would have confessed her own guilt. Her answer was:

> If I am not, may God put me there; and if I am, may God so keep me. I should be the saddest creature in the world if I knew I were not in His grace.[14]

She was condemned as a heretic and executed by burning in Rouen on 30 May 1431. She was only about nineteen years old when she died.

In 1452, twenty-four years after her death, Pope Callixtus III ordered a review to investigate whether the trial of condemnation and its verdict had been handled justly and according to canon law. That same year, the Church declared that a religious play in her honour at Orléans would qualify as a pilgrimage and that an indulgence could be granted for attending that play. The court declared her innocent in 1456. Declared a martyr, she was beatified in 1909 and canonised in 1920.

Bl. Elizabeth of the Trinity (1880–1906)

Elizabeth (Sabeth) Catez was born on 18 July 1880 at the military Camp D'Avor in the village of Jorges-en-Septaine, near Bourges in the district of Cher in France. Her father was an artillery officer in the French army and the family lived in army quarters, her mother (an admirer of Teresa of Avila) belonging to a famous army family in her own right. In November 1882, when Elizabeth was two, the family moved to Dijon in Burgundy and her sister Marguerite (Guite) was born there on 22 February 1883. In her childhood, Elizabeth was subject to temper tantrums. Her sister Marguerite remembers: 'Elizabeth was very lively and quick-tempered. She went into rages that were quite terrible. She was a real little devil!' Spotting one of her own dolls in the crib for Christmas (unknown to her, her mother had lent it for the festivities), she screeched out: 'You wicked priest, give me back my Jeanette'. A friend commented about her, 'That child has a will of iron and must have what she wants'.

Elizabeth's father died suddenly when she was seven and, with a reduced pension, the Catez family moved to a smaller house near the Carmel in Dijon, which Elizabeth could see from her window. Shortly afterwards she made her first confession and began to struggle against her violent temper. The priest who prepared her for her first confession predicted that she would 'grow up to be a saint or a devil'. At the age of eight, her mother enrolled her in the Conservatory of Dijon, probably in order to prepare her for a career as a piano teacher. On 1 January 1889, she wrote a New Year resolution in which she promised her mother:

> I will be very good, very obedient and I will never make you angry with me again. I will not cry any more and I will be a good little girl so as to make you very happy, but you may not believe me. I will do everything possible to keep my promises so that I will not have told a lie in my letter as I have done sometimes. I had a long, long letter in mind but now I can't think of a thing! Just the same you will see that I will be very good.[15]

She made her first communion on 19 April 1891 at the age of eleven. After the ceremony, she said to a friend, 'Jesus has fed me, I am no longer hungry'. She was afterwards to say that from that moment on, Jesus had taken possession of her soul and made his dwelling there. From that time on also, she seemed to have gained the upper hand in her struggle with her temper. She was confirmed two months after her first communion.

During her teens, she played tennis, attended parties and loved dancing. She also played the piano, winning first prize at the Dijon conservatory at the age of thirteen. In 1894, Elizabeth bound herself with a vow of virginity while giving thanks after communion. Over the next seven years (1894–1901), she dedicated herself to interior mortification based on St Teresa of Avila's *Way of Perfection*. She also had a strong devotion to St Catherine of Siena. From the age of fifteen she wrote regularly about her interior development. When Thérèse's *Story of a Soul* appeared soon after her death, Elizabeth read it eagerly and made more than ten pages of notes, as well as copying Thérèse's 'Act of Surrender to God's Merciful Love'. She still had to struggle with her violent temper:

It seems to me that, when someone says something unjust to me, I can feel the blood boiling in my veins; my whole being is in rebellion! But Jesus was with me. I heard his voice in the depths of my heart and then I was ready to bear anything for love of him.[16]

Her mother was opposed to her entering Carmel and Elizabeth was determined to be obedient to her mother. She later wrote that if her mother had not permitted it, she would never have entered. Nevertheless, her own resolution to enter Carmel never faltered and in her diary we find the words: 'I desire so much to go to Carmel'.[17] Like Catherine of Siena, she decided to 'create a little cell in my heart and adore God there'.

May my life be a continual prayer, a long act of love. May nothing distract me from You, neither noise or diversions. O my Master, I would so love to live with You in silence. But what I love most above all is to do your will, and since You want me to still remain in the world, I submit with all my heart for love of you. I offer You the cell of my heart; may it be Your little Bethany. Come rest there: I love You so …[18]

About this time she also wrote: 'Let me live in the world without belonging to the world. I can be a Carmelite within me and that I wish to be.'[19] Her prayer life during this period was one of uninterrupted sweetness and consolation, however, she wrote to a friend:

Pray hard for me, beloved sister; for me too it is no longer a veil which hides him from me, but a very thick wall. It is very hard, isn't it, after feeling him so close, but I am ready to remain in this state as long as it pleases my Beloved to leave me there, for faith tells me that He is there all the same, and what is the use of sweetness and consolations? They are not He. And it is he alone that we seek ... so let us go to him through pure faith.[20]

Meanwhile she continued to live a high-spirited life. She was an accomplished pianist, loved nature, especially the sea, and looked forward to new adventures and experiences like going aboard an ocean liner or watching a cavalry charge. She attended the usual parties and family gatherings. About that time she wrote:

> You know good Master, when I am at these gatherings and festivals, my consolation lies in recollecting myself and enjoying your presence, for I feel you so truly in me, my Supreme Good. In these gatherings people hardly have a thought for you, and it seems to me that you are happy when even one heart as poor and miserable as mine doesn't forget you.[21]

When she was nineteen, her mother finally gave her consent that she enter Carmel at twenty-one. That same year (1899), she made a general confession and was thrilled when the priest assured her that she had never lost her baptismal innocence. He also said that he believed her vocation to Carmel to be genuine. The following year (1900), she met the Dominican Fr Valée who had a special gift for speaking about the Blessed Trinity. It was then she decided to take the name 'Mary Elizabeth of the Trinity', as she wrote to a friend later:

> I think this name points to my special vocation. Is it not beautiful? I delight in the mystery of the Blessed Trinity; I lose myself in its depths.[22]

Having spent what would prove to be three-quarters of her life (1880–1901) outside the cloister, on 2 August 1901, at the age of twenty-one, she finally entered Carmel. A month after entering Carmel, she wrote to her sister Marguerite:

> During the day sometimes think of Him who lives in you and who thirsts to be loved. It is close to Him that you will always find me![23]

Having entered in August, Elizabeth finished her postulancy in December and received the habit (became a novice). Elizabeth's sister, Marguerite, married on 15 October 1902 and, although she had hoped that Marguerite would also enter Carmel, Elizabeth gracefully accepted her sister's marriage and seems to have regarded it as a genuine path to holiness. She finished her novitiate and took her vows in January 1903 at the age of twenty-three. She took the veil nearly two weeks later.

It was on 21 November 1904, the feast of the Presentation of our Lady, that Elizabeth wrote her famous 'Prayer to the Trinity':

> O 'Consuming Fire'! Spirit of Love! descend within me and reproduce in me, as it were, an incarnation of the Word, that I may be to him another humanity wherein he renews all his mystery. And thou, O Father, bend towards thy poor little creature and overshadow her, beholding in her none other than thy beloved son, in whom thou art well pleased.[24]

The following year (1905), during Lent, she began to show the first symptoms of Addison's disease, which was then incurable and which led to the complete collapse of her immune system. It was around Easter 1905, in conversation with Sr Aimée in her cell, that her attention was drawn to a passage from the beginning of St Paul's letter to the Ephesians in which we are described as 'having been destined for the praise of his glory'

(Eph 1:12, 14). Soon afterwards, the sisters were discussing the 'new name' which the elect would have in heaven. She said that hers would be 'The praise of his glory' and that she wished to deserve that name on earth also. During August, her health began to fail noticeably. She had, in fact, been ill with tuberculosis for some months (as Portress she had found it difficult to walk or climb steps), but now her daily routine had to be modified so as not to tire her excessively. Elizabeth also suffered from ulceration, violent headaches, insomnia and was unable to take normal food or drink. She looked on her illness as part of becoming conformed to Christ and, in February 1906, she summed up her vocation as being 'conformed to the death of Christ'.

By the end of March 1906, she was permanently installed in the infirmary. She received the Sacrament of the Sick and Viaticum on Palm Sunday, 8 April. There was a slight improvement at Easter (14 April), but by mid-May her health was again in crisis. At times her suffering was intense. On 16 July, the Feast of Our Lady of Mount Carmel, she wrote to Marguerite (Guite):

> Darling little sister, you must cross out the word 'discouragement' from your dictionary of love; the more you feel your weakness, your difficulty in recollecting yourself, and the more hidden the Master seems, the more you must rejoice, for then you are giving to Him, and, when one loves, isn't it better to give than to receive? … What does it matter how we feel, *He*, He is the Unchanging One, He who never changes: He loves you today as He loved you yesterday and will love you tomorrow. Even if you have caused Him pain, remember that abyss calls to another abyss (see Ps 41:8), and that the abyss of your misery, little Guite, attracts the abyss of

His mercy, oh! you see, He is making me understand that so well, and it is for both of us. He is also drawing me very much toward suffering, the gift of self; it seems to me that this is the culmination of love.[25]

Having been anointed for the second time on 31 October, it seemed that the end had come the following day, 1 November, and she received viaticum. She revived, however, and said to the Sisters:

Everything passes. In the evening of life, only love remains ... Everything must be done for love; we have to forget ourselves all the time: the good God so loves us to forget ourselves ... Ah, if only I had always done that.[26]

After a night of agony, Elizabeth died in the early morning of 9 November 1906. Her last words were, 'I am going to light, to love, to life'.[27] She was twenty-six years old and had been only five years in Carmel.

In 1980, Pope John Paul II listed Elizabeth of the Trinity as among the holy men and women who had the most influence on his life and, when he beatified her as a virgin in November 1984, he described her as 'a brilliant witness to the joy of being "rooted and grounded in love" (Eph 3:17)'. He also said, 'With Blessed Elizabeth a new light shines out for us, a new certain and sure guide is presented to us.'

'I BELIEVE' – 'WE BELIEVE'[28]

Noting that we begin our profession of faith by saying 'I believe' or 'we believe', the *Catechism* describes the Church's faith that is confessed in the Creed as being 'celebrated in the liturgy, and lived in observance of God's commandments and in prayer' (n. 26). It is the same faith, in other words, that is presented in all four parts of the *Catechism* and that faith is man's response to God, who reveals himself and gives himself to man, at the same time bringing man a superabundant light as he searches for the ultimate meaning of his life. (n. 26)

Our Capacity for God[29]

Recognising faith as our response to God's self-revelation, the *Catechism* describes our search for the ultimate meaning of our lives as an expression of our innate capacity for the God who comes to meet us by revealing himself to us. As a young teenager, it was the beauty and grandeur of nature that spoke to Bl. Elizabeth of the Trinity of the good God:

> [O]ne never tires of gazing at that beautiful sea ... Those waves sweeping over the rocks were so beautiful, my soul thrilled before such a magnificent sight![30]

The *Catechism* says:

> Man is by nature and vocation a religious being. Coming from God, going towards God, man lives a fully human life only if he freely lives by his bond with God. (n. 44)

The *Catechism* describes humanity as being 'made to live in communion with God in whom he finds happiness' (n. 45). Wanting to give herself to God and be united to him forever, Elizabeth's life testifies to this bond and she made a vow of virginity while giving thanks after communion at the age of fourteen:

> I felt irresistibly urged to choose him for my Bridegroom and I bound myself to him by a vow of virginity. We did not speak to each other, but gave ourselves to each other with such fervent love that my resolution of being wholly his became stronger than ever.[31]

St Irenaeus believed that the invisible power of God 'bestows upon all a profound mental intuition and a perception of His most powerful and omnipotent presence' and that all people can recognise 'that there is one God and Lord of all, because the reason implanted in their minds moves them and reveals it to them'.[32] These beliefs are echoed in the *Catechism*, which says:

> [When] he listens to the message of creation and to the voice of conscience, man can arrive at certainty about the existence of God, the cause and the end of everything. (n. 46)

Quoting the First Vatican Council,[33] the *Catechism* says that the Church 'teaches that the one true God, our Creator and Lord, can be known with certainty from his works, by the natural light of human reason' (n. 47). Noting that 'every Church throughout the whole world has received this tradition from the Apostles', Irenaeus also recognised this truth:

> Creation itself reveals Him that created it; and the work made is itself suggestive of Him that made it; and the world manifests Him that arranged it.[34]

The *Catechism* also offers a variation on this theme when it quotes Vatican II's *Gaudium et spes* 36, 'Without the Creator, the creature vanishes' (n. 49), and when it says:

> We really can name God, starting from the manifold perfections of his creatures, which are likenesses of the infinitely perfect God, even if our limited language cannot exhaust the mystery. (n. 48)

God Comes to Meet Us[35]
St Irenaeus held that it was 'on account of his great love' that

the Word of God, Jesus Christ our Lord, 'became what we are, so that He might bring us to be what He Himself is'.[36] The *Catechism* also understands the divine self-revelation as motivated by, and being a revelation of, love:

> By love, God has revealed himself and given himself to man. He has thus provided the definitive, superabundant answer to the questions that man asks himself about the meaning and purpose of his life. (n. 68)

Quoting St Irenaeus, the *Catechism* says that 'God communicates himself to man gradually' (n. 53) in deeds and words[37] and that the divine plan for human salvation involves a specific divine pedagogy:

> St Irenaeus of Lyons repeatedly speaks of this divine pedagogy using the image of God and man becoming accustomed to one another: The Word of God dwelt in man and became the Son of man in order to accustom man to perceive God and to accustom God to dwell in man, according to the Father's pleasure.[38]

The *Catechism* describes this gradual communication as beginning with God's manifestation of himself 'to our first parents' both before the fall and afterwards, when he 'promised them salvation (see Gen 3:15) and offered them his covenant' (n. 70). It continued in the 'everlasting covenant' that God made 'with Noah and with all living beings (Gen 9:16)' (nn. 71–2), in the covenant God made with Abraham and his descendants and in the revelation of God's law through Moses. Through the prophets, God prepared his people 'to accept the salvation destined for all humanity'. The Son 'is the Father's definitive Word', however, 'God has revealed himself fully by sending his own Son, in whom he has established his covenant for ever' (n. 73).

Irenaeus says that Christ constituted Himself 'the Head of the Church' so that 'He might at the proper time draw all things to Himself'.[39] He also held that 'the apostles, like a rich man in a bank, deposited with her [the Church] most copiously everything which pertains to the truth'.[40] The *Catechism* recognises the deposit of faith left by Christ to the apostles when it says:

> What Christ entrusted to the apostles, they in turn handed on by their preaching and writing, under the inspiration of the Holy Spirit, to all generations, until Christ returns in glory. (n. 96)

Quoting Vatican II's Constitution on Divine Revelation, *Dei Verbum*, the *Catechism* recognises that:

> 'Sacred Tradition and the Sacred Scriptures make up a single sacred deposit of the Word of God' (DV 10), in which, as in a mirror, the pilgrim Church contemplates God, the source of all her riches. (n. 97)

For Irenaeus, similarly, the Scriptures were a written form of the apostolic tradition:

> What if the apostles had not in fact left writings to us? Would it not be necessary to follow the order of tradition, which was handed down to those to whom they entrusted the Churches?[41]

He also held that it was because the apostles had 'deposited with her [the Church] everything that pertains to the truth' that 'everyone whosoever wishes draws from her the drink of life' (Rev 22:17).[42] Echoing him, the *Catechism* quotes *Dei verbum* 8.1:

The Church, in her doctrine, life and worship, perpetuates and transmits to every generation all that she herself is, all that she believes. (n. 98)

Irenaeus recognised that the Holy Spirit

is in us all, and He is the Living Water (Jn 7:38-39) which the Lord grants to those who rightly believe in Him, and love Him and who know that there is one Father, who is above all and through all and in us all (Eph 4:6).[43]

The *Catechism* outlines one of the effects of the Living Water of the Holy Spirit in us all when it says:

Thanks to its supernatural sense of the faith (*sensus fidei*), the People of God as a whole never ceases to welcome, to penetrate more deeply and to live more fully from the gift of divine Revelation. (n. 99)

One of the other effects of the Spirit in the Church is the hierarchical gift given to bishops. In outlining the apostolic succession of bishops and what St Irenaeus called the 'teaching authority' that the apostles passed on to the Pope and the bishops in communion with him,[44] the *Catechism* quotes Vatican II's Dogmatic Constitution on Divine Revelation, *Dei Verbum* 7.2:

In order that the full and living Gospel might always be preserved in the Church the apostles left bishops as their successors. They gave them 'their own position of teaching authority'. (n. 77)[45]

For Irenaeus, 'The Scriptures are certainly perfect, since they were spoken by the Word of God and by His Spirit.'[46] Recognising that 'God is the author of Sacred Scripture because he inspired its human authors' (n. 136), and that 'because they are inspired, they are truly the Word of God' (n. 135), the *Catechism* says:

> Through all the words of Sacred Scripture, God speaks only one single Word, his one Utterance in whom he expresses himself completely. (n. 102)

Quoting Vatican II's *Dei Verbum* 21, the *Catechism* says that the Church 'has always venerated the divine Scriptures as she venerated the Body of the Lord' and it recognises that both the Scriptures and the Eucharist 'nourish and govern the whole Christian life' (n. 141). It insists, however, that the guidance of the Spirit is needed in reading the inspired Scriptures and that the interpretation of the inspired Scripture 'must be attentive above all to what God wants to reveal through the sacred authors for our salvation' (n. 137). Recognising that the Church 'accepts and venerates as inspired the 46 books of the Old Testament and the 27 books of the New' (n. 128), the *Catechism* points out that the four Gospels 'occupy a central place because Jesus Christ is their centre' (n. 139) and that the Old Testament 'prepares for the New and the New Testament fulfils the Old' (n. 140).

The only texts from Scripture that Elizabeth of the Trinity was provided with when she entered the Carmel in Dijon were the Latin Vulgate version of the Psalms and the New Testament. She hears the voice of Jesus, her 'Master', speaking to her in the Gospels and she so identifies with St Paul that she applies to herself what he says about himself: 'With Christ I am nailed to the Cross' (Gal 2:19); 'I am nailed *(je suis clouée)*'.[47] She had access to some Old Testament texts from other sources, however, and she seems to have intuitively grasped that these texts shed light on her own situation, quoting Hosea 2:17 ('solitude into which God wants to allure the soul that He may speak to it') to explain her own Carmelite vocation.[48]

Our Response to God[49]

Quoting 'According to your faith let it be done to you' (Mt 9:29), Irenaeus said, 'Man has a faith of his own, just as he has judgment especially his own'.[50] The *Catechism* expresses the personal dimension of faith in these words:

> Faith is a personal adherence of the whole man to God who reveals himself. It involves an assent of the intellect and will to the self-revelation God has made through his deeds and words. 'To believe' has thus a twofold reference: to the person, and to the truth: to the truth, by trust in the person who bears witness to it. (nn. 176–7)

Irenaeus professed 'faith in one God, Father Almighty ... and in one Jesus Christ, the Son of God ... and in the Holy Spirit'.[51] The *Catechism* says that 'we must believe in no one but God: the Father, the Son and the Holy Spirit' (n. 178). The *Catechism* also says that, down through the centuries, the Church has constantly confessed the 'one faith, received from the one Lord', as St Irenaeus, 'a witness of this faith', declared when he wrote:[52]

> Indeed, the Church, though scattered throughout the whole world, even to the ends of the earth, having received the faith from the apostles and their disciples ... guards [this preaching and faith] with care, as dwelling in but a single house, and similarly believes as if having but one soul and a single heart, and preaches, teaches, and hands on this faith with a unanimous voice, as if possessing only one mouth. ... For though languages differ throughout the world, the content of the Tradition is one and the same. The Churches established in Germany have no other faith or Tradition, nor do those of the Iberians, nor those of the Celts, nor those of the East, or Egypt, of Libya, nor those established at the centre of the world.[53]

The *Catechism* recognises that believing is 'an ecclesial act' and that the Church's faith 'precedes, engenders, supports and nourishes our faith' (n. 181). St Irenaeus likewise held that the Church's message 'is true and solid' in the sense that 'one and the same way of salvation appears throughout the world'.[54] He also recognised that the Church unceasingly guards the deposit of faith, and is itself constantly renewed by the deposit of faith that it contains:

> We guard with care the faith that we have received from the Church, for without ceasing, under the action of God's Spirit, this deposit of great price, as if in an excellent vessel, is constantly being renewed and causes the very vessel that contains it to be renewed.[55]

Noting that faith is 'a supernatural gift from God', the *Catechism* says that, in order to believe, 'man needs the interior helps of the Holy Spirit' (n. 179). This supernatural gift does not do away with our free will, however, and Irenaeus recognised that 'in faith man's freedom of choice under his own control is preserved by the Lord'.[56] For the *Catechism*, similarly, 'believing' is 'a human act, conscious and free, corresponding to the dignity of the human person' (n. 180). Quoting Pope Paul VI's *Creed of the People of God* n. 20, it says that we believe all 'that which is contained in the word of God, written or handed down, and which the Church proposes for belief as divinely revealed' (n. 182). Noting that the Lord himself affirms that 'the one who believes and is baptized will be saved; but the one who does not believe will be condemned' (Mk 16:16), it says that faith 'is necessary for salvation' (n. 183). Noting that man 'does not by his own power see God', Irenaeus says that the Spirit 'prepares man', that 'the Son leads him to the Father, and the Father gives him incorruption in eternal life, which comes to everyone by the fact of his seeing God'.[57] The *Catechism* says:

Faith makes us taste in advance the light of the beatific vision, the goal of our journey here below. Then we shall see God 'face to face', 'as he is' (1 Cor 13:12; 1 Jn 3:2). So faith is the beginning of eternal life. (n. 163)

THE PROFESSION OF THE CHRISTIAN FAITH[58]

Both the Old and New Testaments recognise that there is one God (n. 228): 'Hear, O Israel, the LORD is our God, LORD alone' (Deut 6:4; see Mk 12:29). St Irenaeus held that the Church 'has received from the Apostles and from their disciples the faith in one God'.[59] The *Catechism* quotes St Joan of Arc who insisted that we 'must serve God first' (n. 223) and it says:

Faith in God leads us to turn to him alone as our first origin and our ultimate goal, and neither to prefer anything to him nor to substitute anything for him. (n. 229)

At her trial, when she was asked if the saints she saw in her visions had 'natural heads' like us, St Joan of Arc said: 'I saw them with my two eyes, and I believe it was they I saw as firmly as I believe in the existence of God.'[60] Echoing St Irenaeus, who held that 'while He [God] comprehends all, he can be comprehended by none',[61] the *Catechism* says, 'Even when he reveals himself, God remains a mystery beyond words' (n. 230).

However, in the light of the mysteries of the Incarnate Word and of the written Word of God, this does not mean that words serve no purpose in trying to name something of God's incomprehensible mystery. For Elizabeth of the Trinity, Jesus 'is all Love!'[62] He is 'the *Only Truth*! ... He sweeps you away, under His gaze the horizon becomes so beautiful, so vast, so luminous'.[63] Describing God's very being as 'Truth and Love', the *Catechism* says that the God of our faith 'has revealed himself as He Who Is; and he has made himself known as "abounding in steadfast love and faithfulness" (Exod 34:6)' (n. 231).

The Creed is divided into three parts, which speak of the first, second and third Persons of the Trinity, and which St Irenaeus recognised as 'the three chapters of our [baptismal] seal'.[64] He recognised faith in the three Persons of the Trinity as something that the Church had received from the Apostles and from their disciples:

> For the Church, although dispersed throughout the whole world even to the ends of the earth, has received from the Apostles and from their disciples the faith in the one God, Father Almighty, the Creator of heaven and earth and sea and all that is in them; and in one Jesus Christ, the Son of God, who became flesh for our salvation; and in the Holy Spirit, who announced through the prophets the dispensations and the comings, and the birth from a Virgin, and the passion, and the resurrection from the dead, and the bodily ascension into heaven of the beloved Christ Jesus our Lord, and his coming from heaven in the glory of the Father to re-establish all things; and the raising up again of all flesh of all humanity, in order that to Jesus Christ our Lord and God and Saviour and King, in accord with the approval of the invisible Father, every knee shall bend of those in heaven and on earth and under the earth, and that every tongue shall confess Him, and that he may make just judgment of them all.[65]

I Believe in God the Father[66]

St Irenaeus recognised that the Creator is Father, Son and Spirit: 'With Him (the Father of the universe) always are the Word and the Wisdom, the Son and the Spirit, through whom and in whom he made all things freely and spontaneously.'[67] Referring to 'the indescribable mysteries of God', he admitted, nevertheless, that the generation of the Son by the Father 'is indescribable'.[68] Bl. Elizabeth of the Trinity told a friend, 'I delight in the mystery of the Blessed Trinity; I lose myself in its depths.'[69] For the *Catechism*:

> The mystery of the Most Holy Trinity is the central mystery of the Christian faith and of Christian life. God alone can make it known to us by revealing himself as Father, Son and Holy Spirit. (n. 261):

Describing him as always 'co-existing with the Father, of old and from the beginning', Irenaeus said that the Son 'reveals the Father to the Angels and Archangels and Powers and Virtues and to all to whom God wishes to give revelation'.[70] He also held that the one who suffered, rose from the dead and is at the right hand of the Father 'is the Word of God, Himself the only-begotten of the Father, Christ Jesus our Lord'.[71] Elizabeth of the Trinity writes:

> [Contemplating] the great distress of the children he loved to excess, the Father in a holy intoxication gave them his adored Word ... the One who reigns in the bosom of the Father and comes to tell us everything about him ... He comes to reveal the mystery, to yield up all the secrets of the Father, to lead us from light to light, right into the bosom of the Trinity.[72]

The *Catechism* expresses the same truth in less poetic language:

> The Incarnation of God's Son reveals that God is the eternal Father and that the Son is consubstantial with the Father, which means that, in the Father and with the Father, the Son is one and the same God. (n. 262)

Echoing St Augustine,[73] Elizabeth believed that our souls can be made

> capable of producing in God the same spiration of love that the Father produces in the Son and the Son in the Father, the spiration that is the Holy Spirit himself![74]

The *Catechism* recognises the mission of the Holy Spirit, who 'is sent by the Father in the name of the Son' (Jn 14:26) and by the Son 'from the Father' (Jn 15:26), as the revelation to us that, 'with them, the Spirit is one and the same God' (n. 263). It also recognises that the grace of Baptism 'in the name of the Father and of the Son and of the Holy Spirit' calls us to share in the life of the Blessed Trinity 'here on earth in the obscurity of faith, and after death in eternal light' (n. 265). Making this mystery her own, Elizabeth prayed that her soul might

> become so pure and transparent that the Blessed Trinity may be reflected in me as in a crystal. The Trinity so loves to contemplate its beauty in a soul; this draws itself to give itself even more, to come with greater fullness so as to bring about the great mystery of love and unity.[75]

Elizabeth recognised, and clearly distinguished between, the three Persons of the Holy Trinity and, writing to her sister Marguerite not long before she died, she invited her to live with them 'within' and she told her that she would bequeath to her

> my devotion for the Three, to 'Love' (see 1 Jn 4:16). Live within with Them in the heaven of your soul; the Father will overshadow you, placing something like a cloud between you and the things of this earth to keep you all His. He will communicate His power to you so you can love Him with a love as strong as death; the Word will

imprint in your soul, as in a crystal, the image of His own beauty, so you will be pure with his purity, luminous with His light; the Holy Spirit will transform you into a mysterious lyre, which, in silence, beneath His divine touch, will produce a magnificent canticle to Love, then you will be the 'praise of his glory' I dreamed of being on earth.[76]

Quoting the Athanasian Creed, the *Catechism* says:

We worship one God in the Trinity and the Trinity in unity, without either confusing the persons or dividing the substance; for the person of the Father is one, the Son's is another, the Holy Spirit's another; but the Godhead of Father, Son and Holy Spirit is one, their glory equal, their majesty equally eternal.[77] (n. 266)

St Irenaeus interpreted 'All things came into being through Him' (Jn 1:3) as meaning that 'the Father made all things through Him [the Word], whether visible or invisible, whether of sense or of intelligence, whether temporal and for a certain dispensation or eternal and through the ages'.[78] The *Catechism* formulates this same principle when it says, 'Inseparable in what they are, the divine persons are also inseparable in what they do' (n. 267).

The *Catechism* quotes Elizabeth of the Trinity's prayer when it says that, even here on earth, 'we are called to be a dwelling for the Most Holy Trinity' (n. 260):

O my God, Trinity whom I adore, help me forget myself entirely so to establish myself in you, unmovable and peaceful as if my soul were already in eternity. May nothing be able to trouble my peace or make me leave you, O my unchanging God, but may each minute bring me more deeply into your mystery! Grant my soul peace. Make it your heaven, your beloved dwelling and the place of your rest. May I never abandon you there, but may I be there, whole and entire, completely vigilant in my faith, entirely adoring, and wholly given over to your creative action.[79]

Both the Old and New Testaments recognise that 'nothing will be impossible with God' (see Gen 18:14; Lk 1:37; Mt 19:26) and Job says that God 'can do all things' (Job 42:2).[80] St Irenaeus held as a 'rule of truth':

There is one almighty God, who formed all things through his Word, and fashioned and made all things which exist of that which did not exist.[81]

Recognising that 'God shows forth his almighty power by converting us from our sins and restoring us to his friendship by grace' (n. 277), the *Catechism* asks the rhetorical question:

If we do not believe that God's love is almighty, how can we believe that the Father could create us, the Son redeem us and the Holy Spirit sanctify us? (n. 278)

The *Catechism* describes the creation of the world and of man as 'the first and universal witness to his almighty word and wisdom' (n. 315). Creation was also 'the first proclamation of the "plan of his loving goodness", which finds its goal in the new creation in Christ'. Describing creation is 'the common work of the Holy Trinity',[82] the *Catechism* quotes St Irenaeus who said that God the Father 'made all things *by himself*, that is, by his Word and by his Wisdom'(n. 292), 'by the Son and the Spirit' who, so to speak, are 'his hands'.[83] St Irenaeus recognised creation from nothing as one of the distinguishing marks of God:

Men, indeed, are not able to make something from nothing, but only from existing material. God, however, is greater than men first of all in this: that when nothing existed beforehand, He called into existence the very material for His creation.[84]

Recognising that 'God alone created the universe, freely, directly and without any help' (n. 317), the *Catechism* teaches that no creature 'has the infinite power necessary to "create" in the proper sense of the word' (n. 318). Describing God as creating the universe 'to show forth and communicate his glory' by sharing 'in his truth, goodness and beauty' (n. 319), the *Catechism* quotes St Irenaeus, who described creation as being ordered to salvation and to the vision of God:

[T]he glory of God is man fully alive; moreover man's life is the vision of God: if God's revelation through creation has already obtained life for all the beings that dwell on earth, how much more will the Word's manifestation of the Father obtain life for those who see God.[85]

Echoing Irenaeus, who held that just as God makes all things 'to be in the beginning, and afterwards gives them con-tinuance',[86] the *Catechism* says:

God created the universe and keeps it in existence by his Word, the Son 'upholding the universe by his word of power' (Heb 1:3), and by his Creator Spirit, the giver of life. (n. 320)

Irenaeus recognised that we are nourished by means of the things God has created, 'causing His sun to rise and sending rain as He wishes'.[87] The *Catechism* echoes his sense of divine providence, describing it as consisting of 'the dispositions by which God guides all his creatures with wisdom and love to their ultimate end' (n. 321) and reminding us:

> Christ invites us to filial trust in the providence of our heavenly Father (see Mt 6:26–34), and St Peter the apostle repeats: 'Cast all your anxieties on him, for he cares about you' (1 Pet 5:7; see Ps 55:23). (n. 322)

Irenaeus recognised that, both in faith and in works, 'man's freedom of choice under his own control is preserved by the Lord'.[88] We are not 'compelled by God' to follow his will but those 'who have not obeyed will not be found worthy to possess the good, and will receive deserved judgement'.[89] Noting that God grants to human beings 'the ability to co-operate freely with his plans' (n. 323), the *Catechism* points out:

> The fact that God permits physical and even moral evil is a mystery that God illuminates by his Son Jesus Christ who died and rose to vanquish evil. Faith gives us the certainty that God would not permit an evil if he did not cause a good to come from that very evil, by ways that we shall fully know only in eternal life. (n. 324)

For St Irenaeus, the angels are also subject to God and serve him:

> [The Father] is ministered to in all things by His own Offspring, and by the latter's Likeness: that is, by the Son and by the Holy Spirit, by the Word and by the Wisdom, whom all the angels serve and to whom they are subject.[90]

When St Joan of Arc was asked during her trial 'whether she did reverence to St. Michael and the angels, when she saw them, she answered that she did, and kissed the ground where they had stood after they had gone'.[91] The *Catechism* describes the angels as 'spiritual creatures' (n. 350) who serve Christ their Lord 'especially in the accomplishment of his saving mission to men' (n. 351). Recognising that 'God willed the diversity of his creatures and their own particular goodness, their interdependence and their order' (n. 353), it points out that the Church 'venerates the angels who help her on her earthly pilgrimage and protect every human being' (n. 352).

We have already noted that St Irenaeus believed that 'the glory of God is man fully alive; moreover man's life is the vision of God',[92] and the *Catechism* recognises that 'Man, and through him all creation, is destined for the glory of God' (n. 353). The *Catechism* says: 'Respect for laws inscribed in creation and the relations which derive from the nature of things is a principle of wisdom and a foundation for morality' (n. 354). This principle of wisdom is not absolute, however, and, when St Joan of Arc was asked during her trial whether it seemed to her that the command she had received to assume male attire was lawful, 'she answered that everything she did was at God's command; and that, if He had bidden her wear a different dress, she would have done so, for it was God's bidding'.[93]

St Irenaeus describes 'the pristine nature of men' as having been 'made in the image and likeness of God'[94] and, addressing God the Father, the *Catechism* quotes the Roman Missal: 'Father ... you formed man in your own likeness and set him over the whole world to serve you, his creator, and to rule over all creatures' (n. 380).[95] Irenaeus distinguishes between our mortal bodies and our spiritual and immortal souls:[96]

> But souls, as compared to mortal bodies are incorporeal: for God breathed into the face of man the breath of life, and man became a living soul (Gen 2:7). The breath of life, however, is incorporeal. And certainly they cannot

say that the breath of life is itself mortal. In this regard David says, 'And for Him my soul shall live' (Ps 21:30), just as if its substance were immortal.[97]

Quoting Vatican II's *Gaudium et spes* 12.4, the *Catechism* recognises that marriage was part of God's plan for humanity from the beginning:

> God did not create man a solitary being. From the beginning, 'male and female he created them' (Gen 1:27). This partnership of man and woman constitutes the first form of communion between persons. (n. 383)

Recognising that 'God made man free from the beginning', placing 'a power of choice' within us 'so that those who obeyed might justly possess the good things which, indeed, God gives',[98] St Irenaeus describes Adam as having 'lost his natural disposition and child-like mind, and come to a knowledge of evil' because of sin.[99] The *Catechism* says:

> Revelation makes known to us the state of original holiness and justice of man and woman before sin: from their friendship with God flowed the happiness of their existence in paradise. (n. 384)

The *Catechism* quotes Vatican II's Pastoral Constitution on the Church in the Modern World, *Gaudium et spes* 13.1, when it describes the fallen state in which humanity finds itself as the fruit of human sin:

> Although set by God in a state of rectitude man, enticed by the evil one, abused his freedom at the very start of history. He lifted himself up against God, and sought to attain his goal apart from him. (n. 415)

The Old Testament Book of Wisdom draws our attention to the role of the devil in our fall: 'It was through the devil's envy that death entered the world' (Wis 1:13; 2:24). Recognising that the angels are rational creatures with free will,[100] and that some of them 'transgressed and became apostates',[101] St Irenaeus describes the devil as an apostate angel who 'is able, as he was in the beginning, to lead astray and to deceive the mind of man for the transgressing of God's commands'.[102] Irenaeus describes Adam as having 'lost by disobedience the mantle of holiness'[103] he had from the Spirit, and Eve, through her disobedience, as being 'made the cause of death for herself and for the whole human race'.[104] Echoing Irenaeus, the *Catechism* says:

> By his sin, Adam, as the first man, lost the original holiness and justice he had received from God, not only for himself but for all human beings. Adam and Eve transmitted to their descendants human nature wounded by their own first sin and hence deprived of original holiness and justice; this deprivation is called 'original sin'. (nn. 416–18)

Irenaeus says that, after his sin, Adam had 'lost his natural disposition and child-like mind, and had come to a knowledge of evil',[105] and he points out that, since 'we are from him, we have inherited his title' to that condition.[106] Quoting Pope Paul VI, the *Catechism* says:

> As a result of original sin, human nature is weakened in its powers, subject to ignorance, suffering and the domination of death, and inclined to sin (this inclination is called 'concupiscence'). 'We therefore hold, with the Council of Trent, that original sin is transmitted with human nature, "by propagation, not by imitation" and that it is ... "proper to each".' (nn. 418–19)[107]

Recognising that 'Jesus Christ ... became what we are, so that He might bring us to be what he Himself is',[108] St Irenaeus believed that, having been formed in the image (body) and likeness (soul) of God, humanity lost its likeness to God through sin and this lost likeness is restored only by means of the Spirit:

> For by the hands of the Father, that is by the Son and the Holy Spirit, man, and not merely a part of man, was made in the likeness of God ... the perfect man consists in the commingling and the union of the soul receiving the spirit of the Father, and the admixture of that fleshly nature which was moulded after the image of God. ... But when the spirit here blended with the soul is united to [God's] handiwork, the man is rendered spiritual and perfect because of the outpouring of the Spirit, and this is he who was made in the image and likeness of God.[109]

Although it does not follow Irenaeus in distinguishing between image and likeness, the *Catechism* adopts a similar perspective when it says:

> Man is predestined to reproduce the image of God's Son made man, the 'image of the invisible God' (Col 1:15), so that Christ shall be the first-born of a multitude of brothers and sisters (see Eph 1:3-6; Rom 8:29). (n. 381)

Although the world that 'has been established and kept in being by the Creator's love' has 'fallen into slavery to sin', it has 'been set free by Christ, crucified and risen to break the power of the evil one':[110]

> The victory that Christ won over sin has given us greater blessings than those which sin had taken from

us: 'where sin increased, grace abounded all the more' (Rom 5:20).[111]

Having outlined the first part of the Creed, which is focused on God the Father, we now turn to the second part, which is focused on Jesus.

I Believe in Jesus Christ, the Only Son of God[112]

Noting that the name Jesus means 'God saves' and that 'there is no other name under heaven given among men by which we must be saved' (Acts 4:12) (n. 452), the *Catechism* quotes St Irenaeus when it recognises that the consecration of Jesus as the Messiah or Christ, which means 'Anointed One', was 'revealed during the time of his earthly life at the moment of his baptism by John':[113]

> [F]or the name 'Christ' implies 'he who anointed', 'he who was anointed' and 'the very anointing with which he was anointed.' The one who anointed is the Father, the one who was anointed is the Son, and he was anointed with the Spirit who is the anointing. (n. 438)[114]

For St Irenaeus, Jesus is 'the Only-begotten of the Father, Christ Jesus our Lord'[115] and, for the *Catechism*:

> The title 'Son of God' signifies the unique and eternal relationship of Jesus Christ to God his Father: he is the only Son of the Father (see Jn 1:14, 18; 3:16, 18) ...The title 'Lord' indicates divine sovereignty. To confess or invoke Jesus as Lord is to believe in his divinity. 'No one can say "Jesus is Lord" except by the Holy Spirit' (1 Cor 12:3). (nn. 454–5)

St Irenaeus recognised that, according to the testimony of the Scriptures:

[Jesus] had in Himself what no other ever had, that pre-eminent generation by the Most High Father; and that He also experienced that pre-eminent birth from a Virgin.[116]

The *Catechism* puts it this way:

At the time appointed by God, the only Son of the Father, the eternal Word, that is, the Word and substantial Image of the Father, became incarnate; without losing his divine nature he has assumed human nature. (n. 479)

Recognising that, in Jesus, man 'conquered the enemy of man' and that, as a result, Jesus 'united man with God',[117] St Irenaeus anticipated, to some extent, the teaching of the Council of Chalcedon, which recognised that Jesus Christ possesses two natures, one divine and the other human – not confused, but united in the one person of God's Son.[118] Although he fully accepted that Jesus was God's Son and therefore divine, St Irenaeus rejected the position of the Docetists, who claimed that Jesus 'suffered only in appearance',[119] and he insisted that, being 'born of Mary who was still a Virgin', he 'rightly received in birth the recapitulation of Adam' and fully shared both Adam's human nature and his state of original grace.[120] St Irenaeus recognised, however, that Jesus himself mysteriously 'allowed that the Father alone knows the very hour and day of judgement' (see Mark 13:32).[121] The *Catechism* formulates the distinction between the human and divine intellects of the Incarnate Word when it says:

Christ, being true God and true man, has a human intellect and will, perfectly attuned and subject to his divine intellect and divine will, which he has in common with the Father and the Holy Spirit. (n. 482)

Quoting St Irenaeus, who described the Son of God becoming human so that human beings might become sons and daughters of God, the *Catechism* says that the Word became flesh to make us 'partakers of the divine nature' (2 Pet 1:4):

> For this is why the Word became man, and the Son of God became the Son of man: so that man, by entering into communion with the Word and thus receiving divine sonship, might become a son of God. (n. 460)[122]

St Irenaeus describes the Virgin Mary, being obedient to God's Word, as having 'received from an angel the glad tidings that she would bear God'.[123] He presents the birth of Jesus 'from the Virgin', implying that he had no human father, as the reason why he is known as Emmanuel, 'God-with-us'.[124] Quoting St Augustine, the *Catechism* says that Mary 'remained a virgin in conceiving her Son, a virgin in giving birth to him, a virgin in carrying him, a virgin in nursing him at her breast, always a virgin' (n. 510).[125] Although St Irenaeus does not, as such, refer to the doctrine that 'from the first instant of her conception, she was totally preserved from the stain of original sin' (n. 508), he held that Jesus was 'the recapitulation of Adam' (and therefore free from original sin) because he was 'born of Mary who was still a Virgin'.[126] The *Catechism* quotes St Irenaeus to show that, by her obedience, the Virgin Mary became the new Eve, the mother of the living:

> Being obedient she became the cause of salvation for herself and for the whole human race. ... The knot of Eve's disobedience was untied by Mary's obedience: what the virgin Eve bound through her disbelief, Mary loosened by her faith. (n. 494)[127]

The *Catechism* quotes St Irenaeus when it describes Christ's whole life as 'a mystery of recapitulation':

> When Christ became incarnate and was made man, he recapitulated in himself the long history of mankind and procured for us a 'short cut' to salvation, so that what we had lost in Adam, that is, being in the image and likeness of God, we might recover in Christ Jesus ... For this reason Christ experienced all the stages of life, thereby giving communion with God to all men. (n. 518)[128]

The 'stages of life' through which Jesus passed, according to St Irenaeus, are those of infants, children, youths and 'old men', in the sense of those who reach the stage of mature adulthood. Having passed through these stages, Jesus experienced death 'so that He might be the firstborn from the dead, having the first place in all things (Col 1:18), the originator of life, before all and preceding all'.[129] Noting that 'Christ's disciples are to conform themselves to him until he is formed in them (see Gal 4:19)', the *Catechism* quotes Vatican II's *Lumen gentium* 7.4 when it comments:

> For this reason we, who have been made like to him, who have died with him and risen with him, are taken up into the mysteries of his life, until we reign together with him. (n. 562)

St Irenaeus describes Jesus as

> becoming a child for children, sanctifying those who are of that age, and at the same time becoming for them an example of piety, of righteousness, and of submission; a young man for youths, becoming an example for youths and sanctifying them in the Lord.[130]

The *Catechism* says:

> By his obedience to Mary and Joseph, as well as by his humble work during the long years at Nazareth, Jesus gives us the example of holiness in the daily life of family and work. (n. 564)

The *Catechism* describes Jesus as being entirely dedicated to serving the will of his heavenly Father:

> From the beginning of his public life, at his baptism, Jesus is the 'Servant', totally consecrated to redemptive work that he will accomplish by the 'baptism' of his Passion. The temptation in the desert shows Jesus, the humble Messiah, who triumphs over Satan by his total adherence to the plan of salvation willed by the Father. (nn. 565–6)

Just as the love of Christ was manifested in the way he gave himself up to the will of his Father, Elizabeth of the Trinity describes the love of Christians as giving themselves up to the will of the Son:

> It is so simple to love, it is surrendering yourself to all His desires, just as He surrendered Himself to those of the Father; it is abiding in Him, for the heart that loves lives no longer in itself but in the one who is the object of that love; it is suffering for Him, gathering up with joy each sacrifice, each immolation that permits us to give joy to His Heart.[131]

Recognising that the kingdom of heaven 'was inaugurated on earth by Christ', the *Catechism* describes the Church as 'the seed and beginning of this kingdom' (n. 567). Elizabeth of the Trinity applies the same doctrine to the individual, recognising that, because 'we bear Him [God] within us', our lives are 'an anticipated Heaven'.[132]

Irenaeus professed his belief in 'the passion, and the resurrection from the dead, and the bodily ascension into heaven of the beloved Christ Jesus our Lord, and his coming from heaven in the glory of the Father to re-establish all things'.[133] The *Catechism* says that the Transfiguration of Christ was aimed 'at strengthening the apostles' faith in anticipation of his Passion' (n. 568). It also points out:

> Jesus went up to Jerusalem voluntarily, knowing well that there he would die a violent death because of the opposition of sinners (see Heb 12:3). (n. 569)

We have already noted that, for Irenaeus, 'The knot of Eve's disobedience was loosed by the obedience of Mary'[134] and that, born of Mary who was still a Virgin, the eternal Word 'received in birth the recapitulation of Adam'.[135] Irenaeus also held that although 'through the first Adam, we offended God by not observing His command, through the second Adam [Christ] ... we are reconciled, and are made obedient even unto death'.[136] In a similar way, the *Catechism* presents Jesus as fulfilling the Law of Sinai

> with such perfection (see Jn 8:46) that he revealed its ultimate meaning (see Mt 5:33) and redeemed the transgressions against it (see Heb 9:15). (n. 592)

Jesus recapitulated in himself the true meaning of the Temple in Jerusalem, the 'dwelling of God among men' that 'prefigures his own mystery', and, when he announced its destruction, it was

> as a manifestation of his own execution and of the entry into a new age in the history of salvation, when his Body would be the definitive Temple.[137]

Describing it as 'a confession of faith that he himself has "received"', the *Catechism* says that St Paul professed that 'Christ died for our sins in accordance with the Scriptures' (1 Cor 15:3) (n. 601). During her trial, St Joan of Arc echoed St Paul when she said that she believed 'what St Michael, who appeared to her, did or said' as firmly as she believed 'that Our Lord Jesus Christ suffered death and passion for us'.[138] For Elizabeth of the Trinity, the soul's 'whole ideal is to fulfil the will of this Father who has loved us with an eternal love' (see Jer 31:3).[139] The *Catechism* makes a similar point when it says:

> Our salvation flows from God's initiative of love for us, because 'he loved us and sent his Son to be the expiation for our sins' (1 Jn 4:10). 'God was in Christ reconciling the world to himself' (2 Cor 5:19). (n. 620)

St Irenaeus describes Jesus as teaching us 'that the adoption of sons by the Father, which is eternal life ... takes place through Himself'.[140] The *Catechism* recognises that 'Jesus freely offered himself for our salvation' and that he came 'to give his life as a ransom for many' (Mt 20:28).[141] By freely accepting death for us 'in complete and free submission to the will of God, his Father', Jesus 'has conquered death, and so opened the possibility of salvation to all' (n. 1019).

> By his loving obedience to the Father, 'unto death, even death on a cross' (Phil 2:8), Jesus fulfils the atoning mission (see Isa 53:10) of the suffering Servant, who will 'make many righteous; and he shall bear their iniquities' (Isa 53:11; see Rom 5:19).[142]

Shortly before her death, Elizabeth of the Trinity wrote to her mother:

I am very absorbed in the Passion, and when you see all He suffered for us in His heart, in His soul and in His body, you have, as it were, a need to give all that back to Him in return; it's as if you wish to suffer all that He suffered. I cannot say I love suffering in itself, but I love it because it conforms me to Him who is my Bridegroom and my love. [143]

Irenaeus recognised that, 'The Lord went away into the midst of the shadow of death (see Ps 22:4) where the souls of the dead were, and afterwards arose in the body.'[144] The *Catechism* says:

During Christ's period in the tomb, his divine person continued to assume both his soul and his body, although they were separated from each other by death. For this reason the dead Christ's body 'saw no corruption' (Acts 13:37). (n. 630)

Irenaeus held that:

The Lord descended into the regions beneath the earth, announcing there the good news of His coming and of the remission of sins conferred upon those who believe in him.[145]

The *Catechism* echoes Irenaeus when it says:

In his human soul united to his divine person, the dead Christ went down to the realm of the dead. He opened heaven's gates for the just who had gone before him. (n. 637)

Irenaeus recognised that the Lord 'arose in the flesh'.[146] The *Catechism* emphasises both the bodily and transcendent dimensions of the resurrection when it says that faith in the resurrection

> has as its object an event which is historically attested to by the disciples, who really encountered the Risen One. At the same time, this event is mysteriously transcendent insofar as it is the entry of Christ's humanity into the glory of God. (n. 656)

For the *Catechism*:

> Christ, 'the first-born from the dead' (Col 1:18) is the principle of our own resurrection, even now by the justification of our souls (see Rom 6:4), and one day by the new life he will impart to our bodies (see Rom 8:11). (n. 658)

Irenaeus also connected Christ's resurrection with the general resurrection of the dead when he wrote that, just as Jesus was 'taken up' after the resurrection, so too the souls of his disciples, after their own bodily resurrection, 'shall come thus into the sight of God'.[147] According to the *Catechism*, 'Christ's Ascension marks the definitive entrance of Jesus' humanity into God's heavenly domain' in order that, as the head of the Church, he 'precedes us into the Father's glorious kingdom so that we, the members of his Body, may live in the hope of one day being with him for ever' (nn. 665–6).

Irenaeus believed that, after the general resurrection of the dead, every knee shall bend to Jesus Christ who will 'make just judgment of them all', sending some 'into everlasting fire' and granting others 'life, immortality' and surrounding them 'with eternal glory'.[148] The *Catechism* recognises that 'Christ the Lord already reigns through the Church, but all the things of this world are not yet subjected to him' (n. 680):

On Judgement Day at the end of the world, Christ will come in glory to achieve the definitive triumph of good over evil which, like the wheat and the tares, have grown up together in the course of history. When he comes at the end of time to judge the living and the dead, the glorious Christ will reveal the secret disposition of hearts and will render to each man according to his works, and according to his acceptance or refusal of grace. (nn. 681–2)

We now move to the third part of the Creed, which focuses on the Holy Spirit.

I Believe in the Holy Spirit[149]

Quoting St Irenaeus, the *Catechism* says that, by virtue of our Baptism, 'the Holy Spirit in the Church communicates to us, intimately and personally, the life that originates in the Father and is offered to us in the Son':

> Baptism gives us the grace of new birth in God the Father, through the Son, in the Holy Spirit. For those who bear God's Spirit are led to the Word, that is, to the Son, and the Son presents them to the Father, and the Father confers incorruptibility on them. And it is impossible to see God's Son without the Spirit, and no one can approach the Father without the Son, for the knowledge of the Father is the Son, and the knowledge of God's Son is obtained through the Holy Spirit. (n. 683)[150]

Again quoting St Irenaeus, who described the Son and the Spirit as the hands of God the Father, the *Catechism* says that, from the beginning to the end of time, 'whenever God sends his Son, he always sends his Spirit: their mission is conjoined and inseparable':

God fashioned man with his own hands [that is, the Son and the Holy Spirit] and impressed his own form on the flesh he had fashioned, in such a way that even what was visible might bear the divine form. (n. 743)[151]

Elizabeth of the Trinity wrote her famous 'Prayer to the Trinity' on the feast of the Presentation of our Lady (21 November) in 1904:

O 'Consuming Fire'! Spirit of Love! descend within me and reproduce in me, as it were, an incarnation of the Word, that I may be to him another humanity wherein he renews all his mystery. And thou, O Father, bend towards thy poor little creature and overshadow her, beholding in her none other than thy beloved son, in whom thou art well pleased.[152]

The *Catechism* says:

In the fullness of time the Holy Spirit completes in Mary all the preparations for Christ's coming among the People of God. By the action of the Holy Spirit in her, the Father gives the world Emmanuel, 'God-with-us' (Mt 1:23). (n. 744)

The *Catechism* says that, by his death and resurrection, 'Jesus is constituted in glory as Lord and Christ' (see Acts 2:36) and that, 'from his fullness, he poured out the Holy Spirit on the apostles and the Church' (n. 746). Based on the text from the letter to the Ephesians, 'might live for the praise of his glory' (Eph 1:12), Elizabeth of the Trinity believed that she was called to be 'the praise of his glory' both here on earth and in heaven:

A praise of glory is a soul that dwells in God, that loves him with a pure disinterested love, without seeking self in the sweetness of this love. A praise of glory is a silent soul that is like a lyre under the mysterious touch of the Holy Spirit so that he may produce in it divine harmonies. A praise of glory is a soul that always contemplates God in faith and simplicity. It is a reflection of God's glory.[153]

For St Irenaeus, the Spirit who is in us all is

the Living Water (John 7:38–39) which the Lord grants to those who rightly believe in Him and love Him and who know that there is one Father, who is above all and through all and in us all (Eph 4:6).[154]

For the *Catechism*, the Church, the assembly of those whom God's Word 'convokes',[155] is 'the sacrament of the Holy Trinity's communion' with us because the Holy Spirit, whom Christ the head pours out on his members, 'builds, animates and sanctifies the Church' (n. 747).

During her trial, when Joan of Arc was asked 'if she would submit to the Church Militant, namely the Church on earth which is so called', her reply appears to recognise that the Church Militant may not always be in full accord with the Church triumphant in heaven:

She answered that she came to the King of France in God's name, and in the names of the Blessed Virgin and of all the Blessed Saints of Paradise, and of the Church Victorious above, and at their command; to that Church she submitted all her good deeds and all she had done or should do. And concerning her submission to the Church Militant she would answer nothing more.[156]

Quoting Vatican II's *Lumen gentium* 48, which recognised that the Church 'will receive its perfection only in the glory of heaven' (n. 769), the *Catechism* recognises that:

The Church is both the means and the goal of God's plan: prefigured in creation, prepared for in the Old Covenant, founded by the words and actions of Jesus Christ, fulfilled in his redeeming cross and his Resurrection, the church has been manifested as the mystery of salvation by the outpouring of the Holy Spirit. (n. 778)

Irenaeus says:

[Jesus] recapitulates all things in Himself, so that just as the Word of God is foremost in things super-celestial, spiritual, and invisible, so also in things visible and corporeal he might have the primacy, and so that, in taking the primacy to Himself, and in constituting Himself the Head of the Church, he might at the same time draw all things to Himself.[157]

Asked during her trial about the Pope, St Joan of Arc stated that she 'believed in Our Holy Father the Pope at Rome'.[158] Recognising that the Church 'is both visible and spiritual, a hierarchical society and the Mystical Body' of which Christ is the head, the *Catechism* says that the Church is 'one, yet formed of two components, human and divine' and that 'only faith can accept' (n. 779) this mystery. Because of its mysterious combination of human and divine components, the *Catechism* recognises that, in this world, the Church 'is the sacrament of salvation, the sign and the instrument of the communion of God and men' (n. 780). Its members have become 'a chosen race, a royal priesthood, a holy nation, God's own people' (1 Pet 2:9) (n. 803) because Christ Jesus 'gave himself for us to redeem us from all iniquity and to purify for himself a people of his own' (Titus 2:14) (n. 802). Quoting Vatican II's *Lumen gentium* 13, the *Catechism* says that all people 'are called to belong to the new People of

God' and, quoting Vatican II's *Ad gentes* 1, it says that, in Christ, all people are called to 'form one family and one People of God' (n. 804). Irenaeus described Christ, the 'Head of the Church', as granting the Spirit to those 'who rightly believe in Him and love Him'.[159] The *Catechism* says:

> Through the Spirit and his action in the sacraments, above all the Eucharist, Christ, who once was dead and is now risen, established the community of believers as his own Body. In the unity of this Body, there is a diversity of members and functions. All members are linked to one another, especially to those who are suffering, to the poor and persecuted. (nn. 805–6)

The records of the trial of St Joan of Arc include the following account of her interrogation:

> Asked if she would submit to the decision of the Church, she answered: 'I commit myself to Our Lord, Who sent me, to Our Lady, and to all the Blessed Saints of Paradise.' And she thought that our Lord and the Church were all one, and therein they ought not to make difficulties for her. 'Why do you make difficulties when it is all one?'[160]

Nuancing St Joan's approach somewhat by implying that the unity of Christ and the Church is already evident but not yet perfectly achieved, the *Catechism* says:

> The Church is this Body of which Christ is the head: she lives from him, in him and for him; he lives with her and in her. The Church is the Bride of Christ: he loved her and handed himself over for her. He has purified her by his blood and made her the fruitful mother of all God's children. (nn. 807–8)

Describing the Spirit as 'the soul, as it were, of the Mystical Body, the source of its life, of its unity in diversity, and of the riches of its gifts and charisms' (n. 809), the *Catechism* quotes St Irenaeus when it says that the Holy Spirit 'makes the Church "the temple of the living God" (2 Cor 6:16)':

> Indeed, it is to the Church herself that the 'Gift of God' has been entrusted. ... It is in her that the communion with Christ has been deposited, that is to say: the Holy Spirit, the pledge of incorruptibility, the strengthening of our faith and the ladder of our ascent to God. ... For where the Church is, there also is God's Spirit; where God's Spirit is, there is the Church and every grace. (n. 797)[161]

Writing to her mother soon after she entered Carmel, Elizabeth of the Trinity recognised that, in the Church, each person's soul was also God's temple:

> Realize that your soul is the temple of God, it is again Saint Paul who says this (see 1 Cor 3:16-17); at every moment of the day and night the three Divine Persons are living within you.[162]

Irenaeus recognised that, 'although scattered throughout the whole world', the Church carefully preserves the preaching and faith it has received 'as if occupying but one house' and 'just as if she had but one soul, and one and the same heart'.[163] Quoting Pope Pius XII's *Mystici Corporis*, the *Catechism* echoes Irenaeus when it attributes the unity of Christ's Mystical Body to the activity of the Holy Spirit:

> To this Spirit of Christ, as an invisible principle, is to be ascribed the fact that all the parts of the body are joined one with the other and with their exalted head, for the

whole Spirit of Christ is in the head, the whole Spirit is in the body, and the whole Spirit is in each of the members. (n. 797)[164]

For St Irenaeus, heretics are 'blind to the truth, walk in various and devious paths; and on this account the vestiges of their doctrine are scattered about without agreement or connection'. The path of those 'who belong to the Church', on the other hand, 'goes around the whole world' because the Church 'has the firm tradition of the Apostles, enabling us to see that the faith of all is one and the same'.[165] Acknowledging the divisions caused by heresy and schism, the *Catechism* recognises, nevertheless, that the Church 'is one' because:

> [It] acknowledges one Lord, confesses one faith, is born of one Baptism, forms only one Body, is given life by one Spirit, for the sake of one hope (see Eph 4:3-5), at whose fulfilment all divisions will be overcome. (n. 866)

For St Irenaeus, the washing of the body and the gift of the Spirit in Christian initiation unites the members of the Church with the holiness of divine life:

> Our bodies have been joined into the unity which leads to incorruption through the washing, our souls have received it through the Spirit. Both are necessary, since both contribute to the divine life.[166]

The *Catechism* teaches that the Church 'is holy' because:

> [T]he Most Holy God is her author; Christ, her bride-groom, gave himself up to make her holy; the Spirit of holiness gives her life. Since she still includes sinners, she is 'the sinless one made up of sinners'. Her holiness shines in the saints; in Mary she is already all-holy. (n. 867)

St Irenaeus implicitly recognised the catholicity of the Church when he described it as being 'disseminated throughout the whole world'[167] and he believed that God has placed 'apostles, prophets and doctors, and all the other means through which the Spirit works (see 1 Cor 12:28)' in the Church.[168] The *Catechism* says that the Church 'is catholic' (i.e., 'according to the whole') because:

> [S]he proclaims the fullness of the faith. She bears in herself and administers the totality of the means of salvation. She is sent out to all peoples. She speaks to all men. She encompasses all times. She is 'missionary of her very nature'. (n. 868)[169]

St Irenaeus recognised that 'the Apostles, like a rich man in a bank, deposited with her [the Church] most copiously everything that pertains to the truth; and everyone whosoever wishes draws from her the drink of life (see Rev 22:17)'.[170] The *Catechism* also recognises that the Church is 'apostolic':

> She is built on a lasting foundation: 'the twelve apostles of the Lamb' (Rev 21:14). She is indestructible (see Mt 16:18). She is upheld infallibly in the truth: Christ governs her through Peter and the other apostles, who are present in their successors, the Pope and the college of bishops. (n. 869)

The *Catechism* quotes Irenaeus:

> For with this church [the Church of Rome], by reason of its pre-eminence, the whole Church, that is the faithful everywhere, must necessarily be in accord. (n. 834)[171]

This same truth was formulated as follows by the Second Vatican Council in its Dogmatic Constitution on the Church, *Lumen gentium* 8:

> The sole Church of Christ which in the Creed we profess to be one, holy, catholic and apostolic ... subsists in the Catholic Church, which is governed by the successor of Peter and by the bishops in communion with him. Nevertheless, many elements of sanctification and of truth are found outside its visible confines.[172]

Bl. Elizabeth of the Trinity recognised the unity of the lay and consecrated life vocations. Writing to her married sister, Marguerite, the April before she died, she told her that she would take her place as the 'Praise of Glory (*Laudem gloriae*)' here on earth:

> You will take my place; I will be '*Laudem gloriae*' before the throne of the Lamb and you, '*Laudem gloriae*' in the center of your soul, we will always be united.[173]

Writing to a young seminarian, she also recognised that all Carmelites, the nuns as well as the priests, share Mary's 'double vocation' of being '"Virgin" – espoused in faith by Christ' and '"Mother" – saving souls'.[174] The *Catechism* recognises that 'those Christian faithful who, professing the evangelical counsels, are consecrated to God and so serve the Church's saving mission' (n. 934) are found among both the clerics and the laity.

The *Catechism* teaches that, in order to 'proclaim the faith and plant his reign, Christ sends his apostles and their successors', giving them 'a share in his own mission' and 'the power to act in his person' (n. 935). Irenaeus teaches that it is 'necessary to obey ... those who have received, with the succession of the episcopate, the sure charism of truth'.[175] Noting that, having founded and built up the Church (of Rome), the blessed Apostles Peter and Paul 'handed over the office of the episcopate to Linus', Irenaeus also lists the eleven successors of Linus, commenting that 'in this order, and by the teaching of the

Apostles handed down in the Church, the preaching of the truth has come down to us'.[176] The *Catechism* says:

> The Lord made St Peter the visible foundation of his Church. He entrusted the keys of the Church to him. The bishop of the Church of Rome, successor to St Peter, is 'head of the college of bishops, the Vicar of Christ and Pastor of the universal Church on earth'. (n. 936)[177]

When he sought to convince Bishop Victor of Rome not to excommunicate Polycrates of Ephesus because he insisted on following the Eastern tradition for dating Easter, Irenaeus cited the precedent of Pope Anicetus, who did not impose the Roman tradition for calculating the date of Easter on Polycarp: 'They parted from each other in peace, and kept peace in the Church both for those who observed and for those who did not observe' the Roman tradition.[178] The *Catechism* says that the Pope enjoys, by divine institution, 'supreme, full, immediate and universal power in the care of souls' (n. 937)[179] including, presumably, the authority to permit local variations from Roman traditions. Noting that he and his contemporaries were 'in a position to enumerate those who were instituted bishops by the Apostles, and their successors to our own times', Irenaeus held that the Apostles 'handed on their authority' to their successors.[180] The *Catechism* says:

> The bishops, established by the Holy Spirit, succeed the apostles. They are 'the visible source and foundation of unity in their own particular Churches'.[181] Helped by the priests, their co-workers, and by the deacons, the bishops have the duty of authentically teaching the faith, celebrating divine worship, above all the Eucharist, and guiding their Churches as true pastors. Their responsibility also includes concern for all the Churches, with and under the Pope. (nn. 938–9)

Because they have received 'the sure charism of truth', Irenaeus recognised that it is necessary 'to obey those who are the presbyters in the Church, those who, as we have shown, have succession from the Apostles'.[182] Noting that God has 'promised through the Prophets, that in the last days he would pour out upon His servants and handmaids the ability to prophesy' (see Joel 2:28), he also implied that God is present and active among the laity. Jesus gave his disciples 'the power of regenerating in God' through Christian initiation and, in this way, God would become accustomed

> to dwell among the human race, to rest with people, to dwell in the workmanship of God, working the will of the Father in them, and renewing them from their old ways to the newness of Christ.[183]

There was a significant development in doctrine on the role and mission of the laity since the time of Irenaeus and, in its summary of that doctrine, the *Catechism* quotes from Vatican II's *Lumen gentium, Gaudium et spes* and *Apostolicam actuositatem*:

> 'The characteristic of the lay state being a life led in the midst of the world and of secular affairs, lay people are called by God to make of their apostolate, through the vigour of their Christian spirit, a leaven in the world' (*Apostolicam actuositatem*, 2.2). Lay people share in Christ's priesthood: ever more united with him, they exhibit the grace of Baptism and Confirmation in all dimensions of their personal, family, social and ecclesial lives, and so fulfil the call to holiness addressed to all the baptized. By virtue of their prophetic mission, lay people 'are called … to be witnesses to Christ in all circumstances and at the very heart of the community of mankind' (*Gaudium et spes*, 43.4). By virtue of their kingly mission, lay people have the power to uproot the rule of sin within

themselves and in the world, by their self-denial and holiness of life (see *Lumen gentium*, 36). (nn. 940–3)

The *Catechism* distinguishes between the vocation of the laity and the Consecrated Life when it says:

> The life consecrated to God is characterised by the public profession of the evangelical counsels of poverty, chastity and obedience, in a stable state of life recognised by the Church. (n. 944)

Writing to a young seminarian, Elizabeth of the Trinity described her Carmelite vocation as sharing in the virginal maternity of Mary:

> I so love what you say about Mary in your letter ... I also think of life as a Carmelite in terms of that double vocation: 'virgin mother'. 'Virgin' – espoused in faith by Christ; 'Mother' – saving souls, multiplying the adopted children of the Father, co-heirs with Christ.[184]

The *Catechism* also recognises the consecrated life as an intimate self-consecration in God's service:

> Already destined for him through Baptism, the person who surrenders himself to the God he loves above all else thereby consecrates himself more intimately to God's service and to the good of the whole Church. (n. 945)

Elizabeth of the Trinity highlights the link between her own vocation and the common destiny of all to become one with the communion of saints in heaven:

> [T]he life of a Carmelite is a communion with God from morning to evening, and from evening to

morning. If He did not fill our cells and our cloisters, ah! How empty they would be! But through him [we] see Him, for we bear Him within us, and our life is an anticipated Heaven.[185]

Quoting *Lumen gentium* 3, the *Catechism* notes that the expression 'communion of saints' or 'communion of the holy' refers first to the 'holy things' (*'sancta'*), above all the Eucharist, by which 'the unity of believers, who form one body in Christ, is both represented and brought about' (n. 960). The expression is also used to describe the communion of 'holy persons' (*'sancti'*) in Christ who 'died for all' (n. 961), so that what each one does or suffers in and for Christ bears fruit for all. Quoting Pope Paul VI's *Creed of the People of God* (n. 30), the *Catechism* says:

We believe in the communion of all the faithful of Christ, those who are pilgrims on earth, the dead who are being purified, and the blessed in heaven, all together forming one Church; and we believe that in this communion, the merciful love of God and his saints is always [attentive] to our prayers. (n. 962)

We have already noted that, for Irenaeus, 'the knot of Eve's disobedience was loosed by the obedience of Mary. What the virgin Eve had bound in unbelief, the Virgin Mary loosed through faith'.[186] Quoting Pope Paul VI's Creed of the People of God n. 15, and noting that, following her Assumption, she 'already shares in the glory of her Son's resurrection' (n. 974), the *Catechism* teaches that Mary continues her maternal role as the new Eve in heaven:

We believe that the Holy Mother of God, the new Eve, Mother of the Church, continues in heaven to exercise her maternal role on behalf of the members of Christ. (n. 975)

Noting that the risen Christ entrusted to the apostles the power to forgive sins when he gave them the Holy Spirit, the *Catechism* says that it is for this reason that the Creed links 'the forgiveness of sins' (n. 984) with its profession of faith in the Holy Spirit. Recognising that the power to forgive sins is exercised both in Baptism and in Penance, the *Catechism* points out:

> Baptism is the first and chief sacrament for the forgiveness of sins: it unites us to Christ, who died and rose, and gives us the Holy Spirit. (n. 985)

Irenaeus refers to some of the women who were disciples of the Gnostic Marcus as later repenting because of their hope of sharing eternal life and publicly confessing their sin in the Church:

> Their consciences branded as with a hot iron, some of these women made a public confession; but others are ashamed to do this, and in silence, as if withdrawing from themselves the hope of the life of God, they either apostatize entirely or hesitate between the two courses.[187]

In fundamental continuity with St Irenaeus, the development of dogma on the sacrament of Penance and Reconciliation is summarised by the *Catechism*:

> By Christ's will, the Church possesses the power to forgive the sins of the baptised and exercises it through bishops and priests normally in the sacrament of penance. 'In the forgiveness of sins, both priests and sacraments are instruments which our Lord Jesus Christ, the only author and liberal giver of salvation, wills to use in order to efface our sins and give us the grace of justification.' (nn. 986–7)[188]

St Irenaeus insisted that 'flesh which is nourished by the Body and Blood of the Lord, and is in fact a member of Him' is capable 'of receiving the gift of God, which is eternal life'.[189] In continuity with Irenaeus, the *Catechism* says:

> We believe in God who is creator of the flesh; we believe in the Word made flesh in order to redeem the flesh; we believe in the resurrection of the flesh, the fulfilment of both the creation and the redemption of the flesh. (n. 1015)

Recognising that it is our bodies that die and decompose 'but not the soul or the spirit',[190] Irenaeus believed that, having been nourished by the Eucharist, our bodies 'shall rise up in due season, the Word of God favouring them with resurrection in the glory of God the Father'.[191] Quoting *Gaudium et spes* 18.2, the *Catechism* says that, as a consequence of original sin, man must suffer 'bodily death, from which man would have been immune had he not sinned' (n. 1018). Like Irenaeus, the *Catechism* recognises that 'Just as Christ is risen and lives for ever, so all of us will rise at the last day' (n. 1016). 'We sow a corruptible body in the tomb, but he raises up an incorruptible body, a "spiritual body" (see 1 Cor 15:42-44).'[192] Irenaeus believed that the righteous will 'receive the promised inheritance ... when they rise again' and that the general judgement would take place afterwards.[193] The *Catechism* says that each person

> receives his eternal recompense in his immortal soul from the moment of his death in a particular judgement by Christ, the judge of the living and the dead. (n. 1051)

Acknowledging that the manner in which the bodies of those who die in Christ's grace will rise from death is accessible only to faith, the *Catechism* quotes St Irenaeus when it presents the Eucharist as a foretaste of that transfiguration:

Just as bread that comes from the earth, after God's blessing has been invoked upon it, is no longer ordinary bread, but Eucharist, formed of two things, the one earthly and the other heavenly: so too our bodies, which partake of the Eucharist, are no longer corruptible, but possess the hope of resurrection. (n. 1000)[194]

Irenaeus believed that those to whom the Lord shall say, 'Come, blessed of my Father, receive the inheritance of the kingdom, which has been prepared for you in eternity' (Mt 25:34), shall receive the kingdom forever.[195] Quoting the Profession of Faith of Pope Paul VI, the *Catechism* says:

We believe that the multitude of those gathered around Jesus and Mary in Paradise forms the Church of heaven, where in eternal blessedness they see God as he is and where they are also, to various degrees, associated with the holy angels in the divine governance exercised by Christ in glory, by interceding for us and helping our weakness by their fraternal concern. (n. 1053)[196]

Bl. Elizabeth of the Trinity implied the possibility of a purification after death when she described her Carmelite vocation as a call 'to be mediatrix with Jesus Christ' who 'is always living to intercede and to ask mercy' (see Heb 7:25).[197] The *Catechism* says:

Those who die in God's grace and friendship imperfectly purified, although they are assured of their eternal salvation, undergo a purification after death, so as to achieve the holiness necessary to enter the joy of God. (n. 1054)

Jean Fabri, one of the witnesses who testified at her retrial, said that shortly before she was burned at the stake, St Joan of Arc 'prayed all the priests there present each to say her a Mass'.[198] The *Catechism* says that, by virtue of the 'communion of saints', the Church 'commends the dead to God's mercy and offers her prayers, especially the holy sacrifice of the Eucharist, on their behalf' (n. 1055). Irenaeus held that those to whom the Lord shall say, 'Depart from me, accursed ones, into the everlasting fire' (Mt 25:41), will be 'damned forever'.[199] Describing 'hell' as the 'sad and lamentable reality of eternal death' (n. 1056), the *Catechism* says that hell's principal punishment 'consists of eternal separation from God in whom alone man can have the life and happiness for which he was created and for which he longs' (n. 1057). It adds:

> The Church prays that no one should be lost: 'Lord, let me never be parted from you.' If it is true that no one can save himself, it is also true that God 'desires all men to be saved' (1 Tim 2:4), and that for him 'all things are possible' (Mt 19:26). (n. 1058)

Quoting the *Profession of Faith of Michael Palaeologus* at the Second Council of Lyons (1274), the *Catechism* says:
> The holy Roman Church firmly believes and confesses that on the Day of Judgement all men will appear in their own bodies before Christ's tribunal to render an account of their own deeds. (n. 1059)[200]

The *Catechism* quotes St Irenaeus who held that, when the Kingdom of God comes in its fullness, the material universe will itself be 'restored to its original state' so that it is 'at the service of the just' (n. 1047) and shares their glorification in the risen Jesus Christ.[201] It also says:

> At the end of time, the Kingdom of God will come in its fullness. Then the just will reign with Christ for ever, glorified in body and soul, and the material universe

itself will be transformed. God will then be 'all in all' (1 Cor 15:28), in eternal life. (n. 1060)

Notes

1. See nn. 30, 32, 92, 102, 119, 129, 158, 281, 300, 311 (twice), 329, 338, 385, 506, 556, 769, 774, 795, 796, 797, 845, 963, 981, 983, 996, 1039 and 1064.
2. See nn. 34, 38, 43, 112, 116, 155, 157, 163, 170, 271, 293, 310 (twice), 311, 404, 412, 460, 555, 556, 627, 795, 904 and 947.
3. See nn. 53, 77, 173, 174 (twice), 175, 190, 292, 294, 438, 460, 494 (twice), 518 (twice), 683, 704, 797, 834, 1000 and 1047.
4. See nn. 127, 826, 956 and 1011.
5. See nn. 223 and 795.
6. See nn. 313 and 356.
7. See nn. 127, 260, 281, 618 and 1011.
8. See Hermigild Dressler, 'St. Irenaeus' in *New Catholic Encyclopedia* (Washington, DC: The Catholic University of America, 2003), 7, 570–2.
9. See Richard A. Norris, *God And World In Early Christian Theology: A Study in Justin Martyr, Irenaeus, Tertullian and Origen* (London: Adam & Charles Black, 1966), 57.
10. See Régine Pernoud, 'St Joan of Arc' in *New Catholic Encyclopedia* (Washington, DC: The Catholic University of America, 2003), 7, 878–9.
11. See W. P. Barrett (ed.), *The Trial of Jeanne D'Arc* (London: George Routledge & Sons, 1931), 149.
12. Malcolm Graham Allan Vale, *Charles VII* (Berkeley: University of California Press, 1974), 55.
13. See Kelly DeVries, *Joan of Arc: A Military Leader* (Gloucestershire: Sutton Publishing, 1999), 96–7.
14. Barrett (ed.), *The Trial of Jeanne D'Arc*, 63.
15. See Conrad de Meester (ed.), *Elisabeth de la Trinité: Oeuvres complètes* (Paris: Cerf, 1991), 222.
16. See ibid., 811.
17. See ibid., 898.
18. Conrad de Meester (ed.), *The Complete Works of Elizabeth of the Trinity*, 3 vols (Washington: ICS, 1984, 1995), 1:16.
19. See de Meester (ed.), *Elisabeth de la Trinité: Oeuvres complètes*, 898.
20. Letter 53 to Marguerite Gollot in ibid., 299.

21. See ibid., 880.
22. Letter 62 to Canon Angles in ibid., 312.
23. Letter 93 in de Meester (ed.), *The Complete Works of Elizabeth of the Trinity*, 2:23.
24. de Meester (ed.), *Elisabeth de la Trinité: Oeuvres complètes*, 908.
25. Bl. Elizabeth of the Trinity, Letter 298 to Marguerite in Conrad de Meester (ed.), *The Complete Works of Elizabeth of the Trinity*, 2:305.
26. Conrad de Meester, *Élisabeth de la Trinité. Biografie* (Paris: Presses de la Renaissance, 2006), 713.
27. Ibid., 716.
28. See the *Catechism*, nn. 26–184.
29. See the *Catechism*, nn. 27–49.
30. de Meester (ed.), *The Complete Works of Elizabeth of the Trinity*, 2:75.
31. de Meester, *Élisabeth de la Trinité. Biografie.*, 112.
32. St Irenaeus, *Against Heresies*, 2.6.1, in Migne (ed.), *PG*, 7:724.
33. See Vatican I, canon 2, n. 1, in Denzinger and Schönmetzer SJ (eds), *Denzinger-Schönmetzer*, n. 3026.
34. St Irenaeus, *Against Heresies*, 2.9.1, in Migne (ed.), *PG*, 7:734.
35. See the *Catechism*, nn. 50–141.
36. St Irenaeus, *Against Heresies*, 5, Preface, in Migne (ed.), *PG*, 7:1120.
37. See the *Catechism*, n. 69.
38. St Irenaeus, *Against Heresies*, 3.20.2, in Migne (ed.), *PG*, 7:944. See the *Catechism*, n. 53.
39. St Irenaeus, *Against Heresies*, 3.16.6, in ibid., 7:926.
40. St Irenaeus, *Against Heresies*, 3.4.1, in ibid., 7:855.
41. St Irenaeus, *Against Heresies*, 3.4.1, in ibid.
42. St Irenaeus, *Against Heresies*, 3.4.1, in ibid.
43. St Irenaeus, *Against Heresies*, 5.18.2, in ibid., 7:1173.
44. See the *Catechism*, n. 100.
45. St Irenaeus, *Against Heresies*, 3.3.1, in Migne (ed.), *PG*, 7:848.
46. St Irenaeus, *Against Heresies*, 2.28.2, in ibid., 7:805.
47. de Meester (ed.), *Elisabeth de la Trinité: Oeuvres complètes*, 162.
48. Bl. Elizabeth of the Trinity, *Heaven in Faith*, 1.2, in de Meester (ed.), *The Complete Works of Elizabeth of the Trinity*, 1:95.
49. See the *Catechism*, nn. 142–84.
50. St Irenaeus, *Against Heresies*, 4.37.5, in Migne (ed.), *PG*, 7:1102.
51. St Irenaeus, *Against Heresies*, 1.10.1, in ibid., 7:550.
52. See the *Catechism*, n. 172.
53. St Irenaeus, *Against Heresies*, 1.10.1-2, in Migne (ed.), *PG*, 7:549-553. Quoted in the *Catechism*, nn. 173–4.

54. St Irenaeus, *Against Heresies,* 5.20.1, in ibid., 7:1177. Quoted in the *Catechism,* n. 175.
55. St Irenaeus, *Against Heresies,* 3.24.1, in ibid., 7:966. Quoted in the *Catechism,* n. 175.
56. St Irenaeus, *Against Heresies,* 4.37.5, in ibid., 7:1102.
57. St Irenaeus, *Against Heresies,* 4.20.5, in ibid., 7:1035.
58. See the *Catechism,* nn. 198–421.
59. St Irenaeus, *Against Heresies,* 1.10.1, in Migne (ed.), *PG,* 7:549.
60. Barrett (ed.), *The Trial of Jeanne D'Arc,* 83–4.
61. St Irenaeus, *Against Heresies,* 2.30.9, in Migne (ed.), *PG,* 7:822.
62. Elizabeth of the Trinity, Letter 161 to Françoise de Sourdon de Meester (ed.), *The Complete Works of Elizabeth of the Trinity,* 2:100.
63. Elizabeth of the Trinity, Letter 128 to Françoise de Sourdon in ibid., 56.
64. St Irenaeus, 'Presentation of the Apostolic Preaching', 100, in L.M. Froidevaux (ed.), *Irénée de Lyon: Démonstration de la prédication apostolique (Sources Chrétiennes,* edited by H. de Lubac and J. Daniélou) (Paris: Cerf, 1959), 170. See the *Catechism,* n. 190.
65. St Irenaeus, *Against Heresies,* 1.10.1, in Migne (ed.), *PG,* 7:550.
66. See the *Catechism,* nn. 198–421.
67. St Irenaeus, *Against Heresies,* 4.20.1, in Migne (ed.), *PG,* 7:1032.
68. St Irenaeus, *Against Heresies,* 2.28.6, in ibid., 7:808–09.
69. Letter 62 to Canon Angles in de Meester (ed.), *Elisabeth de la Trinité: Oeuvres complètes,* 312.
70. St Irenaeus, *Against Heresies,* 2.30.9, in Migne (ed.), *PG,* 7:823.
71. St Irenaeus, *Against Heresies,* 3.16.9, in ibid., 7:929.
72. Bl. Elizabeth of the Trinity, Poem 75, de Meester (ed.), *Elisabeth de la Trinité: Oeuvres complètes,* 996.
73. 'The Holy Spirit proceeds from the Father as the first principle and, by the eternal gift of this to the Son, from the communion of both the Father and the Son', St Augustine, *De Trinitate,* 15.26.47, in Migne (ed.), *PL,* 42:1095. Quoted in the *Catechism,* n. 264.
74. Bl. Elizabeth of the Trinity, Letter 185 to Abbé Chauvignard in de Meester (ed.), *The Complete Works of Elizabeth of the Trinity,* 2:136.
75. Letter 131 to Canon Angles in de Meester (ed.), *The Complete Works of Elizabeth of the Trinity,* 2:60.
76. Bl. Elizabeth of the Trinity, Letter 269 to Marguerite in ibid., 264–5.
77. See Dupuis (ed.), *The Christian Faith,* n. 16.
78. St Irenaeus, *Against Heresies,* 1.22.1, in Migne (ed.), *PG,* 7:669.

79. Bl. Elizabeth of the Trinity, *Notes imtimes,* 15, in de Meester (ed.), *Elisabeth de la Trinité: Oeuvres complètes,* 907.

80. *Catechism,* nn. 275–6.

81. St Irenaeus, *Against Heresies,* 1.22.1, in Migne (ed.), *PG,* 7:669.

82. See the *Catechism,* n. 316.

83. St Irenaeus, *Against Heresies,* 2.30.9; 4.20.1, in Migne (ed.), *PG,* 7:822, 1032.

84. St Irenaeus, *Against Heresies,* 2.10.4, in ibid., 736.

85. St Irenaeus, *Against Heresies,* 4.20.7, in ibid., 7:1037. Quoted in the *Catechism,* n. 294.

86. St Irenaeus, *Against Heresies,* 2.34.2, in ibid., 7:835.

87. St Irenaeus, *Against Heresies,* 5.2.2, in ibid., 7:1125.

88. St Irenaeus, *Against Heresies,* 4.37.5, in ibid., 7:1102.

89. St Irenaeus, *Against Heresies,* 4.37.1, in ibid., 7:1099.

90. St Irenaeus, *Against Heresies,* 4.7.4, in ibid., 7:993.

91. Barrett (ed.), *The Trial of Jeanne D'Arc,* 101.

92. St Irenaeus, *Against Heresies,* 4.20.7, in Migne (ed.), *PG,* 7:1037. Quoted in the *Catechism,* n. 294.

93. Barrett (ed.), *The Trial of Jeanne D'Arc,* 155.

94. St Irenaeus, *Against Heresies,* 5.10.1, in Migne (ed.), *PG,* 7:1148.

95. Roman Missal, EP IV, 118.

96. See the *Catechism,* n. 382.

97. St Irenaeus, *Against Heresies,* 5.7.1, in Migne (ed.), *PG,* 7:1140.

98. St Irenaeus, *Against Heresies,* 4.37.1, in ibid., 7:1099.

99. St Irenaeus, *Against Heresies,* 3.23.5, in ibid., 7:963.

100. St Irenaeus, *Against Heresies,* 4.37.1, in ibid., 7:1099.

101. St Irenaeus, *Against Heresies,* 1.10.1, in ibid., 7:549.

102. St Irenaeus, *Against Heresies,* 5.24.3, in ibid., 7:1188., see the *Catechism,* n. 414.

103. St Irenaeus, *Against Heresies,* 3.23.5, in ibid., 7:963.

104. St Irenaeus, *Against Heresies,* 3.22.4, in ibid., 7:959.

105. St Irenaeus, *Against Heresies,* 3.23.5, in ibid., 7:963.

106. St Irenaeus, *Against Heresies,* 3.23.2, in ibid., 7:961.

107. Pope Paul VI, *Creed of the People of God,* n. 16.

108. St Irenaeus, *Against Heresies,* 5, Preface, in Migne (ed.), *PG,* 7:1120.

109. St Irenaeus, *Against Heresies,* 5.6.1, in ibid., 7:1137.

110. Vatican II's *Gaudium et spes* 2.2, quoted in the *Catechism,* n. 421.

111. *Catechism,* n. 420.

112. See the *Catechism,* nn. 422–682.

113. See the *Catechism,* n. 453.

114. St Irenaeus, *Against Heresies,* 3.18.3, in Migne (ed.), *PG,* 7:934. See the *Catechism,* n. 745.
115. St Irenaeus, *Against Heresies,* 3.16.9, in ibid., 7:929.
116. St Irenaeus, *Against Heresies,* 3.19.2, in ibid., 7:940.
117. St Irenaeus, *Against Heresies,* 3.18.7, in ibid., 7:937. See the *Catechism,* n. 480.
118. *Catechism,* n. 481.
119. St Irenaeus, *Against Heresies,* 3.18.6, in Migne (ed.), *PG,* 7:936.
120. St Irenaeus, *Against Heresies,* 3.21.10, in ibid., 7:954–5.
121. St Irenaeus, *Against Heresies,* 2.28.6, in ibid., 7:808.
122. St Irenaeus, *Against Heresies,* 3.19.1, in ibid., 7:939.
123. St Irenaeus, *Against Heresies,* 5.19.1, in ibid., 7:1175. See the *Catechism,* n. 509.
124. St Irenaeus, *Against Heresies,* 3.19.1, in ibid., 7:938.
125. St Augustine, *Sermons,* 186.1, in Migne (ed.), *PL,* 38:999.
126. St Irenaeus, *Against Heresies,* 3.21.10, Migne (ed.), *PG,* 7:955.
127. St Irenaeus, *Against Heresies,* 3.22.4, in ibid., 7:959A.
128. St Irenaeus, *Against Heresies,* 3.18.1, 7, in ibid., 7:932, 937.
129. St Irenaeus, *Against Heresies,* 2.22.4, in ibid., 7:784.
130. St Irenaeus, *Against Heresies,* 2.22.4, in ibid.
131. Bl. Elizabeth of the Trinity, Letter 288 to Margueritein de Meester (ed.), *The Complete Works of Elizabeth of the Trinity,* 2:291.
132. See Bl. Elizabeth of the Trinity, Letter 123 to Françoise de Sourdon in ibid., 52.
133. St Irenaeus, *Against Heresies,* 1.10.1, in Migne (ed.), *PG,* 7:550.
134. St Irenaeus, *Against Heresies,* 3.22.4, in ibid., 7:959.
135. St Irenaeus, *Against Heresies,* 3.21.10, in ibid., 7:955.
136. St Irenaeus, *Against Heresies,* 5.16.3, in ibid., 7:1168.
137. *Catechism,* n. 593.
138. Barrett (ed.), *The Trial of Jeanne D'Arc,* 124.
139. Bl. Elizabeth of the Trinity, Letter 138 to Madame Angles in de Meester (ed.), *The Complete Works of Elizabeth of the Trinity,* 2:68.
140. St Irenaeus, *Against Heresies,* 2.11.1, in Migne (ed.), *PG,* 7:737.
141. *Catechism,* nn. 621–2.
142. *Catechism,* n. 623.
143. Bl. Elizabeth of the Trinity, Letter 317 in de Meester (ed.), *The Complete Works of Elizabeth of the Trinity,* 2:388.
144. St Irenaeus, *Against Heresies,* 5.31.2, in Migne (ed.), *PG,* 7:1209.
145. St Irenaeus, *Against Heresies,* 4.27.2, in ibid., 7:1058.
146. St Irenaeus, *Against Heresies,* 5.31.2, in ibid., 7:1209.

147. St Irenaeus, *Against Heresies,* 5.31.2, in ibid.
148. St Irenaeus, *Against Heresies,* 1.10.1, in ibid., 7:550–1.
149. See the *Catechism*, nn. 683–1065.
150. St Irenaeus, *Presentation of the Apostolic Preaching,* 7, in Froidevaux (ed.), *Irénée de Lyon: Démonstration de la prédication apostolique*, 41–2.
151. St Irenaeus, *Presentation of the Apostolic Preaching,* 11, in ibid., 48–9.
152. Bl. Elizabeth of the Trinity, *Notes imtimes,* 15, in de Meester (ed.), *Elisabeth de la Trinité: Oeuvres complètes*, 908.
153. Bl. Elizabeth of the Trinity, *Heaven in Faith,* 43, in de Meester (ed.), *Elisabeth de la Trinité: Oeuvres complètes*, 126.
154. St Irenaeus, *Against Heresies,* 5.18.2, in Migne (ed.), *PG,* 7:1173.
155. See the *Catechism*, n. 777.
156. Barrett (ed.), *The Trial of Jeanne D'Arc*, 125.
157. St Irenaeus, *Against Heresies,* 3.16.6, in Migne (ed.), *PG,* 7:926.
158. Barrett (ed.), *The Trial of Jeanne D'Arc*, 76.
159. St Irenaeus, *Against Heresies*, 5.18.2, in Migne (ed.), *PG,* 7:1173.
160. Barrett (ed.), *The Trial of Jeanne D'Arc*, 124.
161. St Irenaeus, *Against Heresies,* 3.24.1, in Migne (ed.), *PG,* 7:966.
162. Bl. Elizabeth of the Trinity, Letter 273 to her mother, in de Meester (ed.), *The Complete Works of Elizabeth of the Trinity,* 2:271.
163. St Irenaeus, *Against Heresies,* 1.10.2, in Migne (ed.), *PG,* 7:552.
164. See Dupuis (ed.), *The Christian Faith*, n. 852.
165. St Irenaeus, *Against Heresies,* 5.20.1, in Migne (ed.), *PG,* 7:1177.
166. St Irenaeus, *Against Heresies,* 3.17.2, in ibid., 7:930.
167. St Irenaeus, *Against Heresies,* 1.10.2, in ibid., 7:552–3.
168. St Irenaeus, *Against Heresies,* 3.24.1, in ibid., 7:966.
169. Vatican II's Decree on the Church's Missionary Activity, *Ad gentes* 2.
170. St Irenaeus, *Against Heresies,* 3.4.1, in Migne (ed.), *PG,* 7:855.
171. St Irenaeus, *Against Heresies,* 3.3.2, in ibid., 7:849.
172. *Catechism*, n. 870.
173. Bl. Elizabeth of the Trinity, Letter 269 to Marguerite in de Meester (ed.), *The Complete Works of Elizabeth of the Trinity,* 2:265.
174. Bl. Elizabeth of the Trinity, Letter 199 to Abbé Chevignard in ibid., 157.
175. St Irenaeus, *Against Heresies,* 4.26.2, in Migne (ed.), *PG,* 7:1053–4.
176. St Irenaeus, *Against Heresies,* 3.3.3, in ibid., 7:851.
177. Code of Canon Law, canon 331.
178. St Irenaeus, *Letter to Bishop Victor of Rome*, quoted in Eusebius, *History of the Church,* 5.24.16–17, in Migne (ed.), *PG,* 20:506.

179. Vatican II, Decree on the Pastoral Office of Bishops in the Church, *Christus Dominus* 2.

180. St Irenaeus, *Against Heresies,* 3.3.1, in Migne (ed.), *PG,* 7:849.

181. Vatican II's Dogmatic Constitution on the Church, *Lumen gentium* 23.

182. St Irenaeus, *Against Heresies,* 4.26.2, in Migne (ed.), *PG,* 7:1053.

183. St Irenaeus, *Against Heresies,* 3.17.1, in ibid., 7:929.

184. Bl. Elizabeth of the Trinity, Letter 199 to Abbé Chevignard in de Meester (ed.), *The Complete Works of Elizabeth of the Trinity,* 2:157.

185. Bl. Elizabeth of the Trinity, Letter 123 to Françoise de Sourdon in ibid., 52.

186. St Irenaeus, *Against Heresies,* 3.22.4, in Migne (ed.), *PG,* 7:959–60.

187. St Irenaeus, *Against Heresies,* 1.13.7, in Migne (ed.), *PG,* 7:592.

188. *Roman Catechism of the Council of Trent,* 1/11:6.

189. St Irenaeus, *Against Heresies,* 5.7.1, in Migne (ed.), *PG,* 7:1140.

190. Ibid.

191. St Irenaeus, *Against Heresies,* 5.2.3, in Migne (ed.), *PG,* 7:1127.

192. *Catechism,* n. 1017.

193. St Irenaeus, *Against Heresies,* 5.32.1, in Migne (ed.), *PG,* 7:1210.

194. St Irenaeus, *Against Heresies,* 4.18.4–5, in ibid., 7:1028–9.

195. St Irenaeus, *Against Heresies,* 4.28.2, in ibid., 7:1062.

196. Pope Paul VI, *Profession of Faith* 29, in Dupuis (ed.), *The Christian Faith,* 30.

197. Bl. Elizabeth of the Trinity, Letter 256 to Canon Angles in de Meester (ed.), *The Complete Works of Elizabeth of the Trinity,* 2:239.

198. Régine Pernoud, *The Retrial of Joan of Arc* (London: Methuen & Co. Ltd, 1955), 188.

199. St Irenaeus, *Against Heresies,* 4.28.2, in Migne (ed.), *PG,* 7:1062.

200. See Dupuis (ed.), *The Christian Faith,* 20.

201. St Irenaeus, *Against Heresies,* 5.32.1, in Migne (ed.), *PG,* 7:1210.

Chapter 6

A LIVING FAITH FOR TODAY

In his apostolic constitution on the publication of the *Catechism* of the Catholic Church, *Fidei depositum* (1992), Pope John Paul II quoted the speech of Bl. John XXIII at the opening of Vatican II in October 1962. In that speech, John XXIII said that the Council would be primarily concerned with the manner in which doctrine was presented, rather than with the substance of doctrine itself. The Church counteracts errors by 'demonstrating the validity of her teaching rather than by condemnations',[1] as he put it. Noting that Vatican II was intended 'to lead all people to seek and receive Christ's love which surpasses all knowledge (see Eph 3:19)', Pope John Paul II said that Bl. John XXIII wanted the Council 'above all to strive calmly to show the strength and beauty of the doctrine of the faith'. He described the *Catechism* as 'a sure and authentic reference text for teaching Catholic doctrine', a means of helping all the faithful 'to deepen their knowledge of the unfathomable riches of salvation (see Eph 3:8)'. It was also a response 'to every individual ... who wants to know what the Catholic Church believes'.

This book is not a compendium of the Church's faith, such as is found in the *Catechism*. It seeks, rather, to present an outline of the principal points of the doctrine in the *Catechism*, illustrating that doctrine by the faith testimony of a representative sample of the Church's saints. The saints that have been chosen as models of prayer, worship, righteousness and belief can be regarded, I think, as representative of the heart and mind of the Church over the two thousand years of its history. In chapters two, three, four and five, we have seen that the doctrine presented in the *Catechism* both reflects their lives of faith and testifies to their communion with the common heart and mind that St Irenaeus attributed to the gift of the Holy Spirit, which Jesus our Lord grants 'to those who rightly believe in him'.[2]

As she lay dying, St Teresa of Avila repeated the phrase from the *Memorare* (Psalm 51), 'A humble and contrite heart You will not despise, O God', and over and over she repeated, 'In short, Lord, I am a daughter of the Church ... I am a daughter of the Church'.[3] In the light of the humble contrition of the phrase from the *Memorare*, she was probably thanking God and asking for his mercy, because she had remained in communion with the Church, her spiritual mother, right up to the end of her life. Her contemporary and fellow Doctor of the Church, St Ignatius of Loyola, formulated a number of rules for 'thinking, judging, and feeling with the Church (*sentire cum Ecclesia*)' if we want to have what he described as 'the genuine attitude which we ought to maintain in the Church militant'.[4] The attitude Ignatius was seeking to cultivate includes both head and heart, thinking and feeling, and it bears fruit in a way of judging and acting that respects and preserves our communion in the Church with the mind and heart of Jesus.

THE 'LITTLE WAY' OF ST THÉRÈSE AS A MODEL FOR OUR PRAYER

The teaching of the *Catechism* on prayer was outlined in chapter two using St John Chrysostom, St Teresa of Avila and St Thérèse of Lisieux as witnesses to the Church's tradition. The first part of the chapter focused on Thérèse and the section on the 'Our Father' focused on Teresa and Chrysostom. In order to explore the contemporary significance of what the *Catechism* has to say about prayer, this section will outline the essential elements of the 'Little Way' of St Thérèse as presented in the Mass for her feast, which is celebrated each year on 1 October.

Thérèse described her 'Little Way' as a 'very straight, very short and totally new'[5] way of becoming a true disciple of Jesus Christ. She compared it to a lift:

> We are living now in an age of inventions, and we no longer have to take the trouble of climbing stairs, for, in the homes of the rich, an elevator has replaced these very successfully. I wanted to find an elevator that would raise me to Jesus, for I am too small to climb the rough stairway of perfection.[6]

In the Gospel for her feast day (Mt 18:1-5), Jesus presents the way a little child related to its parents as the model for those who are greatest in the kingdom of God. Thérèse refers to this Gospel when she describes how, at the age of fourteen, she had her first experience of what the souls of little children were like. She was the youngest in the family and had never spent time with little children until her family had to look after two girls whose mother was dying. Thérèse writes: 'I spent the whole day with them, and it was a great pleasure for me to see with what simplicity they believed everything I said.'[7] For Thérèse, the innocence and trust of the little girls was an insight into the way God wants us to relate to him and she realised that, unless she was totally open and trusting, God would not be free to draw her to himself as he desired.

In the first reading for her feast day (Isaiah 66:10-14), the prophet Isaiah invites the people of Jerusalem to rejoice because, despite their difficulties, God loves them and will succour them like a mother nurses her infant at the breast. For Thérèse,[8] this reading was God's way of telling her that, rather than trying to save herself by doing great things, all she had to do was to accept that she was a little child and that Jesus would care for her like a mother looking after a baby at the breast. He would take her by the hand and lead her to heaven. All she had to do was be willing to accept God's extraordinary love and mercy, and to respond willingly to anything that God asked of her.

Thérèse gradually came to realise that her 'Little Way', the way of childlike abandonment and trust in God, was the key to unlocking the deepest mysteries of God. Commenting on the Gospel text, 'Blessed are you, Father ... for revealing the mysteries of the kingdom to mere children' (see Mt 11:25), which is used as the Gospel acclamation for her feast, she wrote:

> Because I was little and weak He lowered Himself to me, and He instructed me secretly in the *things* of His *love*. Ah! had the learned who spent their life in study come to me, undoubtedly have been astonished to see a child of fourteen understand perfection's secrets, secrets all their knowledge cannot reveal because to possess them one has to be poor in spirit![9]

Although she was very young and inexperienced, Thérèse made her littleness into an asset. She realised that she would get further by depending on God's great love for her, and by trying to respond eagerly to what God asked of her, than by depending on her efforts to get to God.

The second reading for her feast (1 Jn 4:7-16) includes the words, 'God is love [and] ... if God so loved us, we also ought to love one another'. It describes God's love for us as being revealed in Jesus' willingness to die for us while we were still sinners so that we might be liberated and made capable of loving others, as he did, through the power of his Holy Spirit. Commenting on Jesus' commandment to love one another as he loved us, she writes:

Ah! Lord, I know you don't command the impossible. You know better than I do my weakness and imperfection; You know very well that never would I be able to love my Sisters as You love them, unless *You*, O my Jesus, *loved them in me*. It is because you wanted to give me this grace that You made Your *new* commandment.[10]

The Preface of the Mass for her feast sums up her life in the following words:

Father, all powerful and ever-living God ... You reveal the secrets of your kingdom to those who become like little children. Among them you chose saint Thérèse, hidden in Christ, to proclaim the good news of your merciful love. Your Holy Spirit moved her to make her life an oblation of prayer and self-denial for the salvation of all men and women through Christ and his Church.

Although the key to the 'Little Way' of St Thérèse is childlike trust and abandonment into the arms of God who delights in drawing us to himself, it is not simply a matter of 'leaving it all to God', as it were. Out of love for us, Jesus gave himself up to death to redeem us and to unite us to himself through the gift of his Holy Spirit. The Spirit enables us to love God and our neighbour as Jesus did by moving us to make our lives a living and continuous offering of worship and praise of God. In one of her prayers, she describes the Eucharist as a 'mystery of love that only love can repay', and in another she offers herself and her life as 'an act of perfect love' in response to the 'merciful love' of God. The solemn blessing at the end of the Mass for her feast says that, by teaching her 'to offer herself for the kingdom on earth, [Christ] brought her to share his glory in heaven'.

Jesus presented the confident trust of a little child in her parents as the model for how the greatest in the kingdom of God should behave (see Mt 18:1-5). In a similarly paradoxical manner, the way of spiritual childhood that Thérèse lived, and that has become her spiritual legacy to the People of God, has come to be recognised as one of the greatest gifts that our tradition has to offer. It is, perhaps, the kernel of all prayer, the attitude of childlike trust in God that makes it possible for us to address God as 'Our Father'.

THE EUCHARISTIC SPIRITUALITY OF ST THOMAS AQUINAS AS A MODEL FOR OUR LITURGICAL PRAYER

In chapter three of this book, St Thomas Aquinas was the principal witness to the teaching of the *Catechism* on the public worship of the Church. His understanding of the sacraments – of the sacrament of the Eucharist in particular – has become a point of reference for later theology.

For Aquinas, the Eucharist is the most important of the sacraments and all the others are directed to it in some way.[11] Presenting it as the third of the seven, following Baptism and Confirmation, he implies that, from a liturgical point of view, the Eucharist completes the process of Christian initiation.[12] Like all the sacraments, it is a symbolic action, in this case the taking of food and drink as a meal to symbolise the nourishing of our spiritual lives.[13] It is a sacrifice because it commemorates (and is a sacrament of) the passion of Christ. It is called 'communion' because it signifies the unity of the Church as Christ's mystical body. The immediate effect of the sacramental action (the priest speaking the Lord's words, 'This is my body ... this is my blood') is the transformation of the bread and wine into the body and blood of Christ. And the ultimate effect proper to this sacrament is the grace of unity in love between baptised

Christians in the body of Christ.[14] The ultimate effect depends on the intermediate effect, but the intermediate effect does not depend on the ultimate effect. Even if those for whom it is celebrated do not accept the gift of unity in love that the Eucharist makes possible, the bread and wine are always consecrated and become the body and blood of Christ when the Eucharist is celebrated properly.

Aquinas argues that 'transubstantiation' is a suitable name for the way in which the real presence of Christ's body and blood is brought about by the changing (*conversio*) of bread and wine into the body and blood of Christ. For Aquinas, the word 'substance' refers to that which exists independently of anything else. Water, for example, is a substance, but ice and steam are not different substances, since they are merely the accidental characteristics (*accidentia*) of water at different temperatures. It contradicts reason to claim that a thing can be two different substances at the same time, and the substance of bread is no longer present after the consecration because it has been changed into the substance of Christ's body.[15] Our senses of sight and taste continue to perceive the accidental characteristics (*accidentia*) of bread and wine after the consecration, so that, symbolically, we can associate the Eucharist with the notion of nourishment.

On the basis of faith, however, we no longer judge that the Eucharist is actually bread and wine and we affirm that the substance is not that of bread or wine but that of the body and blood of Christ. The divine power, acting through the Word and the Spirit in the liturgy of the Eucharist, changes the substance of the bread into the substance of Christ's body and the wine into the substance of his blood. Christ is now present 'in the way that substance is present (*per modum substantiae*)' and he is unaffected by changes to the accidental characteristics of what continues to look and taste like bread and wine. Any changes to the 'accidental characteristics (*accidentia*)', such as breaking or chewing, do not mean that Christ suffers being broken or chewed. Also, since it is the whole Christ, body and blood, who is substantially present in both the host and the cup, his body is present in the cup and his blood is present in the host.[16]

For Aquinas, the fruitful reception of the Eucharist takes away sin and produces grace and charity. It is the 'sacrament of charity'[17] and:

> The universal spiritual good of the whole Church is contained substantially in the sacrament of the Eucharist.[18]

It brings about the 'union of the Christian people with Christ'[19] and it 'gives us the power to reach glory'[20] by forming the 'society of the saints' that we call the Church, the Mystical Body of Christ.[21] Since the Eucharist is both a sacrifice (because it is offered, *offertur*) and a sacrament (because it is consumed, *sumitur*), it involves a movement in two directions simultaneously. There is a movement from humanity to God in worship, the offering of Christ's passion and death (which is symbolised in the separation of his body and blood),[22] and a movement from God to humanity in sanctification, the giving of grace through sacramental symbols. Noting that those who are to receive are the first people prayed for in the Roman Canon,[23] Aquinas held that for this two-directional movement to take place, those who will receive the body and blood must have a desire for communion with Christ,[24] without which the sacrament cannot sanctify them.[25] Sinfulness is an obstacle to the fruitful reception of the sacrament and Aquinas recognised that the sacrament can be received in a (merely) sacramental way, without the proper dispositions. In order to benefit from the grace of the sacrament, it must be received spiritually, in faith and love. Provided they are united to the Body of

Christ by living in authentic faith and love, which imply a desire for Eucharistic communion,[26] those who are present but do not receive communion can receive the fruits of the Eucharist without actually consuming the host or drinking from the chalice.[27] It is also possible, he says, for those who are not actually present at the celebration of the Eucharist to receive the sacrament spiritually, and to receive its grace in a 'spiritual communion' that does not involve the actual consumption of the body and blood.[28]

For Aquinas, our communion with one another and with Christ comes about through our sacramental commemoration of Christ's saving death, a commemoration that makes his saving death present among us in a way that enables us to share in it, and to allow ourselves to be conformed to him by uniting ourselves with his sacrificial self-offering to God. This same Eucharistic spirituality has been proposed by Pope John Paul II in his encyclical on the Eucharist for Holy Thursday 2003, *Ecclesia de Eucharistia*. Every time we celebrate the Eucharist, 'the sacramental re-presentation' of Christ's saving death and resurrection (n. 11) is really made present for us through the power of the Holy Spirit. By changing the substance of the bread and wine so that they become the substance of his own resurrected body and blood (nn. 14, 18), Jesus makes it possible for the Church to 'draw her life from Christ in the Eucharist' (n. 6). The Church has both a faith-filled remembrance and a real contact with the redeeming sacrifice of Christ on the Cross:

> The Church constantly draws her life from the redeeming sacrifice; she approaches it not only through faith-filled remembrance, but also through a real contact, since this sacrifice is made present ever anew, sacramentally perpetuated, in every community which offers it at the hands of the consecrated minister. The Eucharist thus applies to men and women today the

reconciliation won once for all by Christ for mankind in every age. (n. 12)

The 'Little Way' of St Thérèse has preached the Gospel message that the greatest in the kingdom of heaven have embraced the way of spiritual childhood (see Mt 18:1-5). The 'Little Way' invites us to look to our heavenly Father for the nourishment we need if we are to grow to maturity and, implicitly, it looks to the Eucharist as food that draws us into the true maturity of spiritual childhood. The Eucharistic spirituality of St Thomas Aquinas has, I believe, preached the Gospel message that Jesus is our 'bread of life' (Jn 6:35) and that he nourishes the Church, and gives it a share in his own life, in the Eucharist that is his body and blood. St Thomas Aquinas invites us to unite our lives with his, and to offer our lives to the Father in union with him in the Eucharistic liturgy, so that we may receive, in return, an ever-richer share in the life that he shares with the Father and with the Holy Spirit.

ST AUGUSTINE'S LOVE OF NEIGHBOUR AS A MODEL FOR OUR RIGHTEOUSNESS

In chapter four, St Augustine was the principal witness to the teaching of the *Catechism* on righteousness. At his general audience on Wednesday, 9 January 2008, Pope Benedict XVI described St Augustine as 'the greatest Father of the Latin Church'. On the sixteenth centenary of the conversion of St Augustine in 1986, Pope John Paul II dedicated an Apostolic Letter to St Augustine, *Augustinum Hipponensem*, describing it as 'a thanksgiving to God for the gift that he has made to the Church, and through her to the whole human race'. Pope John Paul II says that it is 'no small merit of Augustine to have narrowed all of Christian doctrine and life down to the question of charity. "This is true love: that we cling to the truth and live righteously".'[29] For Augustine, charity is the good that leads to the possession of all goods, and the good without which all other goods are of no avail: 'Have charity, and you will have them all; because without charity, whatever you have will be of no benefit.'[30]

For Augustine, man is the most social of God's creatures by nature but also the most antisocial by vice,[31] and it is Christ who sets us free from this vice and who opens our hearts to genuine love of neighbour. Augustine accepted that 'faith merits the grace of doing good works', but he insisted that the kind of faith that we ought to have is that by which we might 'obtain that love which alone truly does good works'.[32] Recognising the implications of 'just as you did it to one of the least of these who are my brothers, you did it to me' (Mt 25:40), Augustine reminds us that, although he is rich in heaven, Christ 'is poor and is in the poor' here on earth:

> Christ is at once rich and poor: as God, rich; as a human person, poor. Truly, that Man rose to heaven already rich, and now sits at the right hand of the Father, but here, among us, he still suffers hunger, thirst and nakedness: here he is poor and is in the poor.[33]

Augustine challenges the way in which we ignore Christ's presence in our neighbours, especially among the poor:

> Christ who is rich in heaven chose to be hungry in the poor. Yet in your humanity you hesitate to give to your fellow human being. Don't you realize that what you give, you give to Christ, from whom you received whatever you have to give in the first place.[34]

For Augustine, the care of the poor is a matter of justice, and not only of charity:

The superfluities of the rich are the necessities of the poor. When you possess superfluities, you possess what belongs to others.[35]

He insists, however, that our works can only be described as 'good' when they are motivated by faith and done for the love of God:

Only those are to be called good works which are done for the love of God. But it is necessary that faith be antecedent to them, so that they have their origin in faith, and not that faith have its beginning from them. For nothing is done for the love of God unless first there be belief in God.[36]

The grace of God enables us to recognise with Thérèse that the greatest in the kingdom of heaven have embraced the way of spiritual childhood (see Mt 18:1-5), and, like Aquinas, to accept the spiritual nourishment that Jesus, our 'bread of life' (Jn 6:35), provides for us in the Eucharist. Inviting us to recognise that all our brothers and sisters are also invited to call God 'Father' and that Jesus wants to provide them also with the 'bread of life', Augustine reminds us that it is also the work of grace that enables us to turn away from our antisocial vices and to respect the obligations that human solidarity and a genuine love for our neighbour impose on us. Echoing the concern that St John Chrysostom showed for the spiritual and material needs of the poor, the way in which St Augustine preached the Gospel message of the Last Judgement (Mt 25:31-46) and the example he gave of making this message his rule of life are a constant challenge to the Church – an invitation to make the righteousness of the coming kingdom of heaven our own.

THE RECAPITULATION ANTHROPOLOGY OF ST IRENAEUS AS A MODEL FOR OUR BELIEF

We have already noted that, for St Irenaeus, the Word, through whom all things were created, recapitulated the whole history of the human race during his incarnate life on earth, passing through the period of gestation in Mary's womb, birth, infancy, childhood, adolescence, early and mature adulthood:

> When Christ became incarnate and was made man, he recapitulated in himself the long history of mankind and procured for us a 'short cut' to salvation, so that what we had lost in Adam, that is, being in the image and likeness of God, we might recover in Christ Jesus. ... For this reason Christ experienced all the stages of life, thereby giving communion with God to all men.[37]

Having passed through these various 'stages of life', Christ also experienced death 'so that He might be the firstborn from the dead, having the first place in all things (Col 1:18), the originator of life, before all and preceding all'.[38]

Describing our 'pristine nature' in terms of our having been 'made in the image and likeness of God' (see Gen 1:27),[39] and specifically in the image and likeness of Christ, Irenaeus believed that humanity's sin had disfigured the divine image, but that in Christ its original beauty was restored:

> It is in Christ, 'the image of the invisible of God' (Col 1:15), that man has been created 'in the image and likeness' of the Creator. It is in Christ, Redeemer and Saviour, that the divine image, disfigured in man by the first sin, has been restored to its original beauty and ennobled by the grace of God.[40]

Having been redeemed by Christ, in whom our pristine state of being in the image and likeness of God is restored, all humanity is called to manifest the glory of God by coming to share fully in his life and, in him, to see the face of God:

> [T]he glory of God is man fully alive; moreover man's life is the vision of God: if God's revelation through creation has already obtained life for all the beings that dwell on earth, how much more will the Word's manifestation of the Father obtain life for those who see God.[41]

St Irenaeus offers us a theological vision of our own humanity, a vision that recognises our original share in God's glory, our loss of that glory, and the way in which that glory has been restored to us through our union with Christ. For Irenaeus, it is the Holy Spirit who enables us to recognise Jesus as the Son of God, and it is only those who recognise Jesus as the Son who can approach the Father:

> And it is impossible to see God's Son without the Spirit, and no one can approach the Father without the Son, for the knowledge of the Father is the Son, and the knowledge of God's Son is obtained through the Holy Spirit.[42]

We can only come to see and know God through the work of the Holy Spirit who leads us to Jesus, and through the work of the Son who leads us to the Father. It is only in the vision and knowledge of the Father that we can experience in its fullness the life for which we were created. It is only in Christ, in other words, that we can come to a true understanding of ourselves.

St Thérèse of Lisieux recognised that only childlike trust can open our minds and hearts to the extraordinary gifts of

God's grace (see Mt 18:1-5). St Thomas Aquinas recognised that only the Eucharist can provide us with the spiritual nourishment we need if Jesus is to be our 'bread of life' (Jn 6:35). St Augustine recognised that only the work of grace enables us to recognise Jesus in the least of our brothers and sisters (see Mt 25:31-46) and to treat them accordingly. St Irenaeus recognised that our true glory is found only in Christ and that it is only through the guidance of the Holy Spirit that we can fulfil our true destiny as images and likenesses of his glory (see Gen 1:27).

Notes

1. See *Acta synodalia sacrosancti Concilii Vaticani II*, 1/1:96–7.
2. St Irenaeus, *Against Heresies*, 5.18.2, 1, in ibid., 7:1173.
3. William Thomas Walsh, *Saint Teresa of Avila: A Biography* (Milwaukee: Bruce Publishing Company, 1944), 579.
4. George E. Ganss (ed.), *Ignatius of Loyola: The Spiritual Exercises and Selected Works* (*Classics of Western Spirituality*, edited by Bernard McGinn) (New York - Mahway: Paulist Press, 1991), 211.
5. St Thérèse of Lisieux, *Story of a Soul*, 207.
6. Ibid.
7. Ibid., 112.
8. See ibid., 188.
9. Ibid., 105.
10. Ibid., 221.
11. St Thomas Aquinas, *Summa Theologiae* III, 65.3.
12. St Thomas Aquinas, *Summa Theologiae* III, 72.12 ad 3.
13. St Thomas Aquinas, *Summa Theologiae* III, 73.1–2.
14. St Thomas Aquinas, *Summa Theologiae* III, 75.2.
15. St Thomas Aquinas, *Summa Theologiae* III, 73.1 ad 3, 6.
16. St Thomas Aquinas, *Summa Theologiae* III, 76.5–8; 77.3–8.
17. St Thomas Aquinas, *Summa Theologiae* III, 73.3 ad 3.
18. St Thomas Aquinas, *Summa Theologiae* III, 65.3 ad 1.
19. St Thomas Aquinas, *Summa Theologiae* III, 74.6.
20. St Thomas Aquinas, *Summa Theologiae* III, 79.2 ad 1.
21. St Thomas Aquinas, *Summa Theologiae* III, 80.4.
22. St Thomas Aquinas, *Summa Theologiae* III, 80.12 ad 3.
23. St Thomas Aquinas, *Summa Theologiae* III, 79.7.

24. St Thomas Aquinas, *Summa Theologiae* III, 79.1 ad 1.
25. St Thomas Aquinas, *Summa Theologiae* III, 73.3.
26. St Thomas Aquinas, *Summa Theologiae* III, 73.3.
27. St Thomas Aquinas, *Summa Theologiae* III, 79.7 ad 2.
28. St Thomas Aquinas, *Summa Theologiae* III, 80.1 ad 3.
29. St Augustine, *The Trinity,* 8.7.10, in Migne (ed.), *PL,* 42:956.
30. St Augustine, *Homilies on the Gospel of John,* 32.8, in ibid., 35:1646.
31. St Augustine, *City of God,* 12.27, in ibid., 41:576.
32. St Augustine, *Letters,* 186.3.7, in ibid., 33:818.
33. St Augustine, *Sermons,* 123.4, ibid., 38:696.
34. St Augustine, *Explanation of the Psalms,* 75.9, in ibid., 36:964.
35. St Augustine, *Explanation of the Psalms,* 147.12, in ibid., 37:1922.
36. St Augustine, *Explanation of the Psalms,* 67.41, in ibid., 36:838.
37. St Irenaeus, *Against Heresies,* 3.18.1, 7, in Migne (ed.), *PG,* 7:932, 937.
38. St Irenaeus, *Against Heresies,* 2.22.4, in ibid., 7:784.
39. St Irenaeus, *Against Heresies,* 5.10.1, in ibid., 7:1148.
40. *Catechism,* n. 1701, see *Gaudium et spes* 22.
41. St Irenaeus, *Against Heresies,* 4.20.7, in Migne (ed.), *PG,* 7:1037. Quoted in the *Catechism,* n. 294.
42. St Irenaeus, *Presentation of the Apostolic Preaching,* 7, in Froidevaux (ed.), *Irénée de Lyon: Démonstration de la prédication apostolique,* 41–2.

CONCLUSION

In this book, we have explored the nature and implications of our Christian faith. Recognising Abraham, Moses and Mary as models, we have seen that faith often invites us to leave behind the life with which we have become familiar in order to follow the invitation of God. Drawing us into a relationship with the mystery of God, Father, Son and Spirit, and into a deeper solidarity with our neighbour, regardless of who he or she may be, our faith enables us to share the priestly, kingly and prophetic dimensions of Christ's role and mission.

Taking St Thérèse of Lisieux, St Teresa of Avila and St John Chrysostom as guides, we have outlined the teaching of the *Catechism* on prayer. It is a personal relationship with God in which we are gradually brought to the full maturity of spiritual childhood.

Chapter three presented the *Catechism's* teaching on the public liturgy of the Church, taking St Thomas Aquinas, St Ignatius of Antioch and St Teresia Benedicta a Cruce (Edith Stein) as mentors. The liturgy is an opportunity to unite ourselves with the priestly prayer of Jesus, our Lord, and to unite the spiritual sacrifices of our lives with his in order that we may receive from God the grace of becoming truly one with him in Eucharistic communion.

In chapter four, St Augustine, St Catherine of Siena and Bl. John XXIII were our chosen witnesses to the teaching of the *Catechism* on righteousness. Having become children of God the Father thanks to the extraordinary solidarity of the incarnate Word, who suffered and died to unite us to himself forever, our righteousness is the fruit of our faith, hope and love, and it takes the form of a committed solidarity with all our sisters and brothers in all their needs.

In chapter five, we illustrated the teaching of the *Catechism* on the profession of our faith using St Irenaeus, St Joan of Arc and Bl. Elizabeth of the Trinity. Our belief in God, Father, Son and Holy Spirit, is closely bound up with what we believe about ourselves and our spiritual destiny. Only in Christ is the full grandeur and glory of our creation in the image and likeness of God revealed to us, and it is only in him that we can truly become all that God has intended for us from the beginning.

In this final chapter, we have proposed the 'Little Way' of St Thérèse, the Eucharistic Spirituality of St Thomas Aquinas, St Augustine's love of neighbour and the Recapitulation Anthropology of St Irenaeus as a summary of the teaching of the *Catechism*. St Teresia Benedicta a Cruce described the Holy Spirit, 'God's Moulding Hand', as the master builder of the Church: the 'eternal dome rising from earth and through to very heaven', the one who enlivens its human columns so that they 'rise high and stand firm, immovable', reaching 'high up into the light'.[1] With Jesus as our common foundation (see 1 Cor 3:11) and with columns like St Thérèse, St Thomas Aquinas, St Augustine and St Irenaeus, the Church of our time will not only stand the test of time but will, like them and Bl. Elizabeth of the Trinity, share in the eternal praise of God's glory (see Eph 1:12).

Note
1. See Edith Stein, *The Hidden Life*, 140–5.

BIBLIOGRAPHY

Barrett, W.P. (ed.), *The Trial of Jeanne D'Arc*, London: George Routledge & Sons, 1931.

Batzdorff, Suzanne M. (ed.), *Edith Stein: Selected Writings*, Springfield, Illinois: Templegate, 1990.

Camelot, Th. (ed.), *Ignace d'Antioche: Lettres* (*Sources Chétiennes*, 10, edited by H. de Lubac and J. Daniélou), Paris: Cerf, 1958.

Caprile, G. (ed.), *Il Concilio Vaticano II: Cronache del Concilio Vaticano II*, Rome: La Civiltà Cattolica, 1966–1969.

de Meester, Conrad (ed.), *The Complete Works of Elizabeth of the Trinity*, 3 vols, Washington: ICS, 1984, 1995.

_____ *Élisabeth de la Trinité: Biografie*, Paris: Presses de la Renaissance, 2006.

_____ (ed.), *Elisabeth de la Trinité: Oeuvres complètes*, Paris: Cerf, 1991.

Denzinger, H. and A. Schönmetzer SJ (eds), *Enchiridion symbolorum definitionum et declarationum de rebus fidei et morum*, Rome: Herder, 1976.

DeVries, Kelly, *Joan of Arc: A Military Leader*, Gloucestershire: Sutton Publishing, 1999.

Dressler, Hermigild, 'St. Irenaeus' in *New Catholic Encyclopedia*, Washington, DC: The Catholic University of America, 2003, vol. 7, 570–2.

Dupuis, Jacques (ed.), *The Christian Faith in the Doctrinal Documents of the Catholic Church,* New York: Alba House, 2001.

Foster, Kenelm Francis, 'St Catherine of Siena' in *New Catholic Encyclopedia*, Washington, DC: The Catholic University of America, 2003, vol. 3, 272–4.

Froidevaux, L.M. (ed.), *Irénée de Lyon: Démonstration de la prédication apostolique* (*Sources Chrétiennes*, edited by H. de Lubac and J. Daniélou), Paris: Cerf, 1959.

Ganss, George E. (ed.), *Ignatius of Loyola: The Spiritual Exercises and Selected Works* (*Classics of Western Spirituality*, edited by Bernard McGinn), New York – Mahwah: Paulist Press, 1991.

Graef, Hilda C. (ed.), *Writings of Edith Stein, selected, translated and introduced by Hilda Graef*, London: Peter Owen Ltd., 1956.

Harkins, Paul William, 'St. John Chrysostom' in *New Catholic Encyclopedia*, Washington, DC: The Catholic University of America, 2003, vol. 7, 945–9.

Hebblethwaite, Peter, *John XXIII, Pope of the Council*, revised edition, Glasgow: HarperCollins, 1994.

Herbstrith (Teresia a Matre Dei OCD), Waltraud, *Edith Stein: Ein Lebensbild in Zeugnissen und Selbstzeugnissen*, Mainz: Matthias-Grünewald-Verlag, 1998.

Kavanaugh OCD, Kieran, and Otilio Rodriguez OCD (eds), *The Collected Works of Saint Teresa of Avila*, Washington: ICS Publications, 1987.

Lisieux, Thérèse of, *The Letters of Saint Thérèse of Lisieux*, translated by J. Clarke, 2 vols, Washington, DC: Institute of Carmelite Studies, 1982, 1988.

_____ *Story of a Soul: The Autobiography of Saint Thérèse of Lisieux*, translated by John Clarke OCD, Washington, DC: ICS Publications, 1996.

_____ *The Prayers of Saint Thérèse of Lisieux*, translated by A. Kane, Washington, DC: Institute of Carmelite Studies, 1997.

Migne, Jacques-Paul (ed.), *Patrologia latina*, Paris, 1844–1864.

_____ (ed.), *Patrologia graeca*, Paris, 1857–1866.

Mosley, Joanne, *Edith Stein – Woman of Prayer: Her Life and Ideals*, Leominster, Herefordshire: Gracewing, 2004.

Murphy, Francis Xavier, 'St. Ignatius of Antioch' in *New Catholic Encyclopedia*, Washington, DC: The Catholic University of America, 2003, vol. 7, 310–2.

Noffke, Suzanne (ed.), *Catherine of Siena: The Dialogue* (*Classics of Western Spirituality*, edited by Richard J. Payne), New York – Mahwah: Paulist Press, 1980.

_____ (ed.), *The Letters of St. Catherine of Siena (Medieval & Renaissance Texts & Studies)*, New York: Medieval & Renaissance Texts & Studies, 1988, 52.

O'Donnell OCarm, Christopher, *Prayer: Insights from St Thérèse of Lisieux*, Dublin: Veritas, 2001.

Pernoud, Régine, *The Retrial of Joan of Arc*, London: Methuen & Co. Ltd., 1955.

_____ 'St Joan of Arc' in *New Catholic Encyclopedia*, Washington, DC: The Catholic University of America, 2003, vol. 7, 878–9.

Posselt OCD, Teresia Renata de Spiritu Sancto, *Edith Stein: The Life of a Philosopher and Carmelite. Authorized and Revised Biography by Her Prioress Sister Teresia Renata Posselt, O.C.D. (Text, Commentary and Explanatory Notes)*, edited by Susanne M. Batzdorff, Josephine Koeppel and John Sullivan, Washington, DC: ICS Publications, 2005.

Ratzinger, Joseph, and Christoph Schönborn, *Introduction to the Catechism of the Catholic Church,* San Francisco: Ignatius Press, 1994.

Stein, Edith, *Self Portrait in Letters, 1916–1942 (The Collected Works of Edith Stein),* translated by Josephine Koeppel OCD, Washington, DC: ICS Publications, 1993.

_____ *The Hidden Life: Hagiographic Essays, Meditations, Spiritual Texts (The Collected Works of Edith Stein),* translated by Waltraut Stein, edited by Lucy Gelber and Michael Linssen, Trivandrum: Carmel Publishing Centre, 1998.

_____ *Life in a Jewish Family: Her Unfinished Autobiographical Account (The Collected Works of Edith Stein),* translated by Josephine Koeppel, edited by Lucy Gelber and Romaeus Leuven, Trivandrum: Carmel Publishing Centre, 1998.

_____ *Woman (The Collected Works of Edith Stein),* translated by Freda Mary Oben, edited by Lucy Gelber and Romaeus Leuven OCD, Trivandrum: Carmel Publishing Centre, 1998.

_____ *The Science of the Cross (The Collected Works of Edith Stein),* translated by Josephine Koeppel OCD, edited by Lucy Gelber and Romaeus Leuven OCD, Washington, DC: ICS Publications, 2002.

Teske, Roland J., 'St. Augustine' in *New Catholic Encyclopedia,* Washington, DC: The Catholic University of America, 2003, vol. 1, 850–68.

Vale, Malcolm Graham Allan, *Charles VII,* Berkeley: University of California Press, 1974.

Walsh, William Thomas, *Saint Teresa of Avila: A Biography,* Milwaukee: Bruce Publishing Company, 1944.